THE BEST
TEN-MINUTE PLAYS
2023

THE BEST TEN-MINUTE

Plays

2023

Edited by **Debbie Lamedman**

S&K

Smith and Kraus Publishers

2023

A Smith and Kraus Book

177 Lyme Road
Hanover, NH 03755
To Order: 1.877.668.8680

www.smithandkraus.com

The Best Ten-Minute Plays 2023 Copyright © 2023

Manufactured in the United States of America

ISBN: 978-1-57525-975-8
ISSN: 2164-2435

Cover design/interior formatting by Vickie Swisher, Studio 2020

For information about custom editions, special sales, education and corporate
purchases, please contact Smith and Kraus.

TABLE OF CONTENTS

PLAYS FOR THREE OR MORE ACTORS

FOREWORD

In 1977, The Actors Theatre of Louisville popularized the concept of the 10-minute play with their National 10-Minute Play contest. The Actors Theatre hosted the contest for 28 years, but by the time they discontinued the contest in 2017, the short play concept had caught on like wildfire. Ten-minute play festivals and contests are in abundance all over the world, and it's safe to say this play style is here to stay.

The ten-minute play is its own art form, and if you've ever tried your hand at writing one, it isn't as easy as you might think. Short doesn't necessarily mean simple. I typically receive hundreds of submissions for the 50 coveted slots in this anthology. What am I looking for? To start, the play *needs* to be a play. Not a scene from a larger work. Not a skit one might see on Saturday Night Live. It needs to be as much a play as a full-length piece. Strong characters. Strong conflict. A beginning. A middle. An end. And all that action, dialogue, resolution needs to happen in 10 short minutes.

You will know a good 10-minute play the second you read or see one. You know it's good if it engages you *immediately!* There's no time to court and flirt with your audience … there's no room for pages and pages of exposition and back story! You need to grab their attention fast and keep them riveted throughout the ten minutes. See? Not so easy after all.

The fifty new plays in this volume are excellent examples of well-written 10-minute plays. They are timely, cutting edge, thrilling pieces of theatre, with a bit of absurdity thrown in for good measure! I am convinced there is something for everyone in this varied bunch.

These scripts have the ability to wrench your heart, make you laugh uncontrollably, or ponder what does it all mean? But the best thing about this group of plays is the writers have created dynamic scripts full of diverse characters and challenging situations. These are great pieces to read, act in, and hopefully produce!

These past three years have been some of the most challenging times we have seen in theatre history. But theatre and the people who work in the theatre have always persevered through the most adverse times. You will find the strength and tenacity of those playwrights in the following plays. Let's keep our heads up. Let's keep creating. There are always many more stories to be told.

~ Debbie Lamedman
April 2023

FLAT MEAT SOCIETY

by Tom Coash

CHARACTERS

DEE — Female, 30–60 years old, great cook, Very country. Any ethnicity. Lives in West Virginia, USA

SETTING

The busy, bubbling, cramped kitchen of an old, well-used trailer home in West Virginia. This could be done very simply with just a table/counter and a couple pots or could be more elaborate as desired.

TIME

Late afternoon. The crazy present.

PRODUCTION HISTORY

Flat Meat Society was presented at the Short + Sweet Theatre Festival in Sydney, Australia, October 9–23, 2022. WINNER — Best Script, Best Production, Best Actor. Directed by Emma Carolina-Wolf. The cast was as follows:

DEE: Brooke Ryan

The kitchen of a trailer home, bubbling over with activity. DEE presides over simmering pots, stirring, chopping, singing "On the Road Again" by Willie Nelson. Wears apron with the words "Flat Meat Society — The Real Deal!" Dogs bark outside. A knock is heard at the door.

DEE: *Entrez-vous!*

(DEE talks to audience as if they are the guest.)

> Welcome *et vous*! I'm learning French. Big secret. Thanks for coming all the way out, 'specially during a damn plague. Sorry 'bout the dogs.

(Shouts at dogs ...)

> Quiet! They're my ex's. Damn, I'm excited! NPR right here in my little old trailer. Picture me on NPR! I told Junebug, my cousin, I was gonna be on national radio and she flat out called me a liar. Said, "Dee, you better slow down those meds you're taking."

(Continues preparing various dishes as she talks.)

> Don't worry about the mask, had the darn thing in July. 'Bout coughed up a lung! Laid-out in the hospital for a week. Alone. Anyway, that's when I got my revelation. My brainwave!

(Displays her apron.)

> The Flat Meat Society — The Real Deal! That's trademarked. What do they say? Winners never quit and quitters never stop whining. Well, I was tired of whining. I said, Dee, when you get up outta this bed, you got to turn the mental corner. Expand your horizons. Bitter ain't better.

(Stirring a pot, offers spoon full of something.)

> Here! Something new, for the Cook-Off. Taste.

(Offers more insistently.)

Taste! It's fantastic. Nothing weird, I promise. Yep, yep, that's it … Unbelievable, right?! Possum! Possum grits!

(Guest coughs up a little.)

Oopsie, sorry. Wrong tube?

(Smells spoon.)

Um, um, ummm! Fresh this morning. Lucky find! Doing my UPS deliveries.

(Tastes, then licks spoon.)

Yes, ma'am! Threw in some Serrano peppers, Vermont cheddar, Parmesan, and Hen of the Woods. That's mushrooms. *Grifola frondosa*, that's Latin. Growed right down the hill. Big clump on a stump by the turnoff.

(Offers spoon again.)

More?

(Gets a no.)

Too spicy? No worries, I got something even better cooking. I got plans for you!

(Starts chopping something.)

The Flat Meat Society! Seasonality, regionality, environmentality, goo-de-terre, and plain ol' luck. That's what's important when it comes to flat meats! Necropastoral!

(Tastes again.)

Yes sir! Got that West V-A *goo-de-terre*! That's French. Taste of the earth. Or road in this case. Route 16 near the river. Goo-de-tarmac!

Used to be the Roadkill Festival Cook-Off was the end-all, be-all of my existence, you know? All that mattered. I won that Cook-Off six years in a row. Six straight! Till last year, my streak was broken by cheatin' hucksters flying in flash-frozen Canadian Geese from Nova-damn-Scotia! We're 'sposed to be cookin' roadkill! When's the last time you heard of anybody sideswiped a Canadian goose? Maybe if they was flying a 747! People drive hundreds of miles to this festival to try something different. Authentic. Webster's at the library says, "Roadkill is an animal or animals that have been struck and killed by motor vehicles." Struck and killed by motor vehicles. It's not the Harvest "Hunting" Festival. Not the damn "ship in it from Siberia on UPS" festival! I cook what I scavenge! The real deal! I don't run 'em over on purpose neither, like some!!

(Takes a breath, calms herself.)

Ok, all right, Dee, ok … slow it down … deep breath …

(Takes a chug from an unmarked bottle. Shivers …)

Whew! Medicinal purposes only. Blood pressure. Bitter ain't better.

(Takes another little sip.)

I was even the Roadkill Festival Queen my first year. In my hot tamale days. How I met my ex, Bambi. She was one of my Roadkill Royal Ladies. Cutest thing in Pocahontas County. We were together seven something years.

(Pause.)

Hey, where's my manners?

(Offers bottle to guest …)

Try a taste? Homemade. Natural herbs. Put the bees back in your hive! No?

(Puts cork back in and tucks away.)

Anyway, the whole thing's changed. The Cook-Off. Started out years ago as clean, country fun, you know? Now, it's all about the city coffers. Spreadsheets. Cash flow. Catering to PC buzz-buster tourists. Don't want to offend their delicate, little, Subaru sensibilities.

Humans been eating roadkill since the first ox cart flattened a feral side 'a bacon in ancient Egypt. It's natural. Waste not, want not. People're happy eatin' an apple fell out of a tree, so what's the difference?

Roadkill, or "Flat Meat" I'm calling it, is one hundred percent free of all the antibiotics, hormones, and growth drugs those factory-farms stuff into store-bought meat. Perfect for the pandemic. No human hands touched this meat …

(Taps pot.)

… 'till I picked it up. Which would you rather have in *your* mouth? Corpses of animals that spent their whole lives knee-deep in a crap-filled feedlot, belching climate-destroyin' poison gas, throats cut in a Covid-ridden slaughterhouse, or something been running free, eating wild greens, fresh berries. Drinkin' outta clear mountain streams. That just had the unfortunate misfortune to get caught in some trucker's headlights?

Elk, venison, boar, grouse, wild turkey. For all your Paleo listeners? Are you kidding me, perfect! Survivalists? Listen to the news! Stock up. Animal Rights activists and knowing foodies are onboard and on the road with Flat meat! Ethical, organic, ecological, finger-lickin' good. No G-M-O in this P-O-T! It's not just a choice in the kitchen, it's a lifestyle!

Roadkill *sounds* distasteful, right? Gross. Your mind can't help flashing on one 'a god's little miracles mangled and bloated on the median strip. It's sad! So, I come up with "flat meat." More appetizing, right? Like a sizzling "flat" iron steak. Take away some of the stigmata.

You familiar with that five-second rule, when food's dropped on the floor? Well, we got the five hour rule.

Ideally, you want it still moving, put the poor thing out of its misery. Or in rigor mortis, then you know it's fresh. Stiff as a board, thank the lord. If vultures is on it, cry and drive by.

Anything I won't eat? Pekingese. There's an old country song goes, "Don't ask me how I know."

Course some people just don't take to it. Fred, my ex-husband, ex-biggest mistake of my life? I served him ferret once. Said it smelled like a dirty clothes hamper. I said he smelled like a dirty clothes hamper, which he did, and that was that. Bambi was never actually, really keen, neither. Oh, she liked the glamour, but last spring, after she had a head-on with a White-tailed doe in the fog over to Taylor Mountain, she just couldn't stomach it no more.

It'll mess you up hitting a deer. Beautiful creatures. Hundred twenty, hundred thirty pounds of solid muscle and bone and pure innocence. Crush your fender and your heart at the same time. Said she was standin' there shakin', cryin', tears runnin' down, telling the highway patrol, and that bastard can't keep a straight face. Looking at her license, laughing. 'Cause a woman named Bambi creamed a deer.

So, I said we got to go get that deer. Perfect for the Cook-Off, right? She said, "You're crazy!" Said she was done with roadkill. Well, I *was* a little crazy then, post-imposter-geese-cooking-my-goose fiasco. Bitter as bad vinegar. Obsessed with winning my title back. Waste not, want not, right? Prime venison! I lugged it home, gutted it, was hanging it out back. She hopped in the Chevy and screamed outta here, spitting gravel all the way. Went to Vegas, went vegan, and became one of them run-a-way models.

(Pause.)

I'm proud of her. I am. To get away from here and do something. Not end up roadkill yourself. Layin' in a hospital bed. Run over by life.

(Stirs a pot, bangs a lid or two, takes a moment.)

Bambi said I had lost myself, lost my way. Layin' in that hospital, tubes running out 'a my nose, I wasn't thinking about Possum Paninis or Toad Ala Mode. I was thinking about how she was gone from our kitchen, from our bed. How it was me that drove her away, not that deer.

(Starts to chug from bottle, stops before drinking, considers … makes a decision.)

Nope. Bitter *ain't* better.

(Puts cork back in, puts it away.)

Hell, I don't even care if I win this year. I just want to share my passion. Go out with a good taste in my mouth. Sides, I'm getting too dang busy. Had a video go YouTube viral, courtesy of my 'leven year old hacker niece. Now we got a website, podcasts, T-shirts, aprons. AND big reveal here, drumroll …

(She does a drum roll on pot lids.)

I got a cookbook coming out! And maybe … a live TV show! All sponsored by Michelin. The tire company! *Mais oui!* They're not just tires, they also got that star food thing, right? Three stars, five stars? Tires, flat meat? It's a natural! I said to the Frenchies, *ok, mon freres, ecoutez* … maybe your *companie* isn't doing too good in this present world economic crisis. You need something new. Expand your horizons. Think of your tires as more than just a way to hold cars up. Think of your tire as a metaphor for the Circle of Life. The Cosmic Wheel. Life, death, the journey! The right tires can get you over a hump AND get you a free meal! I cooked 'em a few of my past winners; Southern fried Squirrel with coriander and a squirt 'a chili sauce,

Smidgeon of Pigeon Toast-Toppers, Shake 'n Bake Snake. But what really got 'em, … my *Pee-ass de Résistance* …

(Pushes spoon full of something forward …)

Taste! Go on, expand your horizons!

(Guest tastes.)

Is that flat awesome or what? Calling it Bambi's Revenge. Yep, same deer! Been keepin' a haunch in the freezer. Seared venison with spicy huckleberry dressing. Sides of winter "squash"… get it … squash? And "creamed" corn!

(Guest asks for more.)

More? Told ya!

(Holds out spoon again …)

You being here reminds me of Bambi, sharin' everything. Granny used to say kitchens are for sharin' and sharin's carin'. Maybe I forgot that.

I named this for Bambi so maybe she'll hear about it and see that I'm not crazy. That I'm doing better. That I been thinking 'bout her … missing her … and well … they're wanting me to go to Los Angeles for the TV. That's near Vegas, right? I could take the dogs with me. I could …

(Pause.)

You know what the Michelin company motto is? "A better way forward." Maybe she'll see that *I've* found my way again. A better way, right?

(The stove timer goes off!)

Hot damn! Frog nibbles are ready!

END OF PLAY

CARRY ON

by Jennie Webb

CHARACTERS

BETH, female, 50s–70s (if not older); prides herself on being able to figure out where to put things, making sure they fit. Any race or ethnicity.

SETTING

A place in which to contemplate transitions.

TIME

The present.

NOTE

Carry On is a short play that's not so much about baggage as it is about what we carry and the ways in which we do it.

PRODUCTION HISTORY

Carry On was presented by Ensemble Studio Theatre/Los Angeles as part of "The Early Bird Special" June 18 & 19, 2022. The play was directed by Susan Franklin Tanner. The cast was as follows:

BETH: Angela Bullock

We see a woman of a certain age with a suitcase, which itself has likely seen a lot of miles. She's not holding it by the handle. She embraces it with both arms against her chest, like she's found a runaway child. Or as if it contains a forgotten treasure.

BETH: When did it all start? Well, not start. But when did I start ... acknowledging it? Something like that.

It was days away from the one year ... "anniversary" — which sounds strange, as if it demands some sort of celebration — of my mother's death. And I was, what's the word, preparing myself? Or trying to. Trying to figure out how to prepare?

(She sets the suitcase down on one end.)

Okay. Let me just say this: My brother and I had a very good mother. Exceptional, as a matter of fact. When she died, pretty suddenly all things considered, I was ... devastated. In my experience, losing your mother is devastating in a way that you never expected and no one warned you about because, well, they just couldn't have. It's impossible to comprehend until ... it happens.

(She considers the suitcase.)

Anyway! I had set the date aside. I wanted to be in a sort of self-aware, self-protective space. I had no idea how it would hit me, that year marker, and I wanted to be able to cry for 24 hours if I wanted to!

But as we all know, in life — and probably in death, for that matter (I've no evidence to the contrary) ... shit happens.

This particular shit had to do with my father — who was long divorced from my mother and not aging very conveniently or considerately at that point — and a close friend — who was valiantly fighting the good cancer fight. As it happened, the day's last minute scheduling meant that I'd be at the doctor's with my dad in the morning and spending the afternoon with my friend at the hospital to get the ball rolling for her bone marrow transplant.

Shit.

Not at all what I wanted to fill my "Poor me my mom died one year ago now what?" day with. And I have to admit I was pretty upset about it. Not upset enough to abandon my dad and my friend, but definitely enough to wail to another friend over a few too many cocktails!

(She grabs the suitcase, roughly picking it up by its handle.)

"I cleared my goddamn calendar so I could stay home tomorrow and it was just supposed to be me and my dead mother and now I'm running around town to horrible places I don't want to be. What the fuck?"

Only I'm sure I said fuck a few more times and must have sounded beyond piteous because after a bit, my always dependable, cut-the-shit friend said to me, "Jesus, Beth: Why don't you just take her with you!"

"What?"

"Do what you need to do and just take your mother with you!"

I was about to ask her just what she meant by that. I mean, I did have a small container of ashes that I'd been meaning to spread in my garden, at my mom's request. (Good thing procrastination never seems to bother dead people, right?) So was I supposed to …?

(She takes a new look at the suitcase she's holding.)

But then, something happened.

(She sets the suitcase down.)

As I considered her words — "Just take your mother with you" — my hand moved to my heart …

(Her hand does.)

And in that moment, there she was. My mom. Right there, part of me. It was as physical and, I suppose, spiritual as anything I'd ever experienced.

And I don't give a damn if the martinis had anything to do with it, from that day forward, I've held her in just that way. She's in my heart and wherever I go, I take her with me.

(She's very satisfied with herself. Then she considers the suitcase again, transferring it to another spot.)

Now. Back to my cancer friend, who never even got close to a transplant. Dead the next year. Beyond tragic and I was, of course, feeling her loss. She was a photographer and saw the world in such a marvelous way. A real gift. And one day after she was gone, I was out for a walk and caught a glimpse of some graffiti on a street corner that I must have passed a million times but in that moment, the way the light hit it, it sort of cried out and demanded I stop and, suddenly, bam: I felt her. My friend. I was somehow looking through my eyes, but hers, as well. And every day now when I think of her ...

(She puts her hands to her eyes.)

She's right there.

So for a while I felt very much ... in good company? I didn't have to be sad. I just went merrily along, protected and fulfilled thanks to this new connection: the dearly departed and my body as a piece of carry-on luggage!

(On a positive note, she moves to the suitcase, about to pick it up again, then stops herself.)

But then my brother died. Quickly and traumatically and impossibly and it was unbearable.

Of course, we do bear it. We must bear it. We carry on.

(Perhaps a look at the suitcase, then she continues.)

All right. I know this sounds ridiculous, but after a few months of emotional hairpin turns navigating the bizarre business of death, what did I do but run smack dab into: "Oh fuck! Where do I put my brother?"

(She takes stock of her various body parts.)

At first I wondered …

(She holds her heart.)

In here, with my mother? (See, I'm making this up as I go along, so there are no compartmental rules.) But the truth is that as wonderful as my mother was, I couldn't do that to him. They had a very complicated relationship and it did not feel right to subject either of them to their inescapably explosive heart-to-hearts in perpetuum.

So what about my brother? I agonized over this for quite some time until one day, while I was driving, it struck me …

(She holds her hands in front of her, 10 and 2.)

My hands. My brother could fix anything. He was a do-er. He made things. And so … there he is. With me, every day. In everything I do.

(She moves away from the suitcase.)

Now, this was all a long time ago. But after it started, I began to, shall we say, reunite with others. My dear grandmothers?

(She holds herself tight.)

In my arms, one on each side. A friend who was entirely too full of life to have been taken …

(She touches her mouth.)

She's here every time I smile.

When my father (finally) passed:

(She points to her head.)

> He's here. Emotionally distant through the very end, that's pretty much where he lived.
>
> A lover I lost a few years back? Ha ha. Guess where.

(She wiggles her hips suggestively.)

> At one point, I even began to feel all of those sweet, sweet boys who got sick and died in the 80s when we were all so young and beautiful and nothing could hurt us …

(She runs her hands over her thighs and torso.)

> They're here, in every muscle I used, on every dance floor, tingling with the joy and freedom that inhabited that particular time of music and parties and passion and late nights and illegal substances and such incredible possibility.

(Maybe she tries her best not to look back at the suitcase before continuing.)

> It's a lot to carry with me. I'll admit that. But it's never been a burden. Quite the opposite! It's something that's comforted me. I never feel alone and the people I love will never be truly gone, so why should I dwell on those other times, times when I … can't?

(She might move further away from the suitcase, feeling its presence or pull.)

> Right. And I have to tell you that over the past few years it's become something even more. Bigger than me: my … capacity for holding. Millions upon millions of needless deaths in a pandemic of fear and stupidity? The never-ending list of men and women and children struck down by police violence, mass shootings? Who can even count the lost families at our borders, the victims of warfare and genocide and blind hatred around the world? No, I don't know all of them.

But it's as if, when everything changed — when time irreparably shifted and we were brought together in ways we never imagined — I changed, too. I expanded! And now, I can hold space for them. I can!

(She now returns to the suitcase but notices its frayed edges — perhaps she tries to smooth them out.)

Only here's another thing, something else that's … happening. Whether I'm ready for it or not.

To this body — my body. Which has been able to adapt to all sorts of containment demands, as it were! Overall, we have had a very good ride. Last month, I even started running!

Then just as quickly, I stopped.

It was my knees, you see. They decided this wasn't at all a good idea.

The other day, I looked at my hands. They'd become an old person's hands. How did that happen?

And let's be truthful: My vision's shot. I eat the wrong thing and my mouth hurts. I wake up in the mornings, everything hurts. And my heart: I don't know that it's working correctly, anymore. All too often I feel like it's being torn apart.

So for the first time in my life, it's occurred to me: Not that I'm in any hurry, mind you, but when I am gone — not in this body anymore — what happens to all of the …

(She takes stock of her body again. But what is she searching for? Does she even know? Then she picks up the suitcase by its handle again, holding it in front of her.)

And then there's this, and all it carries! All because I didn't have room, because I didn't have time, because I just didn't have the strength to let go while I was holding it all together …

(She returns the suitcase to her chest, again embracing it—this time with a bit more uncertainty, but most certainly a sense of humor.)

Without me, what is anybody going to do with a suitcase full of tears?

END OF PLAY

SIX FEET

by Claudia Barnett

CHARACTERS

DELPHINE

DAN

SETTING

Here and there.

NOTE

Six Feet was developed at the Experimental Theatre Writing Workshop and Pipeline-Collective's Salon. Special thanks to Suzanne Willett, Nancy Robillard, Yolie Canales, Joel van Liew, Benji Kern, Karen Sternberg, and David Ian Lee.

PRODUCTION HISTORY

Six Feet had a staged reading at the 2nd Seven New Works Festival at Fusion Theatre, Albuquerque, NM, on June 20, 2022. It was directed by Laurie Thomas. The cast was as follows:

DELPHINE: Rachel Wiseman

DAN: Blake Magnusson

At rise. DELPHINE holds two yardsticks and swings them as she walks. DAN approaches.

DAN: Delphine!

(DELPHINE whips one of the yardsticks towards him.)

DELPHINE: Six feet!

(DAN jumps back.)

DAN: Okay, okay.

DELPHINE: *(Motioning with a yardstick.)* This is only three feet. Two together: That's six.

DAN: I can do math.

DELPHINE: It's simple arithmetic, not math.

DAN: Okay.

DELPHINE: This space is my space.

DAN: This land is your land.

DELPHINE: This is public land, but it's my space. The land stays put. My space stays with me.

DAN: I see. Your *turf.* Metaphorically.

(DELPHINE holds the two yardsticks horizontally before her so that they form one long stick. SHE spins in a circle.)

DELPHINE: Each one's a radius.

DAN: And I'd better not cross the circumference.

DELPHINE: Right.

DAN: Or enter the area.

DELPHINE: Exactly.

DAN: I'm just a tangent.

DELPHINE: You're a tangent! Yes!

DAN: And you're the center.

DELPHINE: Of course I'm the center. It's my circle.

DAN: But you're also the center of my circle, Delphine.

DELPHINE: No, Dan. You can have your own circle. You can be the center of your own circle.

DAN: That sounds lonely.

DELPHINE: It sounds safe.

DAN: Does everyone have a circle?

DELPHINE: Everyone could. It's like freedom. You have to insist.

DAN: Is there enough space? In the world? For everyone to have a circle? That might take real math.

DELPHINE: $\pi r2$. 3.14159 times three, squared. Twenty-eight point two seven four three square feet per person. Times all the people in the world.

DAN: How many people are in the world?

DELPHINE: Too many.

DAN: Then everyone can't have six feet.

DELPHINE: Maybe not in India. Maybe not in L.A.

DAN: But we're not in India or L.A.

DELPHINE: So you have no excuse. Stay out of my circle.

DAN: And you stay out of mine.

DELPHINE: Gladly.

DAN: Well, it was nice to see you.

DELPHINE: Are you leaving? You just got here.

DAN: But I'm not actually here. You're "here" at point A. But I'm "here" at point B. So for you, I'm there, not here.

DELPHINE: Okay. But you are leaving? You just got *there*.

DAN: In fact, I'm on my way there.

DELPHINE: But not here.

DAN: Not unless you move.

DELPHINE: I was actually on my way there myself.

DAN: Here?

DELPHINE: No.

DAN: Oh.

DELPHINE: Are you following?

DAN: Of course I'm not following. I'm my own man.

DELPHINE: Independent.

DAN: Absolutely.

DELPHINE: But?

DAN: I love you Delphine.

DELPHINE: Since when?

DAN: Just now.

DELPHINE: Till when?

DAN: Tomorrow. Or forever. Do you love me?

DELPHINE: I don't think so. I don't know. How would I know? Is there a test for love?

DAN: The test of time.

DELPHINE: You're just trying to get in my circle.

DAN: I know: If someone you loved were in danger, you'd try to save them.

DELPHINE: If someone I didn't love were in danger, I'd try to save them.

DAN: If it were someone you loved, you'd try harder.

DELPHINE: Touché.

DAN: Touché?

(DELPHINE points one of the yardsticks like a sword.)

DELPHINE: En garde!

(DAN holds up his hands.)

DAN: Are you challenging me to a duel?

DELPHINE: A test.

DAN: But I'm unarmed.

DELPHINE: Then you're in danger.

DAN: And you won't save me.

DELPHINE: But I will play fair.

(SHE hands him a yardstick.)

DAN: What are the rules?

DELPHINE: Come too close and I'll skewer you.

DAN: What are the stakes?

(SHE points her yardstick at him.)

DELPHINE: We'll see.

(THEY fence. SHE points her yardstick at his throat.)

DAN: OK. I surrender.

(HE throws down his yardstick. SHE swoops it up and steps back, holding both yardsticks in the air, victorious.)

DELPHINE: I win.

DAN: But what did you win?

DELPHINE: Diameter.

(SHE holds out both yardsticks like wings.)

It broadens my circle exponentially.

DAN: If only you could fly.

DELPHINE: Like a condor. I'd own the sky.

(DELPHINE flaps her yardsticks.)

DAN: You know, you encroached on my circle.

DELPHINE: What? When?

DAN: Just then. When you pointed your sword at my throat. Your hand on one end, my neck at the other. *Three* feet in-between.

DELPHINE: Your circle got smaller when I won.

DAN: That's not how it works.

DELPHINE: There's a finite amount of space. When mine got larger, yours shrank.

DAN: You can't have space without giving me space.

DELPHINE: Then what did I win?

DAN: You'll have more space if you share.

DELPHINE: I don't know what you mean.

DAN: Hold out your arms.

(DELPHINE holds out her arms at her sides, a yardstick in each. DAN aligns himself with her and holds out his own arms so they form a line: Dan, yardstick, Delphine, yardstick.)

Look at our diameter now.

(DELPHINE puts her arms down. DAN faces her and kneels.)

DELPHINE: No.

DAN: No what? I haven't even asked.

DELPHINE: I am not knighting you.

DAN: Delphine —

DELPHINE: You may not violate the sanctity of my circle.

DAN: Our circle. We're connected, Delphine. Don't you feel it?

(HE stands to embrace her, but she raises a yardstick in warning.)

DELPHINE: The most we can be is a lemniscate.

DAN: Is that some sort of fish?

DELPHINE: A figure eight.

DAN: Two circles attached at the —

DELPHINE: Nexus.

DAN: Center! We'd share a common center!

DELPHINE: But I'd also maintain my own center.

DAN: Yes of course.

DELPHINE: And you'd respect my autonomy.

DAN: And you'd never leave me.

DELPHINE: How is *that* autonomy?

DAN: It's love, Delphine. We'll be united.

DELPHINE: I don't think so.

DAN: You're saying no?

DELPHINE: I need freedom.

DAN: Love is freedom.

DELPHINE: Sounds more like shackles. Now that I think about it, a figure eight is the shape of handcuffs.

DAN: It's the shape of infinite possibility. If you can't see that, then we're done.

DELPHINE: What? But you love me.

DAN: But you don't love me.

DELPHINE: I mean ... I might. I need time.

DAN: Space *and* time? That's greedy. I'm falling out of love.

DELPHINE: I'm stumbling.

DAN: I'm leaving.

DELPHINE: But you just got here.

DAN: *Here*? ... Not *there*?

DELPHINE: Here. I think ...

DAN: You think ...?

DELPHINE: I think I want you to stay.

(*DELPHINE drops her yardsticks. DAN doesn't move.*)

END OF PLAY

POCKETBOOK

by Cris Eli Blak

CHARACTERS

HARRISON, 30s, Black male. Defense attorney, recent law school graduate.

DOLA, 17, Black female. Smart and quick-witted, in prison for murder.

SETTING

Ross Correctional Institution for Women, somewhere in the South.

TIME

Present Day or Back in the Day. Some Things Never Change.

PRODUCTION HISTORY

Pocketbook was presented by the Kentucky Playwrights Workshop as part of the Play Reading Series in July 2022. The cast was as follows:

HARRISON: Derek Snow

DOLA: Meredith Strayhorn

Lights up on Ross Correctional Institution for Women. Visiting Room. DOLA POST, in prison uniform, sits at a table, her eyes dark with exhaustion, her cheeks chapped from tears she won't let anyone see. Her feet tap anxiously, her palms staying planted on top of the table. HARRISON KARL enters, wearing an old suit that is a size too large.

HARRISON: Miss Post. It's nice to meet you.

(HARRISON extends his hand. DOLA looks him up and down.)

DOLA: Who are you?

(He pulls his hand back, takes a seat, clears his throat.)

HARRISON: My name is Harrison Karl.

DOLA: What's that s'posed to mean to me? That don't mean nothin' to me.

HARRISON: I'm a lawyer.

DOLA: We probably can't afford you.

HARRISON: I'm a public defender. I've been assigned to your case.

DOLA: What? Where's the other guy? The short one. Bald dude.

HARRISON: He'll no longer be assisting you …

DOLA: What're you saying?

HARRISON: *(Nervous)* What I mean is that —

DOLA: He quit.

HARRISON: These things happen.

DOLA: He dropped me.

HARRISON: It's like … a volleyball game, you know? It's back and forth until you find a winner.

DOLA: He dropped me.

HARRISON: I'll be taking over.

DOLA: What's that mean about me, about what he thought
             about me?

HARRISON: I can't tell you. *(Pause)* I'm sorry?

DOLA: He lost hope in me.

HARRISON: Like I said —

DOLA: He thinks I don't have a chance.

HARRISON: I'm not exactly sure why he —

DOLA: You lawyers, all you — you don't care about me.
             You don't care about people like me. Y'all act
             like you wanna help, like it's all about justice and
             helping the little people, the poor folks. People like
             me. People like my mama. Struggling little Black
             girls. All you wanna do is get your win. That's all
             you really care about, your record. Your reputation.
             Where do you go after you leave here? Grab a
             burger? See family? Play ball with some friends?
             Forget about the struggling little Black girls like me?

HARRISON: *(Pause)* I care.

DOLA: They don't have any girl lawyers where you
             come from?

HARRISON: Where exactly do you think I "come from?"

DOLA: Females. Women. I think they'll have a little more
             empathy. Maybe.

HARRISON: That may be true.

DOLA: So get me one of them.

HARRISON: I — can we talk? For a moment.

DOLA: I don't have anything to say to you.

HARRISON: A moment of your time. I won't ask for much from
             you, I promise. I'm only asking for a moment.
             (Changes approach) Have something better to do?

	(she looks up) Because you can go right back to your cell. I can't stop you. *(She mentally weighs her options.)*
DOLA:	You good at what you do?
HARRISON:	I'd like to think so.
DOLA:	You look young.
HARRISON:	I am young.
DOLA:	How long out of school?
HARRISON:	*(Quiet)* Not long …
DOLA:	God, they sent me a baby.
HARRISON:	How old are you?
DOLA:	You don't already know this?
HARRISON:	I do. But I want to hear it from you.
DOLA:	Seventeen.
HARRISON:	Seventeen.
DOLA:	Unless the birth certificate is a liar.
HARRISON:	You're seventeen. A real kid. And yet you had the … passion to do what you did. I have passion too. For the law. For doing what's right, albeit a different kind of passion, but that doesn't change the fact that it's a passion. When I say I can do something, not only do I mean it, I make sure to do it. I make sure to try my absolute best.
DOLA:	You don't get it do you? I don't need your reassurance? I need your help. I need to know that you *can* help.
HARRISON:	I can.
DOLA:	Don't —
HARRISON:	I —

DOLA: Don't! Don't. Don't. Don't. Don't tell me you can do something then don't. I've met too many people like you. People who I can't believe. I need someone I can rely on.

HARRISON: I will do everything I can. *(Pause)* How are they treating you in here?

DOLA: Well … it's prison. Adult prison. Not like what you see on TV though. I haven't played cards once. The food is accurately trash though.

HARRISON: *(Laughs)* I'm sorry to hear that.

DOLA: I'm guilty. You need to know that.

HARRISON: I know.

DOLA: But I don't regret it. And I don't belong here. I'm not a bad person. I was just raised to tell the truth. My mama did a good job with that.

HARRISON: That's good.

DOLA: They threw me in here and I get why but I shouldn't be here. You said it yourself. You said I'm too young.

HARRISON: You didn't steal candy from the supermarket, Dola. You killed a man. You committed murder.

DOLA: It was self-defense.

HARRISON: Can you prove it?

DOLA: Can *you*? You're the lawyer, hotshot. What if it was a drug dealer? What if I had killed a drug dealer, or a gang member — or any other man with skin the same color as mine?

HARRISON: What are you asking?

DOLA: Do you think I'd be in here? You think I'd be in here for as long as they got me in here, for the rest of my life? I'm seventeen and I might not ever eat my favorite meal, walk on grounds that ain't these, ever again. In here I can't walk down an aisle or get a job.

You think it would change if he looked like me, like you?

HARRISON: I don't have a good answer for you. I'm sorry.

DOLA: I got your answer. I killed a white man and that's all it took. That's all it took.

HARRISON: Maybe you should bring your voice down a bit —

DOLA: Who's gonna be shocked by what I'm saying? I don't keep my secrets.

HARRISON: Still —

DOLA: He was hurting her. He was hurting my mama. I did what I had to do.

HARRISON: That may be true —

DOLA: It is. Say it.

HARRISON: Say what?

DOLA: That I don't belong in here, with these grown women. With these beasts. Agree with me. You can't help me if you think I'm as bad as everyone else in this place.

HARRISON: I can —

DOLA: You can't. Not if you don't believe in me. *(he's quiet. She slams her hand on the table)* Say it! Say it or get the hell out. Don't believe me, you won't do a thing but walk outta here and never come back like the last one. I need someone that's gonna have the heart to fight for me, to show a jury, a judge, whoever else, that what I did was justified under the eyes of the law and the Lord. That's what I need. And if you can't provide that you're just gonna have to go on and publicly defend someone who ain't me.

HARRISON: *(Pause)* I believe in you. But we need to work together. And you need to talk to me.

DOLA: About what?

HARRISON: Everything.

DOLA: We couldn't pay the bills, the rent. Could barely
            keep the lights on. Sometimes we couldn't. It was
            winter. Imagine coming home in the winter to
            a cold, dark home. It stops being a home then.
            Becomes worse than a place like this. Becomes a
            shadowland, a pit. Hell. I had a job. Didn't make
            much but made enough to eat. Not nothing super
            healthy but if it fills the stomach why would you
            complain? Times are tough. They're tight. You know
            this. Everyone's falling behind. Everybody I know
            at least. I put in application after application but
            don't nobody call me back. They see my address, my
            name. They see my race and they don't think I'm
            any kind of good worker. They don't call me back.
            I keep trying, keep applying, putting my name in
            wherever it fits. Jobs I never thought I'd be applying
            for, hard jobs, jobs that nobody should be doing,
            especially not me. But I would. If it meant me and
            my mama could eat and have a light on over our
            head in the nighttime — it was worth that. But
            that phone didn't ring. Nobody called. And soon
            enough, well, I couldn't pay for the phone to stay
            on, so even if someone decided to call I wouldn't
            have gotten it no way. So what am I s'posed to do?
            What am I s'posed to do for my family? For my
            mama and me. My mama meets this white man,
            says he can help us out, says his pockets stay heavy.
            He's real nice at first but then he starts on her. New
            bruise every day and I don't like that. Now we got
            lights but neither of us wanna look at what's around
            us. I walk in one night from going around putting
            in paper applications and see him on top of my
            mama callin' her all kinds of names that no Black
            woman should ever be called — no woman at all. I
            don't care who you are. My mama screams and he
            knows I'm there, turns back and looks me straight
            in the eyes and smiles. I can see that smile now. I

haven't smiled since. He's there on top of my mama and I know these hands aren't about to get him off and he's not stopping. He's not stopping.

HARRISON: So you get a gun.

DOLA: I know where my mama keeps it. She always kept it right there in her pocketbook. Her favorite thing in the world, that pocketbook. She sold everything she owned to save your lives, every ring and necklace. But not that pocketbook. It wasn't even designer. I don't know what it was about it but it's her prized possession. And I know just where it is. So I take it, open it up and there it was.

HARRISON: The gun.

DOLA: Yeah. And I pulled that trigger for my mama, just like she gave everything she could for me.

HARRISON: But you didn't know that man was the sheriff's brother at the time, did you?

DOLA: No. Wouldn't have cared if I did. I didn't do it 'cause I didn't like what he was. He was hurting my mama. Haven't shed a tear about it. She's alive. She don't have nobody on top of her right now and that's because of me. I can look at you in the eye sitting right there without blinking once when I say that I would do it twice over again. If you can't handle that then that's just too bad.

HARRISON: *(Taking a breath, crossing his arms)* This is a complicated case.

DOLA: Guess this is where we reach a dead end then.

HARRISON: I like challenges. *(She's surprised)* We'll try. I never make any promises. I'm not that kind of lawyer. But I'm going to try. Whatever it takes.

DOLA: You mean that …?

HARRISON: If I say it I mean it. I'll get started on it tonight.

DOLA:	Okay. *(Pause)* Can you do me a favor?
HARRISON:	Do you want something from the vending machine?
DOLA:	Sure. Chips and a Coke. That's a gourmet meal 'round here.
HARRISON:	I can only imagine.
DOLA:	You really can't. Can you do something else for me?
HARRISON:	Sure. What is it?
DOLA:	Visit my mama. I know she doesn't like places like these. They make her nervous. Brings back memories of when my daddy was inside before he was killed. So it takes a lot to get her down here. She doesn't like it and I don't like it for her. If you can visit her, make sure she's okay, talk to her — I'd appreciate it.
HARRISON:	I can do that. Yeah. I can do that.
DOLA:	I'm supposed to be graduating high school soon, going to prom and all that. Can't now. I know those aren't big deals but they feel like it right now.
HARRISON:	I understand.
DOLA:	Thank you.
HARRISON:	Don't thank me yet. Let me get that gourmet meal for you.

(They look at each other for a beat. DOLA fighting back emotion. HARRISON examining her silent pain. He gives a sympathetic grin. Nods. He stands up and exits, leaving DOLA sitting and waiting. Waiting for so many things.)

END OF PLAY

MOLLIE AND HARRY

by Tom Block

CHARACTERS

MOLLIE: An 88-year-old widower. She has dementia and is slowly slipping off into the Great Night. Any race or ethnicity.

HARRY: Dated MOLLIE in high school. Never married and always harbored a secret love for her. He has not seen her in 65 years since the day MOLLIE and Ellis married. Any race or ethnicity.

SETTING

MOLLIE's bedroom, where she is fading out of life. MOLLIE lies in her bed, exhausted yet mumbling to herself. A single lamp throws a circle of light up near her head. A seat waits next to her.

TIME

2022.

PRODUCTION HISTORY

MOLLIE and HARRY was performed as part of the Cut Edge Collective 10-minute play festival, Tank Theater, 312 W. 36th Street, New York, NY, February 9 and 10, 2023. Directed by Tom Block. The cast was as follows:

MOLLIE: Laurie Sammeth

HARRY: David Baker

MOLLIE's bedroom, where she is fading out of life. MOLLIE lies in her bed, exhausted yet mumbling to herself. A single lamp throws a circle of light up near her head. A seat waits next to her.

HARRY pokes his head onstage, with a hat in his hands. He clears his throat loudly.

MOLLIE: *(Not looking over at the noise.)* Ellis? I thought you were dead.

HARRY: No, Mollie. It's me. Harry.

MOLLIE: Good. Ellis is dead. *(Pause.)* Who's Harry?

HARRY: Moore. Harry Moore.

MOLLIE: Harry no more? That doesn't make any sense *(giggles)*. Ellis is no more. You're right here.

HARRY: No, Mollie. Harry Moore. Don't you remember? Harry Moore. From high school.

MOLLIE: High school! My goodness. That was a long time ago. At least twenty years ago.

HARRY: Seventy years, Mollie. Seventy years ago.

MOLLIE: Are you that old?

HARRY: Yes I am. And so are you.

MOLLIE: Bite your tongue, old man! It's not nice to call a lady old.

HARRY: I still think you are very beautiful.

MOLLIE: Who are you again?

HARRY: Harry. From high school.

MOLLIE: How am I supposed to remember anything from high school? That was a lifetime ago.

HARRY: We were very close.

MOLLIE: Really. What did you say your name was again?

HARRY:	Harry. Harry Moore.
MOLLIE:	Like Emily Bronte?
HARRY:	Right, Mollie. Right!
MOLLIE:	She's English. Dead, too, I think.
HARRY:	Remember we used to study Haiku together. In the park? "The sun falls open, raining light on you and me, pure joy this Monday." Remember?
MOLLIE:	Haiku.
HARRY:	Yes. Japanese poetry. We used to sit under the Oak tree, next to school. Whitman High School. Don't you remember? We'd stay until dusk and then I walked you home. Did you know we wrote seventy two poems together? We'd alternate words. Do you remember?
MOLLIE:	I'm sorry. Does Ellis know you're here?
HARRY:	Mollie. Ellis has been dead for three years.
MOLLIE:	Right. Ellis is dead. Are you the doctor? Because I'm not sure whatever you are doing is working very well. I can't even get out of bed.
HARRY:	Do you remember anything from high school?
MOLLIE:	*(Pause.)* I didn't know Ellis then.
HARRY:	Anything else?
MOLLIE:	Hmmmm. There was a boy. I forget his name. We spent a lot of time together. I wanted him to kiss me.
HARRY:	You did?
MOLLIE:	Yes. We used to sit under a big tree together. For a long time. Until dusk. We wrote some poems. But I could never concentrate on the words. I just thought about him kissing me.
HARRY:	You did? Really?
MOLLIE:	Yes I did. Now who are you again? And why are you asking me these questions?

HARRY: I'm … I'm that boy, Mollie.

MOLLIE: Don't be absurd. You're an old man.

HARRY: Of course I'm an old man. You're an old lady.

MOLLIE: Don't call a lady "old!" What kind of gentleman
          are you?

HARRY: But the boy under the tree. He wanted to kiss you.

MOLLIE: Then why didn't he?

HARRY: He was scared.

MOLLIE: Of what?

HARRY: *(Long pause.)* Being happy?

MOLLIE: That's absurd. *(Pause.)* Whatever happened to that boy?

HARRY: He grew up.

MOLLIE: I see. Did he become happy?

HARRY: He made lots of money.

MOLLIE: Ellis made lots of money. But then he stopped making
          it. He said we had enough.

HARRY: Were you happy?

MOLLIE: Who are you? Why do you know so much about me?

HARRY: I'm –

MOLLIE: If you're the doctor, you're not doing a very good job.

HARRY: I'm not the doctor, Mollie. I'm the boy you wrote
          Haiku with. Harry.

MOLLIE: I thought that I did that with Ellis.

HARRY: Maybe you did. But before that, you wrote Haiku
          with me.

MOLLIE: What is Haiku, again?

HARRY: Were you happy, Mollie? With Ellis.

MOLLIE: If this is couples therapy, you're too late. Ellis is dead. And anyway I told Marilyn that her father and I had come to an agreement. It was too expensive to divorce. So we would just make do.

HARRY: So you weren't happy with Ellis?

MOLLIE: Of course I was happy with Ellis. He was my husband. Why do you keep asking me these questions?

HARRY: I never got married.

MOLLIE: Did you ever try to get married?

HARRY: No.

MOLLIE: Then it's your own fault. *(Tries to lean conspiratorially across to the visitor.)* Want to know a secret?

HARRY: Yes. Yes, I do Mollie.

MOLLIE: How do you know my name?

HARRY: That's not a secret.

MOLLIE: *(Giggles.)* You are a sassy one. You remind me of someone I knew once. His name was Harry.

HARRY: Really? Did you like him, this Harry?

MOLLIE: Oh, very, very much. I loved him.

HARRY: Really?

MOLLIE: Yes. He broke my heart.

HARRY: Really?

MOLLIE: Yes. He didn't kiss me. When we were under the tree. Writing that silly poetry. I hated the poetry, but I loved him.

HARRY: You loved him?

MOLLIE: Yes. I loved him my whole life. I waited.

HARRY: You waited?

MOLLIE: Yes. Every day I thought that he'd come back for me. But he never did. He never told me why he went away.

HARRY: He had to join the army. The Korean War. Well, peace action. Anyway. He had to leave.

MOLLIE: Why didn't he come back?

HARRY: He did. But you were with Ellis.

MOLLIE: How do you know these things?

HARRY: Because I'm Harry. I'm the boy you were waiting for.

MOLLIE: Don't be absurd. You don't look at all like Harry. He was much younger. You're an old man.

HARRY: You're an old lady.

MOLLIE: *(Gasps.)* You shouldn't talk to ladies about their age!

HARRY: Mollie. It's me. Harry. I came back. I came to …

MOLLIE: Yes?

HARRY: To tell you that I love you. I've loved you my whole life. I never loved anyone but you.

MOLLIE: *(Pause.)* That is not an appropriate way for a doctor to talk to their patient.

HARRY: Mollie. Don't you know who I am?

MOLLIE: You're my doctor.

HARRY: I'm Harry! I'm Harry from under the tree. I was too scared to kiss you –

MOLLIE: Why, Harry? Why were you scared? Why? I wanted you to kiss me.

HARRY: I don't know. I was scared. I don't know why.

MOLLIE: Harry Haiku? You're Harry Haiku?

HARRY: Yes, Mollie. Yes. I love you. I still love you.

MOLLIE: You don't look like Harry. He was much younger than you. And he had a service uniform on. He was in the service. What do you do?

HARRY: I was in real estate, Mollie. I owned properties in Atlanta. Got in early and sold when the Olympics came through. Made a ton of money.

MOLLIE: Impossible. Harry didn't have two pennies in his pocket to clink together. And he was going to be a writer. A poet. And maybe a college professor. He loved to teach. And he loved beauty.

HARRY: Something inside of me died when —

MOLLIE: Dead? Harry's dead? *(Starts to weep.)* Oh my God! I loved him my whole life.

HARRY: No! Mollie, no.

MOLLIE: He's not dead? Then why didn't he come to visit me? Ever? Why?

HARRY: He did.

MOLLIE: When? When did he come? I never saw him.

HARRY: He's right in front of you.

MOLLIE: I don't see him.

HARRY: Me, Mollie. Me! I'm Harry!

MOLLIE: Don't be absurd. *(Starts to cry.)*

HARRY: Mollie. Mollie. He sent me. Harry sent me. To tell you.

MOLLIE: He did? Harry sent you? You know Harry? My one and only true love. God I loved him. Harry.

HARRY: Yes. Mollie. He sent me to tell you that he loved you. His whole life. He loved you and only you.

MOLLIE: Really? He did? You don't know how happy that makes me. I'm so happy. I loved Haiku Harry. My whole life.

HARRY: He loved you too.

MOLLIE: *(Long pause.)* I'm sorry. Who are you?

HARRY: I'm going to go. I have to go now. *(Stands creakily up.)*

MOLLIE: Okay. Well thank you for visiting. One so rarely gets visitors.

HARRY: Mollie.

MOLLIE: Yes.

HARRY: I love you.

MOLLIE: *(Sternly.)* That is not an appropriate thing for a doctor to say to a patient!

END OF PLAY

ONCE REMOVED

by Jami Brandli

CHARACTERS

ELLIOT, 30s to early 40s, husband. Any race or ethnicity.

MAGGIE, 30s to early 40s, wife. Any race or ethnicity.

They are both diseased with a deep sadness. And they are really, really trying to move through this sadness.

SETTING

A hotel room with a bed made up perfectly. However, there is a BUMP the size of a soccer ball under the covers, right in the middle of the bed.

TIME

Present day.

NOTE

The production will need a balloon.

PRODUCTION HISTORY

Once Removed was presented by the Savannah College of Art and Design on Nov 4–6, 2022. The production was directed by Scott Alan Smith. The cast was as follows:

ELLIOT: Steven Smith

MAGGIE: Chelsea Jensen

ELLIOT enters wearing a long black trench coat. He isn't entirely surprised by the BUMP in the bed. He approaches, tentatively reaching out, then pulling back. He tries a few more times, but he cannot physically, emotionally or psychologically touch the bump. ELLIOT sits on the edge of the bed and releases a deep, heavy sigh ...

There's a sudden KNOCK at the door. ELLIOT flinches. Then more KNOCKING. Rhythmic. Loud. He looks back at the bump and fumbles to smooth out the covers around it.

ELLIOT: You're early!

(He opens the door to reveal MAGGIE, also dressed in a long black trench coat. She's all seductive smiles.)

ELLIOT: Do you want everyone in the hotel to know we're here?

MAGGIE: I couldn't wait.

(She goes to kiss him.)

ELLIOT: Not yet.

(MAGGIE soldiers on to be playful. ELLIOT isn't ready.)

ELLIOT: We agreed on a time.

MAGGIE: So I'm a little early.

ELLIOT: You know I need to get acquainted with this room first.

MAGGIE: You do everything Doctor James tells you?

ELLIOT: *Maggie.*

MAGGIE: *Elliot.*

ELLIOT: We agreed to do our assignment —

MAGGIE: Homework —

ELLIOT: Our homework *by* the rules and you already broke them.

MAGGIE: Let me see what's under that coat —

ELLIOT: Don't! Rules are important.

MAGGIE: Rules are important ... for mental patients and prisoners.

ELLIOT: And us.

MAGGIE: And us. You're right. Mental patient, meet the prisoner. Prisoner, meet the mental patient. This is the part where you laugh.

(ELLIOT quickly glances at the bump in the bed. MAGGIE catches this, looks at the bump, acknowledges its presence.)

MAGGIE: *(Serious)* There's nothing in that bed.

ELLIOT: I know that.

MAGGIE: Nothing under the covers.

ELLIOT: I know.

MAGGIE: No bump.

ELLIOT: No bump.

MAGGIE: No blood.

ELLIOT: No blood.

MAGGIE: *Nothing.* And I'm completely fine. More than fine.

ELLIOT: I know.

MAGGIE: You're not going to hurt me. I know I made it clear in front of Doctor James, but I just want to be clear about that now.

ELLIOT: Clear as clear can be.

MAGGIE: Good. So ...

(MAGGIE playfully pokes him toward the bed.)

MAGGIE: Let me see what's under there.

ELLIOT: Hey. Stop that.

MAGGIE: LET. ME. SEE.

ELLIOT: Maggie! Seriously. No poking allowed —

MAGGIE: I don't remember a "No Poking" rule —

ELLIOT: Seriously. Maggie. STOP. You don't know when to stop — FUCKING STOP!

(MAGGIE stops. Her playful mood is crushed. Now near the bed, they eyeball the bump. ELLIOT steps away.)

ELLIOT: Doctor James says I need to stop apologizing for everything, so I'm not going to tell you I'm sorry for yelling … Even though I am, sorry.

MAGGIE: ELLIOT. It's been months. As in fourteen. Fourteen months and nine days. I'm going insane.

ELLIOT: Me, too.

MAGGIE: So how about this? How about we forget about our homework and just jump into bed. Jump. Like quick. Like how you run off the high dive and just jump into the pool. Don't think, just jump. Just jump. With me.

ELLIOT: I need to do the homework.

MAGGIE: There is nothing in that bed.

ELLIOT: I know.

MAGGIE: And you're not going to hurt me.

ELLIOT: I *know.*

MAGGIE: So?

ELLIOT: Maggie. It's just. I'm sorry —

MAGGIE: DON'T. Say that.

(Beat.)

ELLIOT: I hate that we have to have homework.

(She then puts her face very close to his, her lips longing to kiss. They're about to touch. But don't. Can't. They want this. Need this.)

MAGGIE: Let's do our homework.

ELLIOT: Okay.

MAGGIE: Okay. You go first.

(ELLIOT, nervous again, takes a small step away from the bed.)

ELLIOT: You go first.

MAGGIE: Doctor James said it would be best if you went first.

ELLIOT: I don't remember that.

MAGGIE: I'm shy.

ELLIOT: You're not shy, Maggie.

MAGGIE: About *this* I am. *I am.* Please?

ELLIOT: Fine.

(He removes his trench coat. He's wearing A SUPERHERO COSTUME, EQUIP WITH A BRIGHT RED CAPE. She's astonished.)

MAGGIE: Elliot. Wow. I mean, WOW.

ELLIOT: You like it?

MAGGIE: Do I like it? You certainly did your homework. Turn around.

ELLIOT: Turn around?

MAGGIE: Yeah. Just do a little …

(ELLIOT turns, gaining confidence.)

MAGGIE: Elliot. This is just. WOW.

ELLIOT: You like it.

MAGGIE: That red cape. My superhero.

ELLIOT: I thought maybe you'd like the superhero look.

MAGGIE: You nailed it. *A*+.

ELLIOT: A+?

MAGGIE: Oh yeah. I don't think I can control myself —

ELLIOT: It's your turn now.

MAGGIE: My turn? Oh. I don't know —

ELLIOT: *Maggie.*

MAGGIE: We don't really need to see mine, do we?

ELLIOT: Doctor James said this will help us.

MAGGIE: I'm not so sure about that. My thing isn't very. It's not very. I don't know —

ELLIOT: *Maggie.*

MAGGIE: I went neutral. Okay? Neutral. I didn't know what to do, so I went neutral.

(She reluctantly takes off her trench coat, places it on the edge of the bed. SHE'S WEARING A FLESH COLORED BODY SUIT WITH A BLACK BRA AND BLACK PANTIES. He's not sure what to make of it.)

ELLIOT: It's. It's. Well. It's —

MAGGIE: LAME?

ELLIOT: It's not lame. It's neutral, just like you said.

MAGGIE: LAME. Look at yours and then look at mine. See the difference? Doctor James should give me an F.

ELLIOT: He's not grading us on this.

MAGGIE: He should! He should so I can gauge my failure.

ELLIOT: You didn't fail.

MAGGIE: This would have been so much easier if I'd worn the metal knight suit. But that was also a lame costume. Lame and heavy. And stupid. Just like this one.

(She grabs her trench coat. ELLIOT rushes to the bed and takes hold of her coat. They tug as they speak.)

ELLIOT: Oh no you don't.

MAGGIE: Give it.

ELLIOT: No. We agreed. Maggie. We *agreed*.

(She releases. He takes the coat.)

ELLIOT: Thank you.

(Eyes on the bump, she moves away from the bed. They're now standing on the opposite sides of the room. She covers her privates with her hands.)

MAGGIE: I picked this clearly lame flesh-colored body suit because I thought that it would be, I don't know, easier. Just like Doctor James said, it'd still be me, but me once removed. You can see me without having to *really* see me. You can touch me without having to *really* touch me. Not that you want to see me or touch me —

ELLIOT: Of course I do, Maggie. It's just —

MAGGIE: I know *It's just*. If I hear that one more time — *It's just* followed by *I'm sorry* — I'm going to kill myself.

ELLIOT: Doctor James told you saying things like that it isn't productive.

MAGGIE: And this is? We get the hotel room, just like he said, and wear these costumes to role play and follow rules. We're *doing* our homework, BUT ARE WE IN THAT BED? Are we, Elliot?

ELLIOT: No.

MAGGIE: No. Exactly. I thought that maybe, just maybe, after everything we've tried over the last year, that *this* would be the thing to finally help us. We might as well be home with you sleeping on the couch and me sleeping on the goddam futon in the office.

ELLIOT: It's still early.

MAGGIE: There's nothing in that goddam bed.

ELLIOT: Maggie —

MAGGIE: Nothing!

ELLIOT: Look. I'm trying here. To work through this. I really
             am. You like my costume.

MAGGIE: I love your costume.

ELLIOT: Good. But.

MAGGIE: But what?

ELLIOT: But. It's just —

MAGGIE: Don't do it.

ELLIOT: It's just —

MAGGIE: Elliot.

ELLIOT: It's just that —

MAGGIE: DON'T.

ELLIOT: I'm *sorry*.

MAGGIE: *(Throwing up her hands)* That's it. I'm going to
             kill myself.

ELLIOT: Well I am *sorry*, Maggie.

MAGGIE: For what?

ELLIOT: What am I sorry for?

MAGGIE: Yes. Just exactly *what* are you sorry for?

ELLIOT: I'm sorry for. I'm sorry for everything.

MAGGIE: Nope. Not allowed to be sorry for everything.
             Against the rules.

ELLIOT: That's not a rule.

MAGGIE: It is now! If you're sorry for everything, then that
             means I had no part in what happened. Like I wasn't
             even there when it happened. How do you think
             that makes me feel? Like a goddam figment of your
             imagination.

ELLIOT: But it wasn't your fault.

MAGGIE: I *know* it wasn't my fault. It wasn't *your* fault either. Elliot, I feel terrible that you woke up in our bed full of blood when it happened, but you need to understand there was absolutely nothing you could have done.

ELLIOT: Maybe … Maybe I could have.

MAGGIE: Maybe you could have *what*?

ELLIOT: Maybe I could have … Maybe I could have saved her.

MAGGIE: *(Concerned) Saved* her? Saved *her*.

(Needs to shake it off) No. No, Elliot. You need to move on and, and, and save me. Goddamit. Save *us*.

(A moment, as a great sadness floods the room. They are desperate to keep afloat. They must keep afloat.)

MAGGIE: Elliot? Elliot … I'm sorry for being —

(ELLIOT suddenly breaks and rushes to MAGGIE. He sweeps her up in his arms. She lets out a yelp of surprise.)

MAGGIE: Hey! I'm trying to apologize to you.

ELLIOT: I know.

(He carries her toward the bed, twirling once or twice.)

MAGGIE: It's kind of hard to apologize when you're holding me like this.

ELLIOT: I know.

MAGGIE: I think you may be breaking a rule.

ELLIOT: I know. Okay?

MAGGIE: Okay.

(He puts her down at the foot of the bed. They look at the bump and then at each other.

ELLIOT removes his cape. A moment. MAGGIE removes her bra and panties. Another moment. He removes the rest of his costume until he's just in his black boxers. She then removes her body suit to reveal yet another black bra and panties. He laughs softly. She's a bit embarrassed.)

MAGGIE: I know. I'm so la —

(He kisses her deeply. She melts. Then she looks at him, absolutely stunned in all the right ways.)

MAGGIE: Oh my God, Elliot … There you are.

ELLIOT: Here I am.

(They each move to their side of the bed. Together, they slowly pull back the covers to reveal A LARGE RED BALLOON in the bed. It begins to float. They watch in awe as the red balloon slowly rises up toward the ceiling. Blackout.)

END OF PLAY

A MAN WHO KNOWS HOW TO HOLD A BABY

by Hal Corley

CHARACTERS

BAXTER, 50s. Any race or ethnicity.

ANDY, 19. Any race or ethnicity.

SETTING

A waiting area near an airport gate, Newark, New Jersey.

TIME

August. Now.

PRODUCTION HISTORY

A Man Who Knows How to Hold a Baby was presented by "Related: Adoption Stories for the Stage," Love Swell Productions, Lauren Bergquist, co-producer, North Park Vaudeville Theatre, San Diego, CA, April 1–3, 2022, directed by Samantha Goldstein, co-producer. The cast was as follows:

BAXTER: Ford Neha Curtiss

ANDY: Reace Pudvah

A storm rages outside as thunder and seemingly near hurricane-force winds sound ominously in the dark. Lights up on BAXTER, 50-something, and ANDY, 19, sitting alone in a long row of seats. ANDY is watching a movie on his phone, notably without sound. Visibly agitated, BAXTER holds a nail clipper, and eyes one finger critically.

BAXTER: "Now *there's* a man who knows how to hold a *baby!*" she said. To the room.

ANDY: Hey. Don't do that here.

BAXTER: The whole *room.* Immediately, my *antennae* rose — as they always do 'round your grandmother, especially in those days — and I think to myself, "Now what was *that* about? 'A man who knows how to hold a baby.'"

ANDY: Uncle Joey you mean? Uncle Joey was "the man?"

BAXTER: Sure, *he'd* produced three kids "the old-fashioned way," he and his nasty do-gooder wife.

ANDY: Nasty, hasn't she done, like, missionary work in Costa Rica?

BAXTER: I'm sorry but she can be just plain unkind at home. And okay — so Joey knew how to change a diaper — whoop-de-*do,* I always loved the irony: folks who wouldn't use paper towels eschewing the cloth variety. Must be a landfill somewhere full of their personal cache of disposables.

ANDY: What is your point?

BAXTER: I'm getting to it — and so, talented-with-a-Huggie Joey *also* knew how to position a baby's head so it wouldn't wobble. So did *I.* That stuff's textbook self-help. Not something in the paternal DNA.

ANDY: Whatever. Don't do that here, Dad, come on.

BAXTER: I'm not clipping random nails, as you might say; I have a hangnail.

ANDY: So don't deal with it in an airport!

BAXTER: I don't chew mine in public like some people. Whose
           musical skills should inspire them to protect their
           precious fingertips —

ANDY: You always, like, trim away, so anybody can see, even
           when you don't have hangnails. Who else carries a nail
           clipper in his pocket?

BAXTER: I purposely brought an old rusty one —

ANDY: Real healthy, rust.

BAXTER: — to clear security, one that didn't have the supposedly
           threatening but useless knife attachment. Got it
           through, didn't I?

ANDY: What a relief.

BAXTER: So anyway — from *that* moment on, your granny
           always made this distinction between *my* skills and
           those of biological —

ANDY: That was, like, twenty years ago.

BAXTER: It was a curse she put out at that family reunion,
           a curse on me.

ANDY: That is so, like, over the top.

BAXTER: So was she, believe me. Feeling justified, questioning
           my daddy talents.

ANDY: She was totally fine about your "daddy talents" later.

BAXTER: Sure, after they were on spectacular display and
           couldn't be denied. She initially failed to acknowledge
           even their potential.

ANDY: Lighten up. Only grandmother I ever had.

BAXTER: Well, I love *that*. That you got a hands-on grandma.
           The — the cookie-baking, over-the-river-n'-through-
           the-woods stuff? Sure, terrific, all that. But boy! When
           a vote of confidence counted, was she ever ready with
           the thinly veiled insults!

ANDY: Since when do you call her "Granny" and "Grandma?" I can always tell when you're nervous about stuff, you start using all these, like, cutesy names for things.

BAXTER: What else did I say that was "cutesy" tonight?

ANDY: "Daddy talents?" Or telling me to eat up at home cause we'll be forced to go to "Mickey D's" the next coupla days. You never say, "Micky D's." Cut that shit out.

BAXTER: I always come back to that reunion when you were five weeks old because I must —

(ANDY lets out an exasperated sigh.)

In addition to drawing this line down the center of their over-decorated living room, with the fruitful parents on one side and your poor barren mom and pop on the other —

ANDY: T.M.I.

BAXTER: — everybody handled you with this sense of entitlement. Like they had the right to paw you.

ANDY: Whatever, like I said, twenty *years* —

BAXTER: We'd just been told by the pediatrician *not* to let every stranger who wanted to coochie-coochie-coo you have at it —

ANDY: Uncle Joey and Aunt Mary Lou weren't strangers.

BAXTER: But they let your cousins put their sticky mitts all over you. They were always eating some cheap garbage candy — Joey bragged about your cousins loving broccoli but ignored their high fructose corn syrup addiction.

ANDY: They did eat a lotta crap growin' up.

BAXTER: And were encouraged to toss ya around like their doll. Like you were common property. "Gimme Baby Andrew!" "No, it's my turn with Baby Andy!" "*I* called dibs on Baby Andy in the car!" Terrible way to start things off. Oh, those *people* —

ANDY: Okay now, Dad. We're done.

BAXTER: Remember when you first started playing? How
            obsessed they were with "where" you got the talent?
            You'd think "from God" would shut 'em up, but no.
            "Your mother and father"— they always italicized the
            words when they said 'em about Mom and me —
            "They can't play the harmonica, and here *you* are, a
            darned Paderewski." Like they know from Paderewski.
            Or harmonicas.

ANDY: Don't get so worked up.

BAXTER: They truly believe we're just stand-in parents. Like
            they'd know how to raise a prodigy. And I tell ya, it all
            started at that fateful reunion —

ANDY: Dad, chill. You're all weirded out.

BAXTER: — when they suggested I didn't know bupkis about
            burping you.

ANDY: *Dad.* Calm down. Just go over there and clip your
            nails, okay?

BAXTER: Why can't you just be patient with me?

(ANDY puts a hand up; silence.)

            I'm sorry. This trip, it just brings all that up.

ANDY: You wanted me to take this trip.

BAXTER: But that doesn't mean it's easy!

            (Because:) I have spent the last nineteen years
            defending my turf.

ANDY: Why?

BAXTER: 'Cause you're my son and there are people, like your
            grandmother used to be, and like your narrow-minded
            aunt and uncle still are, who want to remind me that
            I'm a parent *only* by going an alternate route.

ANDY: You want everybody else to get over it, why don't you?

BAXTER: You're young, predisposed to make complex issues sound simple. You don't get it, your mom and me have been made to feel —

ANDY: Like second class parents! I *know*! But if you aren't — if *you* don't really think you are yourself — stop bringing it up!

(Thunder sounds in the distance.)

BAXTER: This feels like the end of the road somehow.

ANDY: Well, it's not.

BAXTER: I mean, I'm really not threatened by your meeting him. I want you to know him and feel whatever about him you end up feeling. Or so I tell myself. Ask me again on the way home. But uncomfortable or whatever, it just feels the end of something for *me*.

ANDY: So then why don't you not go? *(BAXTER just stares.)* Maybe the storm's a good thing. You don't have to get on the plane.

BAXTER: Ridiculous! My luggage is on! Ours. We shared the suitcase —

ANDY: You don't *have* to go.

BAXTER: But you asked me to come. That meant everything. Now you don't want me to go?

ANDY: Probably wasn't fair.

BAXTER: But what if this guy's a handful?

ANDY: I'll *handle* it. Two days at "Micky D's" and I'm outta there.

BAXTER: I've wanted to run since we got here. Storm hit, I thought phew, ground the planes, we'll jump in a cab and be home in time to eat dinner with your mom. Who's a wreck, I'm sure. You know she's sitting there, a blubbery mess.

ANDY: Mom's sipping chamomile tea, totally, like, glad she's got the house to herself.

BAXTER: Look, in the month since you planned this, do you know how many people have said, "So your boy's finally meeting his real father?"

ANDY: I have *never* referred to him as my real father.

BAXTER: And, of course, this has the potential to be the golden moment of a lifetime. The two of you sitting down to play twin pianos together, tone-deaf me twiddling my well-trimmed thumbs, applauding in the background —

ANDY: Daddy! It's not! The moment! Of a lifetime!

(Silence.)

Did you bring the old, refilled iPod?

BAXTER: I hate that thing. Or those earphones. Like gnats.

(ANDY hands him a traditional headset.)

ANDY: Here. The old-fashioned kind.

BAXTER: I don't want to listen to anything now —

ANDY: I put stuff on you like.

BAXTER: I'm not in the mood to be reminded of the glorious eighties —

ANDY: I put *me* on there. Me.

(BAXTER stares at it.)

Playing.

BAXTER: Really?

ANDY: Me, doing the Debussy Arabesque No. 1.

BAXTER: You did not.

ANDY: So will you listen and shut up a while?

(Silence.)

BAXTER: Did you really think I wouldn't get on the plane with you?

ANDY: Just listen to Debussy, and let me watch my movie, okay?

(BAXTER puts on the headset, ANDY hits the button on the iPod. BAXTER winces, shaking his head.)

BAXTER: Okay, gotta say it: maybe *not* your very *best* recording.

(ANDY throws his hands up.)

I'm sorry, but you put the microphone *way* too close. I've told you, how many times. *(ANDY adjusts in his seat, silently fuming.)* I'm sorry, it just gives it that rinky-dink tinkly player piano sound that doesn't do justice to your work. Also, there's an echo — *(ANDY turns away.)* Well, there is. I'm telling you, 'cause I *have* to. With your gift, you always deserve the unvarnished truth. And I have a right to give it, to be critical of details. I've earned it — *(BAXTER stops, takes off the headset.)* "Now there's a man who knows how to hold a baby."

(BAXTER puts a hand on ANDY's knee.) Andy? It's beautiful.

(He returns to the headset, listening intently. Exasperated, ANDY goes back to his movie. BAXTER steals a glance—and then lingers: He stares at his son with fresh wonder. As Debussy wafts in, it's overtaken by thunder; lights fade.)

END OF PLAY

THE MOST PRECIOUS THING

by Amy Dellagiarino

CHARACTERS

JACQUELINE, female, 30s, A frazzled and broken person who has given up on whatever it is she wanted her life to be. Any race or ethnicity.

CHARLIE, male, female, or nonbinary (director's choice), 30s, A frazzled and optimistic person who has one job and is trying really hard to be good at it. Any race or ethnicity.

SETTING

Inside Jaqueline's mind. There is a desk … That's it.

TIME

Present day.

PRODUCTION HISTORY

The Most Precious Thing was presented by the Santa Cruz County Actor's Theatre January 20–February 18, 2023. The production was directed by Sarah Albertson. The cast was as follows:

JAQUELINE: Manirose Bobisuthi

CHARLIE: Tristan Ahn

A small room with bare walls. The only thing inside of it is a desk. CHARLIE smiles down at JAQUELINE, who sits on the floor rubbing her head.

JAQUELINE: Ow.

CHARLIE: *(Brandishing a pocket watch)* Jaqueline! Welcome! Just in time!

JAQUELINE: *(Looking around)* What ... what is happening?

CHARLIE: *(Consulting the watch)* You have five minutes!

JAQUELINE: Okay. *(Beat.)* For what?

CHARLIE: Oh, right! Sorry! You don't know. So hi, my name is Charlie and I'm here to guide you on your Unconscious Journey for today. Well, for the next five minutes, at least.

JAQUELINE: Am I supposed to know what you're saying?

CHARLIE: Am I not being clear?

JAQUELINE: I'm unconscious?

CHARLIE: *(Excited, she's getting it)* Yes!

JAQUELINE: How did I become unconscious?

CHARLIE: You sort of fell off of a ladder and hit your head when you were trying to put a mannequin torso up on the shelf above the register at The Unspooled Thread.

JAQUELINE: *(It dawns on her)* I'm unconscious *at work.*

CHARLIE: Exactly!

JAQUELINE: Am I ... am I dead? *(In horror)* Did I *die* there?

CHARLIE: No — no! You're very much alive! *(Consults the watch again)* Well ... very much alive for the next five minutes.

JAQUELINE: For the next five minutes I'm alive.

CHARLIE: Yes.

JAQUELINE: So I'm *basically* dead. I've basically died doing retail, is what you're saying.

CHARLIE: No, that's not — sorry, I'm not explaining this right. It's my first day.

JAQUELINE: At *what?*

CHARLIE: *(It is very obvious)* Being your guide. For your Unconscious Journey.

JAQUELINE: *(Overwhelmed)* Oh my god.

(JAQUELINE runs around the room, pounding on the walls, looking for a way out.)

JAQUELINE: Hello? Is anybody there?

CHARLIE: There's nobody there.

JAQUELINE: *(Banging on the walls)* Hello?

CHARLIE: There's nobody there, we're in your mind. It's just the two of us.

JAQUELINE: *(In horror)* Oh no is this hell? Am I in hell?
             (A realization) I *am.* I'm in hell while also being at work — I'm in a hell inside of another hell.
             I'm in a Russian doll of hells.

CHARLIE: I told you, we're in your mind, *not hell.*

JAQUELINE: *That is hell!*

CHARLIE: Okay well that is very sad.

JAQUELINE: *Get me out of here! How do I get out of here?*

CHARLIE: You'll be out in *five minutes,* that's what I've been saying — You're kind of at the crossroads, which is where *I* come in.

JAQUELINE: The crossroads of *what?*

CHARLIE: Of life! And — and death.

JAQUELINE: So I *am* dying.

CHARLIE: Not necessarily!

JAQUELINE: How can I be at the crossroads of life *and death* and yet *not necessarily* be *dying?*

CHARLIE: We just have to look in the desk, that's all, okay? Easy.

(JAQUELINE is taken aback. It's as though she's just noticed the desk for the first time, even though it's the only thing in the room.)

JAQUELINE: The — the desk?

CHARLIE: Yeah — am I being unclear again? *(To himself)* I *feel* like I said that clearly ...

JAQUELINE: Why?

CHARLIE: Because! Inside are the contents of what you think your life is worth. The higher the value, the more the guarantee you wake up to — well, to life. The lower the value ... That's where the watch comes in.

JAQUELINE: What do you mean?

CHARLIE: If the worth of your life is quite ... low then you still have some time to argue about why it's a life worth living.

JAQUELINE: And for that you get *five minutes?*

CHARLIE: *(Consulting the watch again)* Well ... *four* minutes now, actually.

JAQUELINE: *What?!*

CHARLIE: Don't worry! I'm sure you won't need it. It's a "just in case" thing.

JAQUELINE: But — but the desk looks empty.

CHARLIE: That's just on *top*, that doesn't necessarily mean anything. Sometimes people compress their life's value into *one* thing, like a really big diamond or something, and put it in one of the drawers. I wouldn't worry about it, seriously. There's probably something really great in here, like a Fabergé egg.

(CHARLIE pulls open the drawer and stares down into it.)

CHARLIE: Oh. *(Beat.)* Oh wow.

JAQUELINE: What? What is it?

CHARLIE: I've just … never seen this before.

JAQUELINE: Seen *what?*

(CHARLIE reaches into the drawer and brings out …. one quarter. He places it on the desk with a plink.)

JAQUELINE: A quarter.

CHARLIE: … Yes.

JAQUELINE: You think my life is worth *one quarter.*

CHARLIE: No! *No — you* think your life is worth one quarter.

(Beat.)

CHARLIE: *(Consulting the watch)* It's okay — you still have like three and a half minutes to convince yourself otherwise.

(Beat.)

JAQUELINE: Oh my god, I'm gonna die at work.

CHARLIE: Not necessarily!

JAQUELINE: Oh my god.

(JAQUELINE sinks down to the floor.)

CHARLIE: Wait — so you're just … giving up? That's *it?*

JAQUELINE: Yes, why is that *so surprising?* You've *seen the evidence*, my life is worth only *one quarter*, it's *hopeless.*

CHARLIE: So *change your mind.*

JAQUELINE: You act like it's *that* simple.

CHARLIE: It *is* that simple!

JAQUELINE: How would *you* know? You've never done this before, you have no idea what you're doing!

CHARLIE: Well that's very hurtful.

(Beat. Both JAQUELINE and CHARLIE sulk in silence for a
moment. Slowly, JAQUELINE reaches out her hand for the quarter.
Understanding, CHARLIE hands it to her. She stares at it in her
palm, turning it over and over in her hands for a moment.)

JAQUELINE: My dad would be so pissed at me right now. He was
             always telling me I could be whatever I wanted to
             be. Like he really *believed* it, you know?

CHARLIE: But you didn't?

JAQUELINE: I don't know. It seemed ... like a lot to believe
             I guess.

CHARLIE: Why?

JAQUELINE: It just seemed easier not to, honestly. It can be a lot
             of pressure — all that belief.

CHARLIE: What do you mean?

JAQUELINE: Oh, who knows.

(But she does. Beat.)

JAQUELINE: My mom died when I was seven. She was hit by a
             car while running, isn't that so dumb? That seems
             like the kind of stuff that only happens in movies
             or sappy TV dramas or something. She was always
             a very conscientious runner, too. She wore reflective
             clothing and looked both ways multiple times when
             crossing the street and all that junk. She only ever
             ran with one headphone in, so she could be on
             alert. It didn't seem fair, you know? That someone
             could be that careful and have it still not matter.
             And I was their only child, so when Mom died, it
             was just me and Dad. I was the only place he put
             his love. So much love. It felt like I was drowning in
             it. It felt like it was swallowing me up. Like I would
             die in love. And at the same time ... he was so sad.
             Just the saddest, most broken man. So it was like ...
             even though he was pouring all of his love into me,

I still wasn't quite enough to save him. From all that sadness.

(JAQUELINE looks at the quarter in her hand.)

JAQUELINE: You know what's so stupid? This quarter — it reminds me — there was this little claw machine outside the grocery store we used to go to, filled with cheap toys and shit. Oh man, I used to love it. I would *beg* my parents to let me play. And this one night — it was maybe a year after my mom died — this one night I snuck out of the house with my piggy bank to go find that machine to win a stupid toy for my dad. I was like *convinced* that would fix him. Man … that machine ate *all* my quarters. But I didn't mind, because I had this one lucky one that I had painted with red nail polish, and I just *knew* that would be the one that …

(JAQUELINE sits up suddenly.)

JAQUELINE: That would be the one that would win.

(JAQUELINE stares down at the quarter in her hand.)

CHARLIE: … Uh, what? What is it?

JAQUELINE: This quarter. It's the same quarter. With the red nail polish.

(She holds it out to CHARLIE.)

JAQUELINE: See?

CHARLIE: Uh … okay.

JAQUELINE: It's the same one I used. My last quarter. The lucky one. The one that won that janky green plush rabbit. My dad still has that rabbit. It's on his bookshelf. He says …

(She begins to become emotional.)

JAQUELINE: He says it's the best gift he's ever got. That cheap, janky, gross old rabbit. *(In wonder)* Rabbits aren't even *green*. And he loves it.

(She looks up at CHARLIE.)

JAQUELINE: He loves it, Charlie. *(A realization)* This isn't just *a* quarter. This is *the* quarter. The quarter that brought my dad's smile back. Oh my god. Charlie. This is the most precious thing.

(They stare at each other for a beat. Charlie consults his watch.)

CHARLIE: Time's up.

END OF PLAY

THE PITY MOURNER

by Paul Donnelly

CHARACTERS

MARGARET HENSLOW — Late Middle-aged, female, somewhat astringent.

ARCHIE ST. CLAIRE — Later Middle-aged, male, a bit more gregarious.

SETTING

A small viewing parlor in a funeral home. Can be represented with a settee and small side table with a box of tissues.

TIME

The present

PRODUCTION HISTORY

The Pity Mourner was presented by the Lauderdale-by-the-Sea Seaside Players Sea Shorts Short Play Festival in Lauderdale-by-the-Sea, FL, June 3–12, 2022. The production was directed by Brenda Aulbach. The cast was as follows:

MARGARET HENSLOW: Judy Goldstein

ARCHIE ST. CLAIRE: Fred Rallo

MARGARET HENSLOW, *a woman in late middle age, sits alone in a viewing parlor. MARGARET fidgets. SHE stands and crosses to the doorway. SHE waits for a bit then returns to the settee and sits. SHE remains distracted. After a few uncomfortable beats, ARCHIE ST. CLAIRE, a man in slightly later middle age, enters. MARGARET leaps to her feet to greet him.*

MARGARET: Thank you so much for coming.

ARCHIE: Very sorry for your loss.

(An awkward silence. Then simultaneously:)

MARGARET: I don't believe we've ...   ARCHIE: It must have been ...

(An awkward silence. Then simultaneously:)

MARGARET: I'm so sorry.   ARCHIE: I'm sorry.

(An awkward silence. Then simultaneously:)

MARGARET: Please go ahead.   ARCHIE: Please go ahead.

(After a beat.)

MARGARET: I don't believe we've met.

ARCHIE: Archie. Archie St. Claire.

MARGARET: So nice of you to think of us.

ARCHIE: Oh it seemed the least I could do.

(Another moment of awkward silence.)

(ARCHIE looks off R.)

ARCHIE: I see you went with the closed casket.

MARGARET: Mother insisted.

ARCHIE: Much less upsetting I think.

MARGARET: That was hardly her concern.

(ARCHIE looks puzzled.)

MARGARET: She didn't want people to see her with more make up than she had worn in her entire life. For someone with no vanity, she was surprisingly vain.

(ARCHIE nods.)

MARGARET: But then you must have known how she was.

(ARCHIE nods)

MARGARET: It's really so good of you to be here.

ARCHIE: I'm surprised there are no other …

MARGARET: So am I. But I guess I really shouldn't be. Aunt Enid's not well enough to travel and Pepper has to stay to look after her. I didn't quite get why cousin Tony couldn't come, but he's not here.

ARCHIE: Small family, then.

MARGARET: That's the lot of us.

(An awkward silence.)

ARCHIE: Those are two lovely floral arrangements.

MARGARET: One from my firm and one from my father.

ARCHIE: Oh.

MARGARET: You sound surprised.

ARCHIE: Since he isn't here I thought maybe he had passed first.

MARGARET: No. I'm surprised the card didn't read, "Ha. Ha. I'm still here!"

ARCHIE: Bit competitive were they?

MARGARET: They divorced when I was in sixth grade.

ARCHIE: Just a few years ago then.

MARGARET: You're too kind, Mr. St. Clair.

ARCHIE: Archie, please.

MARGARET: How did you know Mother?

ARCHIE: Oh, from around.

MARGARET: She hadn't been out of the nursing home in years. Of course none of those people will come. Too close to home. Who's next and all that. I don't remember you from the old neighborhood …

ARCHIE: No.

MARGARET: And Mother wasn't much of one for church …

ARCHIE: I guess I should come clean.

MARGARET: Yes?

ARCHIE: Truth be told I didn't know your mother.

MARGARET: Oh?

ARCHIE: I came to pay my respects to Lucy Buchanan across the hall.

MARGARET: Then how did you end up here?

ARCHIE: Well Lucy has a full house.

MARGARET: How nice.

ARCHIE: Then I saw you sitting over here by yourself and I thought "that poor woman, it's just not right that she should have to sit there alone."

MARGARET: I see.

ARCHIE: I hope I haven't given offense.

MARGARET: It is a bit odd. A pity mourner. Tells you all you need to know about Mother that that's the only kind she's got.

ARCHIE: What about your friends?

MARGARET: Isn't that the question of the day?

ARCHIE: It's early yet.

MARGARET: I'm not expecting a closing rush.

(An awkward silence.)

ARCHIE: I guess I should be going back …

MARGARET: You don't have to rush off. I appreciate the company.

(An awkward silence.)

ARCHIE: Guess you never know what fate's going to throw your way.

MARGARET: Isn't that the truth?

ARCHIE: I mean here we are. Strangers not five minutes ago …

MARGARET: And now strangers still.

ARCHIE: Nothing like one of these occasions to remind you that life is short.

MARGARET: If you say so.

ARCHIE: So don't pass up any opportunity however unlikely.

(An awkward silence.)

ARCHIE: I really should be going to pay my respect to Lucy.

MARGARET: I suppose.

ARCHIE: Since you don't have much of a crowd would you like to pop over with me?

MARGARET: I'm not going to abandon my mother, Mr. St. Claire.

ARCHIE: Archie.

MARGARET: Even if that makes me the only one who doesn't.

ARCHIE: No. Of course. And I've no doubt people will turn up.

MARGARET: We live in hope.

ARCHIE: I do. It's what lets me ask, would you care to have dinner later?

MARGARET: Mr. St. Claire?

ARCHIE: These things should be over by eight.

MARGARET: I don't think so.

ARCHIE: No point in you having to dine alone after …

MARGARET: Is this usually how you go about meeting women? Beats the internet I suppose.

ARCHIE: It's nothing of the kind.

MARGARET: It seems odd …

ARCHIE: You're not feeling that it's Kismet throwing us together like this?

MARGARET: This is hardly the time or place …

ARCHIE: Your mother's way of making sure you're not left all alone?

MARGARET: I'm not … What makes you think …

ARCHIE: If you had a fella he'd be here wouldn't he?

(MARGARET does not respond.)

ARCHIE: If I had a girl she'd be here with me, so we're even.

MARGARET: You should get to your friend's viewing.

ARCHIE: And leave you here alone like this …

MARGARET: I'm used to it.

ARCHIE: And I'm saying you shouldn't have to be.

(A beat.)

MARGARET: Do you really want to see me again?

ARCHIE: Yes, I do.

MARGARET: Are you free tomorrow?

ARCHIE: Sure.

MARGARET: During the day?

ARCHIE: I can get free.

MARGARET: Then meet me here at 10:30 tomorrow morning.

ARCHIE: Here?

MARGARET: That way I won't have to go to the internment alone.

(A beat.)

MARGARET: Never mind. It was a stupid idea.

ARCHIE: Not at all.

MARGARET: I'm not at all myself.

ARCHIE: I'd be honored to ...

MARGARET: You'll do it?

ARCHIE: If we might lunch after ...

MARGARET: That's certainly to be expected, isn't it?

(A beat.)

ARCHIE: All right then. I will see you here tomorrow morning at 10:30.

MARGARET: Very good. Now you really should go pay your respects to your friend.

ARCHIE: Shame she's not here to hear about this one. She'd be tickled pink.

MARGARET: I will see you tomorrow, Mr. St. Claire.

ARCHIE: Archie.

(A beat.)

MARGARET: Archie.

ARCHIE: Perhaps I should know your name.

MARGARET: Margaret. Margaret Henslow.

ARCHIE: Pleased to meet you, Margaret. Very sorry for the circumstances.

MARGARET: I can't say it isn't odd.

(A beat.)

ARCHIE: Well then, goodbye for now.

MARGARET: Yes. And Archie ...

ARCHIE: Yes?

MARGARET: Thank you for dropping by.

ARCHIE: Until tomorrow.

(ARCHIE exits.)

MARGARET: Well how do you like that, Mother?

(Lights fade to black.)

END OF PLAY

INTIMATE MATTERS

by Mikki Gillette

CHARACTERS

JENNA — 25, a trans woman; she's attractive and confident, with a wry sense of humor, and a weariness born from some hard experiences.

NIALL — 25, a cis man; open, guileless and easily embarrassed, he's prone to making *faux pas*, and attempting to smooth them over

SETTING

A restaurant in a U.S. city. The romantic ambiance at time clashes with the tone of the pair's talk.

TIME

Present day.

PUNCTUATION NOTES

A stroke (/) marks the point of interruption in overlapping dialogue.

A dash (-) marks the halting of a thought.

PRODUCTION HISTORY

Intimate Matters was produced by Fuse Theatre Ensemble at the Old Moody Stages in Portland, OR in September 2021. The production was directed by Asae Dean. The cast was as follows:

JENNA: Juliet Mylan

NIALL: Heath Hyun Houghton

A Restaurant. NIALL and JENNA sit at a table.

NIALL: I enjoyed meeting you at the party. Thanks for coming out tonight.

JENNA: Of course. I'm glad / you asked

NIALL: Oh, when I said, "coming out," I didn't mean, like, because you're transgender. I / just meant here

JENNA: Right.

NIALL: Sorry . . . I don't mean to be weird about, you know . . . I think it's great, personally.

JENNA: Um, thanks? . . . Have you eaten here before? The menu looks good.

NIALL: Yes . . . I hope that wasn't awkward just now when I said I / think it's great

JENNA: *(becoming annoyed)* It was . . . fine.

NIALL: Oh, good.

JENNA: How do you know Vince and Aubrey?

NIALL: Aubrey and I went to school together. How about you?

JENNA: I met Vince through work. I was glad he invited me. They're good party hosts.

NIALL: Definitely. When Aubrey invites me, I'm there . . . *(Beat)* So, J.K. Rowling — what the fuck, huh?

JENNA: I'm sorry?

NIALL: You know, with the / anti-trans stuff

JENNA: Are you bringing up J.K. Rowling because I'm trans and it's the first thing you think of when, like, you look at me, or something?

NIALL: Oh, I mean, um . . . maybe. That's bad, isn't it?

JENNA: It's kind of weird. I guess it's good that you didn't ask me about surgeries before our appetizers came, though.

NIALL: Haha, right. Totally.

JENNA: You weren't just about to ask me about surgeries, /were you?

NIALL: No . . . I mean, um — honestly, yes, I / was

JENNA: Wow.

NIALL: I was sort of . . . working my way toward — I should just stop / talking

JENNA: Jesus . . . Vince mentioned / you were kind of awkward

NIALL: In my defense, you and I are on a date, so . . .

JENNA: So . . . what, exactly? You thought, "Why not / bring up

NIALL: No. I, you know, thought we might . . . at some point, maybe, become "intimate," and . . .

JENNA: You didn't think I would have shared . . . some things before that happened?

NIALL: *(embarrassed, flustered)* Oh, was I supposed to wait?

JENNA: I don't know. There's not, like, an authoritative etiquette guide on the matter. I think you're always on safe ground not asking people about their / genitals

NIALL: Right, sorry . . . We are on a date, though . . .

JENNA: Yes, I believe you / mentioned that

NIALL: Right.

(Pause.)

JENNA: I feel like you're just sitting there obsessing on my groin now.

NIALL: I don't mean / to, it's

JENNA: What if I spent our whole dinner speculating indirectly about the size of your penis?

NIALL: Oh . . . I guess I'd feel a little self-conscious.

JENNA: I'm not / surprised

NIALL: Did you want to know the size of / my penis

JENNA: No! It was a hypothetical / question

NIALL: Right. Sorry.

JENNA: It would be nice to just get to know you a little as
           people before, you know, discussing "those things."

NIALL: Oh, okay.

JENNA: What were you like in high school, for instance?

NIALL: Me? I was kind of quiet.

JENNA: Aww. Were you a daydreamer?

NIALL: *(suddenly)* Were you a boy in high school?
           Oh my / gosh

JENNA: What?!

NIALL: Sorry. It just occurred to / me that

(Jenna gathers her things, upset.)

JENNA: I can't do this.

NIALL: No, wait. Please. I promise I wasn't trying to upset you.

JENNA: You asked what gender I was in high school, but you
           "weren't trying to / upset me?"

NIALL: No, I wasn't . . . I was just curious, I swear.

JENNA: Okay . . . but it did upset me, do you understand that?

NIALL: Oh. I'm sorry. Do you want to say / why it

JENNA: I'm a woman. I don't want to be asked about when
           I was forced to act like / I was a boy . . .

NIALL: That makes sense. Sorry . . . will you stay? On our
           date, I mean?

JENNA: *(sighs, wary)* I guess.

NIALL: Thanks . . . in high school I was mainly quiet because
           my mom died and when I tried to talk about it, people
           got annoyed.

JENNA: Oh, I'm sorry. That sounds hard.

NIALL: Thanks. I saw a counselor, which helped, and by college things were better.

JENNA: That's good. I like counseling.

NIALL: Oh, did you see a counselor — oops.

(NIALL covers his mouth spontaneously. JENNA appears confused and stunned, then laughs.)

NIALL: Sorry about that. I, um . . . never mind.

JENNA: You were going to ask if / I saw a

NIALL: I stopped myself, though. I realized / it might

JENNA: I feel like an asshole now.

NIALL: No. You shouldn't.

JENNA: I'm some first date fascist, who's taught you to censor / yourself

NIALL: No, it's good. I don't want to be rude / to you

JENNA: I did see a counselor in order to get a letter for my hormones.

NIALL: Right . . . I thought that might have been the case. You didn't need to say that if you didn't / want to, though

JENNA: Fuck. This is the most awkward evening, isn't it?

NIALL: No . . . it's, um, we're getting to know each / other

JENNA: Besides the topic I've said I don't really want to talk about, are there other questions / you had

NIALL: No . . . I was wondering when you thought you might be open to / sharing about

JENNA: Seriously?

NIALL: Just because, you know, it seems like we're getting along so far, so . . .

JENNA: Your optimism is bordering on the delusional.

NIALL:	Huh? . . . I mean, I shared about my mom, / and
JENNA:	Sorry, I shouldn't have said that.
NIALL:	It's okay.
JENNA:	*(with difficulty)* I transitioned in freshman year, and even though I was a girl for almost all of high school, no guy would date me, because they were afraid it would "make them gay."
NIALL:	Oh, sorry. That's awful.
JENNA:	Why would a guy liking a girl be "gay," you know?
NIALL:	It isn't. They were just stupid.
JENNA:	*(upset)* And it's not "stupid" that you're fixated on the status of my genitals now?
NIALL:	Oh, um . . . it's a little different, I think?
JENNA:	In what way?
NIALL:	Well, I agree that you're a woman, and I don't think my being here, regardless of, you know . . . whatever equipment — no, that's dumb, um, / . . .
JENNA:	You don't think dating me makes you gay.
NIALL:	Right. Exactly . . . Having said that, though, I — and this is probably a fault of my own — can't really imagine, you know, any kind of . . . sexual activity I could pleasurably take part in / that would involve ...
JENNA:	That is so basic, Niall.
NIALL:	It's true, though!
JENNA:	I hate when guys say that.
NIALL:	I like intercourse . . . between my penis and a vagina, I mean.
JENNA:	You should speak up. I don't think they heard you in the kitchen.
NIALL:	*(embarrassed, softer)* Oh, right. It is how I feel, though.

JENNA:	Have you even tried anal? On a woman, I mean? It's similar.
NIALL:	It's . . . messy.
JENNA:	Really? . . . Okay, there's oral sex. There's you getting pegged while she wears a / strap on
NIALL:	Jenna.
JENNA:	All right, it sounds like you don't want to / do that . . .
NIALL:	I don't think having . . . a boundary around something like that is — that's okay, isn't it?
JENNA:	It's hurtful. A lot of trans women will never be able to afford surgery.
NIALL:	I understand that.
JENNA:	And you don't care? You're just / like, "I only want . . .
NIALL:	I do care. I've donated to people's GoFundMe's. I think insurance should / cover . . .
JENNA:	So you asked me out just to roll the dice, and see / what I might have down there . . .
NIALL:	No . . . I enjoyed meeting you, and thought you were attractive.
JENNA:	But if I did have a / penis . . .
NIALL:	Arrgh . . . can't you just tell me?
JENNA:	Oh my god.
NIALL:	Sorry. I / shouldn't have said . . .
JENNA:	I had my surgery, Niall. Are you happy?
NIALL:	Um, I mean . . . sort of, or — I meant, I'm happy for you, because I'm / sure you . . .
JENNA:	Yes, I can tell my potential dysphoria was on the top of / your mind.
NIALL:	Do you hate / me?

JENNA:	No . . . your social ineptitude is kind of / charming.
NIALL:	Really? You don't think I'm unbearably dumb?
JENNA:	No.
NIALL:	Oh, wow. I thought from the moment I brought up J.K. Rowling, you'd been looking at me with contempt.
JENNA:	Nope . . . good to know that's the vibe I give off, though, / I guess . . .
NIALL:	Wow, so you're enjoying our date? Oops, that sounded really / desperate . . .
JENNA:	That was a shockingly direct / question.
NIALL:	Right. Sorry. Maybe we should look at / our menus . . .
JENNA:	I've had worse . . . dates, I mean.
NIALL:	Really? Oh, so . . . that's good / then, right
JENNA:	I still think your "preferences" indicate a lack of imagination, on your part.
NIALL:	Oh, um . . .
JENNA:	I guess as a cis male, that's not your / fault, though.
NIALL:	Maybe you . . . could try the "pegging" thing you mentioned — I mean, if / you want . . .
JENNA:	Oh, wow.
NIALL:	I just thought that, since / you brought it up . . .
JENNA:	Right. Let's see where the evening takes us.

(Both lift their menus, smiling.)

END OF PLAY

SOULMATE

by Deirdre Girard

CHARACTERS

LORNA, Female, 30s. Attractive, sophisticated, a bit mysterious. Any race or ethnicity.

JERRY, Male, 40s. Friendly and enthusiastic with a working class attitude and accent. Any race or ethnicity.

SETTING

A Local Train.

TIME

The Present.

PRODUCTION HISTORY

Soulmate was presented by Lowell Arts Theatre in Lowell, MI on October 27–30, 2022, where it was voted Best of Show by a panel of theater professionals. The production was directed by Laurel Conrad. The cast was as follows:

JERRY: Mike Golczynski

LORNA: Mandee Thiell

LORNA *is sitting on a train, reading, heading home after a long day of work. JERRY looks around and then chooses the seat next to her.*

JERRY: Do you mind?

LORNA: *(Not looking up from her reading)* Of course not.

JERRY: Some people, you know how it is, they stack stuff up, put a coat on the seat, pretend the person with them just hit the restroom or something. That's why I always like to ask.

LORNA: The seat's free.

JERRY: *(Sitting)* Great. I know the train's mostly empty, but I never liked sitting alone. I get enough of that at home. *(No response)* Hey, you look familiar …

LORNA: *(With a touch of sarcasm)* Do I?

JERRY: It's not a line, I'm no good at that stuff. I just swear I've seen you somewhere …

LORNA: Perhaps. I take this train pretty frequently.

JERRY: No, it's not that …

LORNA: We'll just have to live with the mystery. *(Beat)* Though I suppose you're used to that.

JERRY: What?

LORNA: Mysteries. You're a police officer aren't you?

JERRY: How did you know that?

(LORNA shrugs.)

JERRY: Please tell me I don't look that much like a cop …

LORNA: I've probably seen you in uniform somewhere.

JERRY: No, I've been plainclothes for years … *(Beat)* Wait! Wait just a minute here! I've got it! I knew I saw you before, I never forget a face. You're Lady Lorna! Oh my God, I can't believe I'm sitting next to you! I saw your show like five, six years ago, an old girlfriend dragged me and I thought it was all bull until you told me about my dad. And there's just no way...Wow. Lady Lorna.

LORNA: Not anymore.

JERRY: What, did you like stop seeing things psychically or something?

LORNA: No, I saw too much and it became ... difficult I guess. I just wanted to tune out. Live with my own thoughts, not everyone else's. But sometimes, with people like you, I just can't tune out.

JERRY: That's how you knew I was a cop! What else can you see?

LORNA: I'm retired.

JERRY: Oh, sorry, sorry. Didn't mean to be rude there.

LORNA: It's fine.

JERRY: Ever since I seen you that one time, I'm a believer. I even thought about going to one of those people but ...

LORNA: But as a cop you know there are a lot of unscrupulous people who claim to be psychics?

JERRY: Yeah. And I feel a little embarrassed too. You know, asking personal questions and whatnot. Look at me, chatting away like a groupie, when you're trying to read. Sorry Lorna.

(LORNA goes back to reading and JERRY reaches into his duffle bag, pulls out a big box of crackers, holds them out to LORNA who shakes her head "no," and then he eats a few.)

JERRY: Sad to say, this is my supper.

(The train suddenly lurches and LORNA is thrown toward JERRY, grabbing his arm. The train settles but LORNA hangs onto JERRY, her face becoming grim.)

JERRY: Hey, hey, you okay there? That was a bit of a bump, huh?

(*LORNA closes her eyes and doesn't respond.*)

JERRY: Lorna?

LORNA: Shhhhhh …

(*After a few moments, LORNA opens her eyes and slowly releases JERRY.*)

JERRY: What's happening here Lorna? I'm not thinking you're into me or nothing, so are you like having one of those premonitions?

LORNA: Yes, I … when I touched you …

JERRY: Oh wow, cool. So like what did you see? (*No response*). Is it that bad?

LORNA: Sometimes the images are confusing …

JERRY: Don't bullshit me here, you look like you're about to burst into tears …

LORNA: Not at all, I just get overwhelmed sometimes, too much coming at me all at once.

(*JERRY coughs a bit. LORNA reaches into her tote bag and takes out a bottle of juice, and hands it to JERRY.*)

LORNA: Here, wash down those crackers.

JERRY: (*Taking the bottle and drinking*) Thanks, this is delicious.

LORNA: It's my own secret recipe.

JERRY: Well, tell me! I want to know! What did you see when you grabbed my arm?

LORNA: I … nothing Jerry, not really.

JERRY: Nothing? I never even told you my name was Jerry! That's amazing! What else? Don't hold back!

LORNA: I … uhm … do you have any questions? Maybe …

JERRY: Well, yeah. I mean, truth to tell, I always thought I'd be married by now, wife, kids, house in the burbs, the whole bit. And I just never met the right person. Sometimes I think I'm off-putting or whatever, and it's never going to happen. Can you tell me if, you know, I'll ever have those things.

LORNA: I'm not sure ...

JERRY: You mean "no," right? I can see it in your eyes. I'll always be alone, right until the end.

LORNA: No!

JERRY: I'm a cop Lorna, I know when someone's lying to me. Wish I didn't.

LORNA: You won't be alone Jerry.

JERRY: You're a nice lady and all but —

LORNA: I know how much you want to find love, and you will. I was just too uncomfortable to spell it out ...

JERRY: I don't understand ...

LORNA: You'll meet someone special on a train.

JERRY: No way! Are you sure? When?

LORNA: You already have.

JERRY: I don't remember meeting a woman on a train. Oh God, not that one last week who was complaining to the conductor that her seat was dirty and the floor was a mess?

LORNA: *(Laughing)* No.

JERRY: Then I can't imagine who ...

LORNA: Really?

JERRY: I can't think of one woman on a train in the last year who I'd even be slightly ... *(a few beats)* No ... no way...

LORNA: Am I that awful looking?

JERRY:	You're way too beautiful! It can't be you!
LORNA:	I'm afraid it is.
JERRY:	You mean we're going to go on a date or something?
LORNA:	Several.
JERRY:	I can't believe this! I feel like I hit the lottery! Okay, okay. Just to prevent some future heartache here, like how long are we going to date? I mean, if you're going to dump me eventually, I don't want to get my hopes up.
LORNA:	I'm not going to dump you.
JERRY:	Well, I mean, I can already tell you I'm never dumping you, so one of us would have to dump the other one.
LORNA:	Not at all. We get married.
JERRY:	Are you shitting me?
LORNA:	I'm not sure I should tell you the rest.
JERRY:	Divorced right? Oh man … it's okay … I'm sure it's all my fault. And I was getting so excited too. Figures I'd blow it.
LORNA:	Will you stop?
JERRY:	Okay, okay. Just rip off the bandage. Tell me everything.
LORNA:	We date for a year, and then you propose.
JERRY:	And for reasons I can't even figure, you apparently say "yes"…
LORNA:	Because you're funny, and self-deprecating and kind. You work hard and see the best in everyone. You make me happy Jerry.
JERRY:	I'm going to have to trust you on that one. So what's next?
LORNA:	We get a dog. A basset hound named Eddie.

JERRY: I always wanted a Basset Hound named Eddie!

LORNA: We save for a small house. Small but perfect, with a lovely garden. I grow flowers, but all you want to grow is —

JERRY: Tomatoes! Like my grandpa!

LORNA: Yes, exactly. And then in another couple of years we have our first child. It's a girl.

JERRY: *(Tearing up)* I'm sorry, I'm getting all kinds of emotional here. This can't be my life ... I don't deserve ...

LORNA: It is. And then we have a second daughter.

JERRY: Are they good kids?

LORNA: The best. Sara becomes a teacher like your mom and Becca follows in your footsteps. She's so damned proud of you.

JERRY: A cop? Seriously?

LORNA: She makes Captain.

JERRY: Is all this stuff for sure, like 100 percent, or is all like a vague "maybe" — because I'm afraid to let myself believe here.

LORNA: Believe. We are soulmates, and from this moment, we will never leave each other. I promise. It's the future you deserve.

JERRY: It's all so crazy, but I feel better than I've ever felt in my life, just knowing it's all going to turn out okay for me.

(LORNA takes his hand.)

LORNA: Should we get the first kiss out of the way?

JERRY: Right here? In public like?

LORNA: Right here.

(LORNA takes his face into her hands and gently kisses him.)

JERRY: That was the best kiss I've ever had.

LORNA: I'm glad.

JERRY: It's like in the movies, when a kiss is full of promises, you know?

LORNA: Yeah. Are you happy Jerry?

JERRY: I'm crazy happy.

(LORNA takes his hand again.)

JERRY: I'm starting to feel kind of funny …

LORNA: It's okay. I'm right here with you. Keep holding my hand and just close your eyes.

JERRY: So sleepy …

LORNA: Just let go …

(JERRY closes his eyes. After a moment, LORNA reaches over, takes the drink she gave him and puts it back into her bag.)

LORNA: I wish I could change the things I see, but I can't. The rest of your life would have been a misery … losing your job … drinking … profound and bitter loneliness that kills that last little bit of hope you had left in your beautiful heart. With my special juice, you'll just drift quietly into painless death, your last moments filled with joy. *(Kissing the top of his head)* Goodbye soulmate. You were truly loved in the end.

OFF-STAGE VOICE, CONDUCTOR: Last Stop Folks.

(LORNA exits the train. JERRY'S body slumps down over both seats.)

END OF PLAY

הבהא | AHAVAH

by Dana Hall and David Lipschutz

CHARACTERS

SAUL GOLDBERG, Male, 30s, Jewish

ALICE HOBBS, Female, 30s, SAUL's gentile partner

SETTING

Sitting room of the home of Saul's Bubbie and Zayde.

TIME

Present day

NOTES

- / indicates an abrupt cut-off of the line.
- | indicates overlapping lines.

PRODUCTION HISTORY

Ahavah had its premiere production with The Farmington Players in Farmington Hills, MI, June 24–26, 2022. The production was directed by Mike Gingerella. The cast was as follows:

SAUL GOLDBERG: Lance Alan

ALICE HOBBS: Denise Kallas

*At Rise: Lights up on SAUL and ALICE in a small front room.
They are in SAUL's Zayde and Bubbie's home where Bubbie's
reception (shiva) is taking place in the next room. ALICE is in a
bright-colored dress. SAUL is in dark clothing. He is carrying a small
tied-up grocery bag. ALICE is reading a little note card with a photo
of Bubbie that has a short blurb on it.*

ALICE: Should we go in?

SAUL: Just give it a minute. I can hear my Zayde kvetching
            about me.

(SAUL sits, puts the bag down, and takes out his phone.)

ALICE: *(mouths "kvetching")* Ok. How do I look?

SAUL: *(looking at phone)* Fine.

ALICE: Really, you've hardly looked at me.

(ALICE tries to get his attention then feels defeated.)

ALICE
[CONT.]:   Maybe I shouldn't have come /

SAUL: No. No, it's not you. It's just. Bubbie was as frum
            as they come /

ALICE: What? I don't understand /

SAUL: *(gestures to ALICE's outfit)* Frum. Kosher. She was,
            uh, traditional.

ALICE: So.

SAUL: Soooo if she saw you in that dress she'd, she'd plotz.

ALICE: But *you* love this dress.

SAUL: I do. *(sees ALICE's disbelieving reaction)* I really do!

(SAUL puts his hand in ALICE's.)

SAUL
(CONT.):   Sorry, I haven't seen the rest of my family in a while,
            and I just want everything to be perfect.

ALICE: Just be yourself honey /

SAUL: Right. *(laughs to self)*

ALICE: What?

SAUL: Hmm?

ALICE: What's so funny?

SAUL: Oh. Nothing. Just. Funny you should say that I should be myself. Cuz, speaking of when we go in there, I'm a lawyer.

ALICE: You're a paralegal.

SAUL: Not today. They *(pointing at exit)* think I passed the bar exam. If they knew I was schlepping around work for actual attorneys, I'd never hear the end of it. I've actually been trying to figure out how to ask you to do this for me.

ALICE: *(In disbelief, pulls away)* Seriously?

SAUL: Alice, come on. I'm still me. Except this version of me is Junior Partner at Feinberg, Feinberg, and Gorman LLC. Oh, and I live in the West Village /

ALICE: Of course you do.

SAUL: *(hesitating)* One more thing …

ALICE: Can't wait to hear this.

SAUL: You converted.

ALICE: What?! I'm Jewish now?

SAUL: *(faux excited)* Mazel Tov.

ALICE: What the fuck[1], Saul? Where is all *this* coming from? First, I don't think I've ever heard you utter a Yiddish word | before today —

SAUL: That's just | mishegas.

---

1 Director's discretion to change to "hell" or a non-curse word.

ALICE: — and now all of these lies to your family. I just. Listen, I'm so sorry for your loss. I am. And I'm trying to be patient because I know how close you were with your Bubbie. But I can't believe she would want you to be this fake version of yourself.

SAUL: You're right. You're definitely *not* a Jew.

ALICE: And you're not a lawyer. *Yet* | I mean.

SAUL: Wow. | Ok.

ALICE: Not that there's anything wrong with that. So you didn't pass the bar the first time. So what? You've been able to take time off to be sure this was even something that *you* wanted. Besides, you're sitting for the bar again soon. I mean, don't you want your family's support? Like their real support?

SAUL: Fine. You're right. I'll avoid the whole conversation.

ALICE: That is not what I said.

SAUL: Listen, I just want to get through today, ok?

ALICE: Sure. Fine. Whatever.

(ALICE goes towards the door.)

ALICE
[CONT.]: Oh, I sent a beautiful arrangement of flowers. I wonder if they arrived yet.

SAUL: You *what*?!

ALICE: Yeah, I sent roses. I knew Bubbie was special to you, so I got the "ethereal elegance package" with these white ribbons down the side. Oh, and the roses are in the shape of a heart /

SAUL: Food, Alice. Not flowers, or bows, or ethereal packages. You bring food.

(SAUL holds up the grocery bag; it contains a wrapped container of Matzah Ball Soup.)

SAUL
[cont.]:   See! Matzah Ball Soup.

ALICE: Oh, that's what that smell was /

SAUL: Yes, Alice. That's the smell of love and exile and *(trails off)* a bissele of this and a bissele of that. I don't really know all the ingredients, it's from this place off 3rd Avenue. Their soup is second only to Bubbie's. She'd make it for me whenever I was sick, or sad, or looking too thin; it's basically Jewish penicillin.

ALICE: *(opening cap of the container and looking into the bowl)* Yum, yummy, oh, and look at the little balls floating. *(Mustering up enthusiasm)* Mmmm, delicious, honey.

SAUL: Don't try and cheer me up.

ALICE: There's more food in there, right? *(heading towards the door)* We should head in /

SAUL: *(gently grabbing ALICE's hand)* Wait. So you'll go along with *everything*, right?

ALICE: They'll see right through me.

SAUL: You're right. Ugh! What was I thinking? I'm such a schlub.

(SAUL begins pacing around.)

SAUL
[cont.]:   Is it getting hot in here? It feels warm, right? Wait. Is that? D'you hear that? *(a realization)* Rabbi Abramowitz is in there! What am I saying? Of course, he's here! He visited Bubbie every week at the hospital to replay his Shabbat sermon. I can't lie to him or even around him. I'm done for. *(SAUL starts loosening his tie a bit)* Oy, I'm schvitzing.

ALICE: Hey, hey. It's okay. Just be yourself in there. Your sweet, awkward self.

SAUL: But that's just it. The Rabbi will see right through me. He always has /

ALICE: I'm sure that's not true.

SAUL: Listen, Al. This man knows me. He was my Sunday
           school teacher aged 4 to 18, he was my Bar Mitzvah
           tutor, and he was my mohel. In fact, he moheled three
           generations of my family. He did me, he did my uncle
           Jack, and my nephew Zev. So when I say he'll see right
           through my lies ... he will.

ALICE: Ok. That *is* a rather ... intimate connection, but I, I
           think you might be in your head too much about this.
           (grabs soup container) Maybe you should have a bite to
           calm your nerves.

SAUL: *(looking at container)* No thanks. I can't eat at a time
           like this.

(SAUL pushes the container. In the process, he spills on his pants.)

SAUL
[cont.]:   Damn! Great. | Just great.

ALICE: I'm | sorry!

SAUL: It looks like I pissed my pants.

ALICE: I don't have anything to wipe it with.

*(SAUL starts emptying his pockets. He takes out a few things
including checks. ALICE also checks her pockets to no avail.)*

SAUL: Perfect. All I have is this stuff and one of Bubbie's
           checks.

ALICE: Check? *(takes it)* $13.00?

SAUL: *(distracted while wiping pants)* Hmm? Oh. Yeah. I've
           got a bunch of these checks from her.

ALICE: You never cashed them?

SAUL: Nah. I thought maybe Bubbie was getting a little
           forgetful.

*(SAUL takes more checks out of his wallet. ALICE is looking
at checks.)*

ALICE: $13.00, $13.00, they're all for $13.00.

SAUL: I guess so.

ALICE: Oh damn. *(handing check to SAUL)* Look in the memo of this one.

SAUL: *(reading check)* "Alice."

ALICE: Why?

SAUL: I dunno. Look. She wrote "Bar" on this one. And this one just says "Ahavah" /

ALICE: More like "I'll have a" *(pronouncing it mockingly like "Ahavah")* little more money than $13.00 thank you Bubbie.

SAUL: Jesus /

ALICE: Sorry. I know; too soon for jokes.

SAUL: No. Rabbi Abramowitz. He said in his last visit to her, she spoke of Ahavah and the importance of love. I guess it was the topic for his sermon that week. *(a thought)* Wait. No. 13. 13 …

(SAUL takes out his phone and is intently searching the internet.)

SAUL
[cont.]:   *(Realizing)* Oh Bubbie.

ALICE: What? What'd you find?

SAUL: I just realized something about Ahavah and 13. So I googled the two words together. And guess what? *(reading from phone)* "Ahavah" means "love" in Hebrew.

ALICE: Oh.

SAUL: Yeah. According to this, "the Jewish mystics remark on the affinity between the word *ahavah* and the numerical value of the letters being 13. Oneness, unity, is the aspiration of love, it is without conditions. Love is Giving."

(*SAUL hands the phone to ALICE.*)

ALICE: (*reads phone*) "The more we give, the more we show love without condition." Damn. Wait. (*rifles through checks*) "Bar." Saul, look. She must have known about your bar exam results.

SAUL: What? How could she? I never told her. (*takes the check*) But she, she never said anything.

ALICE: And yet she loved you anyway.

SAUL: (*looking through checks*) She knew about everything. (*Then he takes the check that was in his pocket*) And she didn't just love me here.

ALICE: What?

SAUL: (*handing check to ALICE*) Al. She loved you, too.

ALICE: (*reading check*) "Alice."

(*ALICE turns to say something to SAUL but sees he is crying. She holds him in her arms. SAUL holds her tighter.*)

SAUL: I just. I miss her so much.

ALICE: I know, honey. I know.

SAUL: (*after finally gaining his composure back*) She loved you. She didn't care if you were Jewish, or not Jewish, or anything about that. She knew I loved you, and that, that was good enough for her.

ALICE: She was a beautiful woman.

SAUL: She was. I, I don't like talking about her in the past tense. Feels strange to think she isn't here.

ALICE: I'm pretty sure she'll always be with you. (*refers to checks*) She always has been.

(*SAUL smiles at the thought of this and after a moment he gets an idea.*)

SAUL: You know what I think?

ALICE: What's that?

SAUL: I say, let's go in there. As ourselves. Me and /

ALICE: Your shiksa goddess.

(They share a laugh. SAUL reaches for her hand.)

SAUL: I was going to say my *girlfriend*. *(He kisses her hand)* No lies. Just the *real* us. This is what Bubbie would've wanted. Me to just be me.

(They start to exit. SAUL turns around abruptly.)

SAUL
[cont.]: Balls! /

ALICE: Yes, it takes a lot of *chutzpah* to be yourself.

SAUL: No, we forgot the Matzah Balls. *(gestures to where they were left)* I may be brave but I'm not stupid enough to go in there empty-handed. *(grabs the soup container, as they start to exit again)* Also, can we talk about how you used not one but two Yiddish terms just now?

ALICE: You noticed that huh?

SAUL: Hard not to. Hey. I love you.

ALICE: I love you, too.

SAUL: Good. Now let's go in there and schmooze.

(They smile at each other, hold hands, and exit.)

END OF PLAY

THE GRAPE NERDS REUNION

by Alli Hartley-Kong

CHARACTERS

ALYSSA, a 28-year-old woman. She dresses impeccably, in a nice blazer and slacks, and is clearly uncomfortable with the vibes of the bar. Any race or ethnicity.

MIKE, a high school rocker gone to seed, also 28. A prominent scar on his head, bad tattoos, ripped jeans, a black band t-shirt, and metal-studded jewelry. Any race or ethnicity.

SETTING

A bench outside of a small town suburban bar that is clearly thumping.

TIME

Present day

NOTE

This play contains brief mentions of a character's past suicidal tendencies.

PRODUCTION HISTORY

The Grape Nerds Reunion was presented as part of *Jersey Voices 2022* by Chatham Community Players in Chatham New Jersey, July 29th–August 7, 2022. The production was directed by Sarah Pharaon. The cast was as follows:

ALYSSA: Ali Archetti

MIKE: Anthony Bentrovato

At rise, MIKE sits on a bench outside a thumping bar, scrolling through his phone. The door opens, and ALYSSA walks out. She looks around then beelines towards MIKE.

ALYSSA: Michael ...! Mike ...?

MIKE: *(slightly uncomfortably)* Hey ... I ....

ALYSSA: I've been looking for you all over! I ran into Maya inside — can I sit with you?

(Without waiting for a response, ALYSSA sits down and throws her arms around him for a hug.)

MIKE: I'm sorry ...

ALYSSA: Alyssa Meekin?

MIKE: Drama club, middle school ...?

ALYSSA: Marching band, eleventh grade ...

MIKE: Sorry, I had a traumatic brain injury. Motorcycle accident —

ALYSSA: Senior year, Labor Day Weekend —

MIKE: You remember? Huh. We must've been friends.

ALYSSA: You really don't remember me?

MIKE: My brain is weird, after the accident. I don't remember anyone. Only — smells, sometimes, and tastes. Faces — people — the important stuff? Nothing.

ALYSSA: Must be strange to be at a high school reunion — and not remember high school.

MIKE: My wife insisted we come.

ALYSSA: She wasn't even in our grade ...

MIKE: She kept in touch with a lot of my friends, after the accident. *(Awkward pause)* Alicia, right?

ALYSSA: Alyssa.

MIKE: Maya never mentioned you.

ALYSSA: We were friends before you got together. You started dating her in December of junior year. *(Beat)* Sorry. I have a really good memory.

MIKE: Did we ever eat breakfast together? I look at you … and I taste omelets.

ALYSSA: Friday nights after marching band, we'd go to the diner. Breakfast for dinner.

MIKE: I can kind of piece that together. Brain injury or not, it's been a long time.

ALYSSA: Ten years. It's crazy. How have you been? Are you happy? Are you working?

MIKE: I'm alive. That's something, right? *(Beat)* I'm still playing bass. We played Bamboozle this year again. Just like high school. Only I could remember it.

ALYSSA: Shut up, they still do Bamboozle?

MIKE: We were the oldest people there.

ALYSSA: I saw you play Bamboozle the summer before the accident … I didn't talk to you after the show. I just wanted to see you play.

MIKE: Were we friends? It doesn't sound like we were friends.

ALYSSA: You only did one season of marching band … You were a rocker wanna-be, I was president of the History Club. But remember those ridiculous red saddle shoes you had?

MIKE: I've seen pictures.

ALYSSA: One day we were walking around the mall. I dared you to buy them. I was the one who picked those out.

MIKE: Why has no one ever mentioned you before? I hear stories and I think — I was such an ass in high school. You seem nice. A bit creepy. But nice. Did I do something bad to you?

ALYSSA: We had our history.

MIKE: Good history?

ALYSSA: All history is something, isn't it?

MIKE: That's deep.

ALYSSA: You know in high school, you were the deep one.

MIKE: Really …? Brain injuries make you kinda flat,
            sometimes …

ALYSSA: You weren't flat back then. Anything but.

MIKE: Sometimes I feel like I'm acting in a play. Figuring out
            how normal humans would react and doing it.

ALYSSA: We used to talk about everything back in the day.
            Actually … you know that hill next to the high school
            —? Wait … sorry … memory loss.

MIKE: I know that hill. My mom still lives here. When I
            drive by, I sometimes get this weird … nostalgia. Did
            something happen on that hill, between us, you know?
            Like … boy and girl, teenagers?

ALYSSA: No. We just … talked. I mean, it was a big talk …
            Maybe it wasn't that big, maybe it just felt that way
            because when you're sixteen, everything feels big.
            I don't know.

MIKE: What did we talk about?

ALYSSA: Mostly me … sorry. We were sixteen. Who wasn't
            self-centered? And … my dad had cancer.

MIKE: Oh, god. I'm sorry.

ALYSSA: It's okay, he's fine. Twelve years in remission. It was just
            … it was hard being a kid, living with that …

MIKE: I get it. My mom was sick in middle school.

ALYSSA: That's what we talked about that day. Her story gave
            me hope. Is she still doing okay?

MIKE: Fifteen years out. No recurrence. Nothing.

ALYSSA: Good. I worry about her. She's been through enough … Anyways, my dad was sick, and I was so fixated on doing well in school, getting into an Ivy. I thought … if I got straight As I could make it better. It was just a rough time. And you listened. You were the only person who got it.

MIKE: I got what it was like to want to go to an Ivy League school?

ALYSSA: Maybe that was it. You were different, you weren't a Type A overachiever. You just listened without trying to top me.

MIKE: I'm sorry, this is gonna sound weird. We didn't kiss that day, did we?

ALYSSA: Not that day, no.

MIKE: Oh.

ALYSSA: It was perfect. Even without a kiss. It's perfect because we didn't kiss. When I was done talking, you said, I'm tired, I don't want to walk. I don't know why you were so tired, I was the one baring my soul.

MIKE: That sounds tiring to listen to.

ALYSSA: You know — I never thought about it from your perspective … Huh. Anyways, after I was done talking, we rolled down the hill.

MIKE: What?

ALYSSA: Like kids in elementary school. We had grass stains on our clothes and everything. *(Beat)* We had nothing in common, besides band. But for that hour … you were my friend.

MIKE: And then I messed it up, didn't I?

ALYSSA: I was hoping … if I explained, the memory would come back.

MIKE: I always hope too. It never does. I'm sorry. Sounds like I was an ass.

ALYSSA: It's not your fault you can't remember me —

MIKE: I meant in high school. You said we didn't kiss that day on the hill ...? We did kiss at some point though. When I look at you ... I taste grape nerds.

ALYSSA: What?

MIKE: You know little purple candies that kind of look like aquarium rocks?

ALYSSA: Huh. They always gave us candy on the way home from marching band competitions.

MIKE: Did we kiss ever ... that's the only reason I can think why I would look at you and taste something ...?

ALYSSA: Once, on the band bus. You were actually my first kiss. And then ... that next night you texted me that it had been a mistake. You were texting someone else.

MIKE: And then ...?

ALYSSA: We never really talked again. The other girl was Maya — so I guess it worked out for you ...

MIKE: Oh. God. Sorry.

ALYSSA: It's fine. I turned out okay. I went away for college.

MIKE: Ivy League?

ALYSSA: No, didn't get in. But I went to somewhere even better ... for me. Williams. I became a writer. I have a book deal.

MIKE: That's impressive.

ALYSSA: You know what's even more impressive? I'm happy. Everything turned out much better than I imagined it would. I'm married.

MIKE: Did he come with you to the reunion?

ALYSSA: She. No ... the only reason I'm here is you.

MIKE: I feel really bad. You came here today to confront me — and I remember nothing ...

ALYSSA: I'm not here to confront you. Actually — I came here tonight to thank you.

MIKE: For what? I sounded like I treated you horribly.

ALYSSA: That day on the hill ... I had a plan. I'm okay now. Don't worry. That was ten years ago. But ... I wasn't okay then. I woke up that morning and thought, I just don't want to be here anymore. Not ... in high school. Like ... on this planet. Alive.

MIKE: Oh. *Oh.*

ALYSSA: I can't even say it out loud, what I wanted to do.

MIKE: You were gonna hurt yourself.

ALYSSA: More than hurt myself. It seems so stupid, now. I mean, my problems were real to me, then, but ... they were so temporary. It's just so stupid ...

MIKE: It's not stupid Alyssa, I'm glad you didn't do anything.

ALYSSA: Me too. Oh my god, me too. It's just. I thought I was so alone. I guess most teenagers think that. But that day — on the hill — I wasn't alone. I was just there with you.

MIKE: And then I messed that up ...

ALYSSA: No ... I mean. Yes. But it's fine. If your high school crush dumps you for another girl, at least it's his future wife? On the day I needed you ... you were there. So it's fine. It's more than fine. *(Beat)* You know, I had wanted to visit you in the hospital ... but I was scared about seeing you like that. How I'd feel. So I didn't.

MIKE: I probably wouldn't have remembered you anyways.

ALYSSA: That's what scared me. Because you were so meaningful to me. *(Beat)* It all got so weird after we kissed. I thought over time it would get less weird, but we never talked again — and then the accident happened ...

MIKE: I'm so sorry, Alyssa. You sound like you were a wonderful person back then.

ALYSSA: You don't have anything to be sorry about. We were sixteen. Dumb.

MIKE: Yeah, but you seem —

ALYSSA: Happy. I'm happy now. So that's what I wanted to say. I mean … you don't remember. And even if you did, you'd have no idea you meant to me. How can we ever know what anyone else is going through? Just … thank you.

MIKE: No, thank you. For telling me your story. I'm glad you're here, Alyssa. Not at this reunion. Just — here.

ALYSSA: It's really good to be alive, isn't it?

MIKE: Can I ask you something? Can I kiss you? Not make out, we're both married. Nothing crazy. Just a kiss. Would that be okay?

ALYSSA: I think so. Michael …?

(MIKE checks over his shoulder that no one is watching, then pecks her on the lips chastely.)

MIKE: There. So I can remember too. I hope.

ALYSSA: I don't still taste like Grape Nerds, do I?

MIKE: You taste happy. Confident. Lipstick and Chardonnay. I should go home to my wife.

ALYSSA: Me too.

MIKE: I hope things work out in your life.

ALYSSA: They already have.

(MIKE walks back inside the bar, leaving ALYSSA sitting. She lifts her fingers on her lips, touching where he kissed her.)

END OF PLAY

DOMESTIC HELP

by Julianne Jigour

CHARACTERS

FELIX, male, 20s, a clown.

MARGARET, female, 40s.

SETTING

The study in MARGARET's house.

TIME

Now.

PRODUCTION HISTORY

Domestic Help was presented as a staged reading and selected as a finalist in the 2022 Samuel French Off Off Broadway Short Play Festival at the Peter Jay Sharp Theater in NYC, August 16–20, 2022. The reading was directed by Corey Atkins with stage directions read by Amelia Bethel and Kaia Parnell. The cast was as follows:

FELIX: Connor Johnson

MARGARET: Soomi Kim

SCENE ONE

MARGARET's study. She sits at her desk, writing in a notebook. A knock at the door.

MARGARET: Yes?

(FELIX, a clown, enters. He wears a big painted smile on his face, but he doesn't actually smile. He stays close to the door and shifts his weight from one foot to the other.)

FELIX: It's raining. Outside.

(A pause.)

MARGARET: Is that all?

FELIX: Yes.

(FELIX hurries out, shutting the door behind him. MARGARET continues writing.)

(Another knock at the door.)

MARGARET: Yes?

(FELIX enters.)

FELIX: It's raining really hard.

(MARGARET resumes writing. FELIX surveys the room and then looks down at his big clown feet.)

FELIX: Do you have children?

MARGARET: No, I don't believe I do.

FELIX: There are children in your backyard. Outside. They look cold. And wet.

MARGARET: Oh. Well, they're not mine.

(MARGARET goes back to writing. FELIX exits, shutting the door behind him.)

(Another knock at the door.)

MARGARET: Yes?

(FELIX enters.)

FELIX: Should I let them in? I think they want to come in.

MARGARET: Oh, no. I don't let strangers into my house. That's a very important rule here. No strangers in the house. That's how things get dirty, Dominic.

FELIX: My name is Felix.

MARGARET: I don't like that name.

(FELIX nods. MARGARET goes back to writing.)

FELIX: What're you writing?

MARGARET: My to-do list. I'm on #49,218: Write a letter to Aunt Nadine. Oh! That reminds me *(as she writes)* . . . #49,219: Find out whether Aunt Nadine is still alive. I vaguely recall some illness occurred. Anyway, there's so much to do. I've been working on this list for months. That's why I contacted the agency. To get some help. Otherwise, I forget to eat. Forget to sleep. They said you were quiet, Dominic. That's good because I need quiet.

(FELIX makes a point of being quiet. MARGARET studies him.)

MARGARET: I don't want your makeup to soil my towels.

FELIX: Oh, it's not makeup.

(FELIX rubs his face and shows MARGARET a clean hand.)

MARGARET: Well, that's a relief. Curious. I would've thought the agency would've placed you in a circus rather than a domestic help position.

FELIX: My parents were in the circus. But when they realized I wasn't funny, they gave me to the agency.

MARGARET: I'm glad you're not funny. I find laughter rather vulgar.

(FELIX smiles for the first time.)

FELIX: I'm definitely not funny. I don't know any jokes.
          It's in my records. I tried to learn some when I first
          got to the agency because I thought if I did, my
          parents might want me back. But nobody ever came
          to get me. Turns out the agency doesn't allow take-
          backs anyway, and I could never really get the jokes
          down to begin with. That's why the agency couldn't
          place me in entertainment. I can't even make
          balloon animals!

MARGARET: Entertainment is a waste of time.

(FELIX moves closer to MARGARET.)

FELIX: But I like doing what people tell me to do. I'm good
          at that.

(MARGARET studies FELIX.)

MARGARET: What's the worst thing you've ever been asked to do?

(FELIX thinks. He becomes uncomfortable.)

MARGARET: Will you leave please?

(FELIX exits. MARGARET resumes writing.)

SCENE TWO

*MARGARET writes in her study. FELIX enters with a cup of tea
and sets it on her desk.*

MARGARET: Is it bedtime already?

(FELIX nods. MARGARET drinks her tea.)

MARGARET: Time just escapes me. To be forward-thinking as
          I am, one really can't bother with the present.

FELIX: Excuse me, ma'am, but . . .

MARGARET: What is it?

FELIX: I don't want to be a pest about it, but —

MARGARET: Oh, no, I don't want you to be a pest about anything.

FELIX: But. The children are still outside.

(MARGARET drinks her tea.)

MARGARET: Did I eat dinner tonight?

FELIX: Yes.

MARGARET: What did I have?

FELIX: Salmon. With greens.

MARGARET: Hm. When you do this sort of work, really high-level work, the little things in life tend to fall away. Your brain just doesn't have room to hold onto them.

FELIX: They're crying.

MARGARET: Pardon?

FELIX: The children outside. They're crying.

MARGARET: Well, children will do that. I know it's a nuisance, but it's natural for them to cry.

FELIX: I think they're waiting to come inside.

MARGARET: Why?

FELIX: I think they think they live here.

MARGARET: They don't.

FELIX: Should I leave the outdoor lights on?

MARGARET: Why would you do that?

FELIX: In case they're afraid of the dark.

MARGARET: I have an electricity bill, Dominic. You're not going to leave the lights on for some misplaced children in my backyard.

(FELIX nods. MARGARET sips her tea.)

MARGARET: I can see myself to bed.

(FELIX hesitates, turns to leave, and then turns back.)

FELIX: May I sleep in your room?

MARGARET: You have your own bedroom.

FELIX: I know.

MARGARET: Are you saying you don't like the bedroom I've
              provided for you?

FELIX: No, it's nice. I've never had my own dresser before.

(A pause.)

FELIX: I just. I can hear the children from my bedroom.
              They're right outside my window.

*(MARGARET opens a desk drawer and searches for something.
She finds it and presents it to FELIX.)*

MARGARET: Ear plugs.

SCENE THREE

*MARGARET writes in her study. FELIX, disheveled and exhausted,
enters with a tray of breakfast. He has blue tear drops on his face.*

FELIX: Good morning.

MARGARET: Oh, it is a good morning! I've already added
              five items to my list. I'm on #49,463: Contact
              government official about excessive holidays on
              the national calendar.

(FELIX sets the breakfast tray on MARGARET's desk.)

MARGARET: What's that on your face?

(FELIX turns his face away.)

MARGARET: Come here. Look at me.

(FELIX presents his face to MARGARET.)

MARGARET: Have you been crying?

FELIX: . . . No.

MARGARET: There are big blue tear drops all the way from your eye to your chin.

FELIX: I was just. Feeling a little sad.

MARGARET: You don't have time to be sad, Dominic. You're my domestic help.

FELIX: I couldn't sleep.

MARGARET: Why not?

FELIX: The children kept crying.

MARGARET: I gave you ear plugs, did I not?

FELIX: They hurt my ears. So I took them out.

MARGARET: Did they not fit properly? I don't know much about clown anatomy.

FELIX: I have sensitive ears.

MARGARET: Well, I can't have you crying on the job.

(MARGARET bites into her breakfast. FELIX stands there, listening. A pause.)

FELIX: Do you hear that?

MARGARET: What?

FELIX: The children. They've been screaming for the last hour.

(MARGARET listens and hears something.)

MARGARET: Oh. I thought that was the birds chirping. Are you sure those aren't birds?

(FELIX nods. MARGARET eats more breakfast and thinks to herself.)

MARGARET: I had a parakeet once. Simon. He ate part of an avocado and died.

FELIX: Would it be okay if I put some food and water out for the children?

MARGARET: If you leave food out, they'll keep coming back.

FELIX: But what if they have nowhere else to go?

MARGARET: They'll just have to wait to be collected by whoever owns them.

FELIX: But what if —?

MARGARET: Stop. Talking. About. The children.

(A pause. FELIX turns to leave. Then he turns back, bracing himself.)

FELIX: What if nobody ever comes to get them?

(A pause.)

MARGARET: I thought you said you were good at doing what you're told.

FELIX: I am, but —

MARGARET: Your preoccupation with these children is negatively impacting your job performance.

FELIX: I'm sorry, ma'am, it's just —

MARGARET: I'm beginning to think I should call the agency to tell them they didn't properly place you.

FELIX: Please —

MARGARET: Perhaps they should reevaluate your utility.

(MARGARET picks up a phone and begins to dial.)

FELIX: Please don't —

MARGARET: If there's one thing I can say about the agency, they're efficient. Why I bet they could send one of their drivers over within the hour.

FELIX: Don't call the agency.

(A pause.)

FELIX: Please.

(A brief pause.)

FELIX: Once the children are gone, I'll be able to focus,
              I'll —

MARGARET: Then make them go away.

FELIX: How?

MARGARET: Think of something.

SCENE FOUR

*MARGARET writes in her study. FELIX enters. His clown hair and
clothes are dripping wet.*

MARGARET: Dominic! You're getting water in my study!

FELIX: I called the agency.

MARGARET: You must get a towel and dry off immediately.

FELIX: I called the agency to take the children away.

MARGARET: You're going to have to mop this floor.

FELIX: I went outside when the agency arrived.

MARGARET: The children didn't touch you, did they?

FELIX: The children are very ill.

MARGARET: You must go wash yourself.

FELIX: They're very hungry and scared.

MARGARET: Hot water and soap.

FELIX: The children said they live here.

MARGARET: That's ridiculous.

FELIX: They said you locked them outside.

MARGARET: You're going to take the word of some stray children
              over mine?

FELIX: They seemed very certain.

(MARGARET thinks.)

MARGARET: If I had children, I'd have made a note of it
             somewhere.

(MARGARET shakes her head and flips back through pages in her notebook. She hits a page and stops. She rereads it, holds it closer to her face, and then farther away.)

MARGARET: Oh dear . . . #48,763: Let the children back in.

(MARGARET lingers on the page and then looks up.)

MARGARET: Well. An honest mistake.

(MARGARET flips to her current page in the notebook and resumes writing.)

(FELIX stands there, dripping and watching MARGARET. MARGARET looks up.)

FELIX: They're gone now. The children.

MARGARET: I asked you to go dry off, Dominic.

(A pause.)

FELIX: Why did you forget them?

(MARGARET pauses a long while, confused.)

MARGARET: Why are you standing there wet like that?

FELIX: It's raining. Outside.

END OF PLAY

BULLETPROOF

by Rebecca Kane

CHARACTERS

SHAWN: Male, 20s, any race. Looks somewhat put-together.

PJ: Male, 20s, any race. Looks like an overgrown teenager.

SETTING

A clearing in southern California, vaguely near Los Angeles.

TIME

Midday. Summer, late 1990s.

PRODUCTION HISTORY

Bulletproof was presented by Playwrights' Round Table in Orlando, FL, July 22–31, 2022. The production was directed by Rochelle Curbow Sebesta. The cast was as follows:

PJ: Benjamin Mainville

SHAWN: Contona Thomas

Lights up on PJ and SHAWN, sweating in the sun. They're somewhere in a deserted patch of California, just far enough away from civilization that they could get away with plenty of noise.

SHAWN is setting up a video camera on a tripod. He holds a gun.

PJ has on a bulletproof vest under his t-shirt. He keeps adjusting it.

SHAWN: P.J., what's the problem?

PJ: Huh? I don't have a problem.

SHAWN: You keep messing with it.

PJ: It's not as comfortable as I thought it would be. Cops have to wear this all the time. You'd think it'd be a little more breathable.

SHAWN: It's not supposed to be comfortable. It's supposed to do its job.

PJ: "Supposed to." Damn, let's hope. *(He cackles like a crazy person. SHAWN does not smile.)* I'm sweating like an animal in this thing.

SHAWN: I'm sweating like an animal and I'm not even in it.

PJ: That's pretty sexy, Shawn. I tell ya if I wasn't a kept man … *(He laughs again. SHAWN does not respond.)* Can we hurry up? There's a gas station only like half a mile back. What if someone drives —

SHAWN: I can't shoot you.

PJ: You have to.

SHAWN: You're engaged. What if it goes wrong? How the fuck am I gonna face Susie? I'm the one who introduced you guys.

PJ: How can it go wrong? Just don't shoot me in the head.

SHAWN: You mean just don't shoot you anywhere except square in the chest. How do we know my aim is that good?

PJ: How bad could it be? Just concentrate.

SHAWN: Yeah, just concentrate. I'm only going to shoot one of my oldest friends in the chest for the sake of some dumb article for a dumber magazine. What could possibly throw me off?

PJ: See, being sarcastic isn't gonna help you focus. Let's just get it over with.

SHAWN: Does it have to be right this second? Can you give me some time?

PJ: I'm sweating my ass off. Please, Shawn? We already did so much work. We talked it up all week. Josh is expecting it. We'll get nailed if we pussy out.

SHAWN: We won't get nailed. He can't replace us, P.J. We're the last functioning non-junkies who write coherent articles about skateboarding and other stupid crap for miles around.

PJ: I don't know how much of a functioning non-junkie I am.

SHAWN: That's not ... you're not the only person in the office who ... you won't get fired if you don't write this, PJ.

PJ: No, YOU won't get fired if you don't write it. You're half the content every month. I've never gotten anything to publication.

SHAWN: You've been here for months. Why would he fire you now?

PJ: Because he said he would.

SHAWN: Wait, really?

PJ: "Get me a real story or you're fired" he said.

SHAWN: I don't think this is what he meant.

PJ: Look, I'm getting fired one way or another, right? Get it?

(SHAWN clearly gets it. He's not amused. They hear the noise of a car approaching. SHAWN quickly pockets the gun and both men force as

casual a pose as possible. It doesn't work very well. The car passes.)

PJ: How do you think the shot looks on the camera?

SHAWN: It looked fine when I set it up. Is it safe for us to get any closer?

PJ: I don't know.

SHAWN: You don't know? You didn't do any research?

PJ: I thought you would.

SHAWN: It's not my article, idiot.

PJ: Good point.

SHAWN: No research? None? How did you even get one of those?

PJ: Josh got it for me.

SHAWN: Of course he did.

PJ: Look, I called this shooting range that said —

SHAWN: You called? You didn't even go to see them?

PJ: They said it would feel like getting hit by a hammer, which I thought was reassuring. And pretty interesting, right?

SHAWN: No. Can we stand further apart?

PJ: We'll lose detail in the shot, I think.

SHAWN: I don't need detail. I need you to live.

PJ: Chill out, dude.

SHAWN: I can shoot you or I can chill out but I can't do both.

PJ: Then let's do it. Right now. We'll do this super quick and we'll go get beers at Bar Louie and chill out. Take aim. Let's do this. Tell me when to count off.

(SHAWN braces himself and raises the gun. PJ turns away. SHAWN adjusts his aim. A lot.)

PJ: Are you just … aiming?

SHAWN: Yeah.

PJ: I thought you've done this before.

SHAWN: Shoot someone? Seriously?

PJ: But you said you've shot a gun.

SHAWN: I went to a range when I was sixteen.

PJ: Yeah, right, for your birthday. I remember. Not since then?

SHAWN: Nope.

(PJ pauses. Maybe out of real worry. Then:)

PJ: I bet you're a natural!

SHAWN: Do you want me to check the camera one more time?

PJ: You're stalling.

SHAWN: I want to be your best man.

PJ: I know.

SHAWN: I can't do that if I kill you. You finally found a woman patient enough to deal with your shit, who you're marrying next month, and now you're writing some feature where you get shot in the chest.

PJ: "In which," I thought.

SHAWN: What?

PJ: I think the correct grammar would be writing a feature "in which" I get shot, not "where" I get shot.

SHAWN: How can you be so cavalier about this?

PJ: Because I'm wearing a vest whose whole purpose is to let me be cavalier about this!

SHAWN: Cops are not cavalier about getting shot, even with a vest.

PJ: It'll work.

SHAWN: If you're so sure it's gonna work, how come you

proposed this article as "testing" it?

PJ: Dramatic effect, maybe?

SHAWN: Great. A drama. I hope me killing you isn't the climax.

PJ: I'm not gonna die, Shawn. I'm never gonna die. The worst that could happen is you get me in the arm or something by accident. I'll live through that. Lots of people do.

SHAWN: What if it malfunctions?

PJ: The gun?

SHAWN: The vest.

PJ: How does Kevlar malfunction?

SHAWN: Maybe Josh got something cheap.

PJ: Josh is our editor. He wants this article to work out, and he doesn't want his magazine to go down in a pile of burning lawsuits, he just wants to try writing about something shocking and cool and innovative. He wouldn't green light this if he really thought we were gonna die. I trust him ...

(PJ looks away from SHAWN and the gun.)

SHAWN: Finish that sentence.

PJ: With my life. Yeah, with my life.

SHAWN: I wouldn't. We're talking about a man who wants to turn this fucked up idea into a web series.

PJ: If I die, he won't be able to publish it.

SHAWN: Obviously you don't know Josh like I do.

PJ: Would you please shoot me already?

(SHAWN preps the gun. He aims it. PJ fights laughter.)

PJ: Did you ever think anyone would say that to you?

SHAWN: I should never have convinced him to hire you.

PJ: In three ... two ... one.

SHAWN: I can't do it!

(SHAWN puts the gun on the ground. As he talks, PJ picks up the gun.)

SHAWN: Just find another job, dude! There's other magazines to work at. I know you think this one is most rad or punk or whatever stupid bullshit you think is cool these days, but there has to be some sort of compromise. This is not some skateboarding video with some impossible flip, this is serious. This is getting hurt for real. Besides, fuck, whoever said you had to work at a magazine? Find a record company or something!

(PJ has turned the gun on himself.)

SHAWN: That's not funny.

PJ: It's hilarious. Everything about this is hilarious.

SHAWN: Nothing is funny about you for sure dying now.

PJ: I'm not going to die, Shawn.

SHAWN: I know you think you're immortal but please put that down. (No response.) I'm not fucking around, put it down!

PJ: It's going to work. I'll show you.

SHAWN: That range is so dangerous. P.J., please. Peter? Please. I'll do it. I promise.

(After a long pause, he hands SHAWN the gun.)

PJ: I'm never gonna die.

SHAWN: I know.

(PJ and SHAWN lock eyes. SHAWN raises the gun. Blackout.)

END OF PLAY

HOT BLOOD SUNDAE

by Aly Kantor

CHARACTERS

JESS, she/her, 20s, an ice cream lover. Any race or ethnicity.

BEX, she/her, 20s, a casual raw vegan. Any race or ethnicity.

SETTING

Somewhere in America.

TIME

Daytime.

PRODUCTION HISTORY

Hot Blood Sundae was presented by New Ambassadors Theatre Co. in NYC, October 26–30, 2022. The production was directed by Mia Y. Anderson. The cast was as follows:

JESS: Starr Kirkland

BEX: Maile Binion

JESS:	You said you got tested, right?
BEX:	Yeah, why?
JESS:	Can I ask you a question?
BEX:	Um. About …?
JESS:	Nothing too personal. Just, like —
BEX:	Go ahead.
JESS:	Was it, like, itching, burning?
BEX:	It was more like —
JESS:	Or just pain?
BEX:	Just pain. Heat. The kind of heat that makes you stop and go, "Oh. This might be infected."
JESS:	But not, like burning burning? Like, an "I need Monistat" level of burning?
BEX:	No.
JESS:	Okay.
BEX:	Why?
JESS:	What?
BEX:	Did you —
JESS:	No. Just curious. When do you find out?
BEX:	Tomorrow.
JESS:	Shit. And when's the …
BEX:	Another three weeks.
JESS:	Yeah. That makes sense, since …
BEX:	Did you hear Lila was positive?
JESS:	No shit?! I haven't seen her in like —
BEX:	I know, right?

JESS: Where even is she? Is she, um. Is she out about her …
           status … and everything? Like, do people know?

BEX: No, she's totally out about it. She's, like, great. It's
           like a whole new lifestyle for her, but she's crazy happy.
           I called her up when, um … Before I got tested.

JESS: That's so crazy. That she's happy like that?

BEX: SO crazy.

(A beat.)

JESS: This is gonna sound weird, but … can I, like, see?
           Can I see where he …

BEX: Like, the spot? It's kind of …

JESS: You don't have to.

BEX: You can look. Just be gentle. It's still sort of … tender.

(Relax. BEX shows JESS a spot on her neck, under her hair.)

JESS: Wow. It's still warm. Do you think — did they seem
           pretty sure that you're …?

BEX: They don't know. But that kind of heat, I just feel like …

JESS: Sorry.

BEX: Ow.

JESS: .   Sorry! Sorry!

BEX: … Touch it again?

JESS: What?

BEX: Push it with your fingers until it — YES! YES!
           OHHHHHHHHHHHHHHH!

JESS: What the literal fuck Rebecca?

BEX: Was that weird? It felt really good.

JESS: No! It's cool! It's cool that I made you feel that good.
           I didn't even have to do anything, really. I mean,
           compared to, like — going down on a guy, or …

BEX:	I know! I'm really sick of giving next-level, crazy indulgent blow jobs and getting thirty seconds of 'eh' in return. It's bullshit.
JESS:	I don't even know what good sex is. When people say the female orgasm is a myth I, like, totally get it. And I hate that I get it! But I get it! Have I ever even had an orgasm?
BEX:	How would we even know?
JESS:	Even when it's good, I feel like it needs to be really good to deserve its own word. Right?
BEX:	You know, I've actually been having dreams since he —
JESS:	Like, wet dreams?
BEX:	No! Like, nightmares? Except … nightmares are supposed to be bad, right? But my nightmares are actually exciting? Wet dream meets nightmare. Like, just for example — don't get grossed out — in my dream I'm eating a cow and it's still alive.
JESS:	Aren't you vegan?
BEX:	I'm casually raw vegan, but mostly I just fast.
JESS:	Yeah, me, too. I do intermittent fasting. I only eat lunch now. It's … fine.
BEX:	It's, like, a spiritual thing.
JESS:	I do meditate more now.
BEX:	I meditate, but I'd still eat an entire fucking cow. If nobody was looking, I'd eat an entire fucking cow right now, swear to Christ.
JESS:	Who's looking?
BEX:	I mean, the cow would be looking. I'd have to blind the cow. I'd have to do an Equus.
JESS:	Sometimes I dream I'm eating ice cream, and all I do in the dream is eat ice cream. It's like a nine-hour,

	cinematic dream of me eating soft-serve in slow motion. It's literally the most pleasure I have ever experienced in my bed.
BEX:	And, okay, does your boyfriend make you —
JESS:	I don't have a boyfriend.
BEX:	Wait, really?
JESS:	Not anymore.
BEX:	No?
JESS:	I dumped him. He shamed me for sleeping in. I couldn't do it anymore.
BEX:	Well, I was going to ask if he makes you shave.
JESS:	Does Brian?
BEX:	I dumped him, too.
JESS:	No shit?!
BEX:	Yes, shit! He didn't disclose! That's fucked! And that hairy motherfucker made me shave EVERYTHING.
JESS:	I haven't seen anyone in weeks and I still shave. Why do I do that? In my head, it's like, "Oh, just in case!" In case of what? In case I need to work food service naked? Like..?!?
BEX:	I've had that nightmare, too, actually. I've never even worked in food service.
JESS:	If I had my way, I'd never shave again. Not my legs, not my pits, nothing. Just let it grow and give zero fucks whatsoever.
BEX:	If I had my way, I'd eat a steak every day. Rare. Someone else can blind the cow. I want blood on my mashed potatoes! I want to scrape them off a ceramic plate with the side of my fork. Whoops! Cleaned the plate! WHAT ARE YOU GONNA DO ABOUT IT, BRIAN?

JESS:	Oh my god, I want mashed potatoes! I forgot they existed! How does that happen to a person? I live in an alternate universe where potatoes don't exist!
BEX:	I just want to eat food! I don't even care what it is!
JESS:	… Can we get ice cream? I never get ice cream because I'm always cold. Are you always cold? I'm always cold and I always want ice cream. Not Halo Top, either. Halo Top tastes the way cramps feel. I think it's synthesized from human tears.
BEX:	WHAT IF THERE WAS ICE CREAM MADE OUT OF BLOOD?
JESS:	Um.
BEX:	SORRY BUT HOLY SHIT I AM SO ANEMIC. I AM LITERALLY BLEEDING AS WE SPEAK.
JESS:	You too?!
BEX:	Did we sync up?!
JESS:	That explains a lot, actually.
BEX:	But … no. No. I'm not going to let that be an excuse! I'm not going to wake up in four days and suddenly want to get my butthole waxed! I'm not going to be happy starving myself because I am not actively shedding my motherfucking uterine wall or whatever at that particular moment! And guess what! I don't even want a baby! Ever!
JESS:	I don't want a baby, either! I want four small dogs and maybe like a ferret?
BEX:	YOU DESERVE A FERRET. AND ICE CREAM. AND PLEASURE.
JESS:	I DO! I REALLY DO! SO DO YOU!
BEX:	I WANT TO MOAN AGAIN.
JESS:	What?
BEX:	I WANT TO HOWL.

JESS:	… What?
BEX:	I WANT TO HOWL. AT. THE. FUCKING. MOON.
JESS:	What moon?
BEX:	WHO CARES? LITERALLY FUCK THE MOON.

(BEX howls. JESS joins in. They howl until they're spent.)

JESS:	That was. Awesome. Why was that awesome?
BEX:	I have been holding that in for… a while.
JESS:	I could keep going, honestly.
BEX:	Hey, Jess?
JESS:	Yeah?
BEX:	I hope it's positive.
JESS:	What?
BEX:	If it's positive, I could do this every month. I could get hairy and devour meat and run through the woods until it feels like my heart is about to explode and just … let everything go.
JESS:	But then you'd be a werewolf.
BEX:	Yeah.
JESS:	You'd be a literal monster. You want to be a monster?
BEX:	I want to … want anything. I want to want anything and get it. Monsters get what they want. So, yeah, I guess I want to be that.
JESS:	Yeah. *(A beat.)* Hey. Would you …
BEX:	Would I what?
JESS:	Would you ever. Um.
BEX:	What?
JESS:	Would you infect me?
BEX:	… For real?

JESS:	I am so serious. I am 100 percent serious.
BEX:	I mean, of course! Obviously!
JESS:	Really? Because I can't keep doing this. I know it's, like — personal and —
BEX:	Wolves are pack animals. We need each other.
JESS:	Would you do it right now? If you break the skin, you can even lick the blood. I promise it won't even be weird for me. My ex was into some really esoteric shit.
BEX:	Are you sure? Didn't you dump him?
JESS:	Yeah, but that's not why.
BEX:	Okay, I guess. Okay, just … say when.
JESS:	Okay. Okay. Three, two —

(A phone begins to ring. BEX checks it.)

BEX:	Shit. Um.
JESS:	Is it Brian?
BEX:	It's the lab.
JESS:	The lab? What lab?
BEX:	The lab where I had the blood panel done. But they're not supposed to call until tomorrow. Do you think it's my results?
JESS:	Answer it!
BEX:	I'm scared!
JESS:	Let me answer it!
BEX:	They won't tell you anything! It's a HIPAA violation! I'm letting it go to voicemail!

(They let it go to voicemail. They wait for the little DING! It's agonizing. BEX checks the message immediately.)

JESS:	Well?!
BEX:	Fuck.

JESS:	Fuck yes or fuck no?
BEX:	I'm negative.
JESS:	Oh.
BEX:	Yeah.
JESS:	So do we just …?
BEX:	Just buy stock in Nair?
JESS:	I got some in my mouth once. It kind of tastes like Halo Top.
BEX:	Just … split a single seaweed snack to take the edge off?
JESS:	I'm still cold. I'd probably be warmer if I had actual body hair.
BEX:	I'd probably be warmer if there was any amount of iron in my blood whatsoever.
JESS:	You can still bite me if you want.
BEX:	It would just make me sad.
JESS:	I still really want ice cream.
BEX:	Yeah.
JESS:	Maybe I'll dream about it tonight. It's fine.
BEX:	I was so ready to be a monster.
JESS:	Me too. But.
BEX:	What?
JESS:	You told people you were getting tested, right?
BEX:	A few people. I told you. I told Lila. I told fucking Brian. He'll be thrilled.
JESS:	How about your mom?
BEX:	I had to tell my mom.
JESS:	So a lot of people know, actually. That you got tested.
BEX:	I guess?

JESS: But not that you're negative.

BEX: Right.

JESS: So maybe you're positive. They can't call and check. That would be ...

BEX: ... a HIPAA violation.

JESS: That would be a HIPAA violation.

(A beat. Two diabolical grins.)

BEX: Oh dear.

JESS: I'm so sorry to hear about your diagnosis.

BEX: Sorry I infected you. It couldn't be helped!

JESS: What a shame.

BEX: What a tragedy!

JESS: Two promising women turned monsters!

BEX: Should we do something? To make us feel better about this tragic diagnosis?

JESS: Ice cream?!

BEX: Steak house then ice cream.

(They begin to exit.)

JESS: And I'm sleeping in tomorrow!

BEX: You have to! The shock! You're incredibly ill!

JESS: I'm losing control!

BEX: Can't hold back!

(They howl. They howl long and loud as they exit, until they're out of earshot.)

END OF PLAY

AWESOME POSSUM

by Elizabeth A.M. Keel

CHARACTERS

AMY, a female vet tech and frequent animal rescuer. Any race or ethnicity. 20s and up.

DR. ROMAN, a veterinarian. Any race or ethnicity and any gender. 20s and up. (Pronouns may be adjusted to the actor.)

SETTING

An exam room in DR. ROMAN's veterinary clinic.

TIME

3 a.m. on a weeknight.

NOTE

The contents of the box should never be seen.

PRODUCTION HISTORY

Awesome Possum was presented by Rec Room in Houston, December 3, 2022. The performance was directed by Bree Bridger. The cast was as follows:

AMY: Lindsay Ehrhardt

DR. ROMAN: Anjana Menon

After hours in a veterinary clinic exam room. DR. ROMAN snaps on the light as AMY guiltily withdraws her hands from a medium-sized cardboard box. She is wearing thick elbow-length gloves for protection, along with pajama pants and muddy Wellies.

DR. ROMAN: You're fired.

AMY: Sure.

DR. ROMAN: For real this time.

AMY: Thanks for coming, Dr. Roman.

DR. ROMAN: It's 3 a.m.

AMY: The witching hour, already?

DR. ROMAN: 3 a.m. *again.*

AMY: It's nocturnal.

DR. ROMAN: Can't you rescue anything during *business hours?*

AMY: I'm sorry I didn't shut the alarm off fast enough. I promise I was trying to let you sleep for once.

DR. ROMAN: Don't agonize. I was up. It's still too quiet without her.

(Beat.)

AMY: I'll get all the mud cleaned up, too.

DR. ROMAN: Hmph.

(DR. ROMAN goes to wash their hands. AMY, trying not to be smug in her victory, shakes some kitten kibble into a shallow dish and sets it in the box. She clucks to what's inside.)

AMY: Hungies? Hungie, baby?

DR. ROMAN: Is it mammalian, then?

AMY: … Well, I know birds aren't your favorite.

DR. ROMAN: Has it taken any water?

(AMY recloses the flap on the box.)

AMY: I found it in the pond, actually. At the edge of it.

DR. ROMAN: What were you doing out there?

AMY: Walking.

DR. ROMAN: Amy.

AMY: Believe it or not, I don't *look* for them. They come
                   find me when they need me.

*(She hands DR. ROMAN matching gloves. They pull them on.
DR. ROMAN Chuckles.)*

AMY: What?

DR. ROMAN: Only one of the people in this room holds the state
                   record for most janky, fucked up possums rescued,
                   and it ain't / me.

AMY: I've had *help*.

DR. ROMAN: And you will buy *this* help some breakfast when
                   we're done. Now let me see your newest, dear
                   didelphidae.

*(As they move to open the flap of the box, AMY backs up to block
the doorway.)*

AMY: Dr. Ro?

DR. ROMAN: Hmm? What are you doing back there?

AMY: Just ... be careful.

(There is a slight but audible rustling of wings.)

DR. ROMAN: Why did that sound like wings?

AMY: Um. I don't *think* it can fly.

*(Now something inside the box mews. DR. ROMAN peers inside.
They hold very, very still. With the air of someone who doesn't want
to set off a bomb:)*

DR. ROMAN: Not a possum. Not a possum. Not a possum. Amy.

AMY: Yeah.

DR. ROMAN: The *pond?*

AMY: Yeah, the pond. In the cattails. I think it …
crashed.

(A soft, distinct mooing.)

AMY: *(Baby-voiced, to the creature.)* I'm still here. Love
you, you're okay. *(To DR. ROMAN.)* At first I
thought they were eating each other and got stuck,
but —

DR. ROMAN: There's no seam. That is *one* creature.

AMY: Is it taking the food?

DR. ROMAN: NO, NONE OF ITS *FOUR FUCKING FACES*
IS IN THE KIBBLE BITS.

AMY: You're gonna scare it! You can be mad at me, but
use the nice, customer-service tone.

(Beat.)

AMY: *Please.*

(Beat.)

AMY: I wasn't sure if it *could* eat. I mean, there's nowhere
for waste elimination. It's just hooves and feathers
and —

(A human baby laughs. Beat.)

AMY: I think it likes us.

*(DR. ROMAN moves a finger back and forth, over the top of the
box, like a coach checking for a concussion. The creature follows the
movement.)*

DR. ROMAN: All of its eyes blink together.

AMY: It's lucid.

(The creature moves suddenly, startling them.)

DR. ROMAN: Shit! Oh, shit! There's a tail under the fourth wing!

AMY: Chill out!

DR. ROMAN: *(With restraint.)* Why didn't you *leave it* where you found it?

AMY: A warm, glowing light told me not to.

(DR. ROMAN laughs in disbelief, then falls silent, then begins to weep. AMY hugs her friend.)

AMY: Hey. It's okay. It's okay.

DR. ROMAN: I asked for a sign. After she — After I lost her —

(Beat.)

AMY: Well, look at you, lucky duck. You got one.

(AMY plucks a tissue for them. DR. ROMAN takes time to dry their face and glasses. Once they're pulled together enough:)

AMY: I weighed it, on the scale. It weighs *nothing*. I took a picture, and only got a glare.

DR. ROMAN: Did you do a blood draw?

AMY: I tried. The needle melted.

(Beat.)

AMY: I think he's still a … "cub" of their kind. But when he was outside, in the reeds, he was just kind of lethargic and sad and lonely …

DR. ROMAN: I see where you're going with this.

AMY: Then the light came and told me to bring him in. To you. "Who saved who?" If the kittens and the skunks and the golden retrievers couldn't reach you, these last few months, then maybe, maybe, one of these? Could?

DR. ROMAN: One of these.

AMY: They deliver mercy. According to Google.

DR. ROMAN: Google! Why not the Vatican.

AMY: Cause he's wild and free.

DR. ROMAN: Right.

(Beat. DR. ROMAN takes AMY's smart phone and scrolls whatever article she found.)

DR. ROMAN: I thought cherubs were fat pink babies.

AMY: It's ... one fourth baby.

DR. ROMAN: Is that part — cow?

AMY: Ox, technically.

DR. ROMAN: Huh.

AMY: I figure the other ... *cherubim* ... will probably come for him soon.

DR. ROMAN: Thank you, Amy. We'll take good care of him, till then.

(They remove their gloves and feed the cherub kibble by hand. We hear the eagle and the ox head crunching away as the lion head purrs in contentment. The box fills with light, illuminating them both.)

END OF PLAY

THE MICHAELSON MODEL

by Alexis Kozak

CHARACTERS

FRED, male, 40ish to 60ish. A veteran teacher. Any race or ethnicity.

LOGAN, male, early-20s. A first-year teacher. Overtly sure of himself. Any race or ethnicity.

SETTING

An American high school classroom.

TIME

The present. Shortly after the end of the school day.

NOTE

Like teachers do, both of these people are capable of charming someone to death, by tai chi-ing and twisting even the most serious of things into a joke. This "charm-and-joke" version of shock-and-awe can be used as both a defense and as a weapon. In fact, maybe it is the only way to survive.

PRODUCTION HISTORY

The Michaelson Model was presented by Sheila Duane and Playwrights at Night at Jersey Shore Arts Center in Ocean Grove, NJ, on October 5th, 2022. The production was directed by Alexis Kozak. The cast was as follows:

FRED: James Benner

LOGAN: PJ Benson

High school classroom. FRED — a veteran teacher — sits at his desk, working on a computer. He wears glasses and looks over the tops of his lenses at his computer screen. After a moment, LOGAN — a first-year teacher — pops his head in at the door. He is on his way out of the building: jacket, bag, and smart phone in hand.

LOGAN: Burning the candle at both ends?

FRED: Just the person I wanted to see.

LOGAN: Be still my beating heart.

FRED: Come in here, kid.

LOGAN: Just popping in to say, "Have a nice afternoon."

FRED: These Student Growth Objectives are killing me — you know how to do this, right?

LOGAN: The S.G.O.'s were due by lunch.

FRED: *(Charming, a joke.)* Yeah, well, some of us teach for a living.

LOGAN: You are working with a basic spreadsheet?

FRED: I used to total it up by hand and make a table in a Word document.

LOGAN: A Word document? Jeez. Do they even *make* those anymore?

FRED: Everybody swears this will save me a couple of hours.

LOGAN: Oh, minimum.

FRED: The way this totals things up automatically, it makes me nervous. I don't even really know what it's doing.

LOGAN: You want me to take a look?

FRED: I signed on for coffee, summers off, not *this* crap.

LOGAN: You're using the one administration emailed out, right?

FRED: Trying to.

LOGAN: *(Indicating FRED's chair, "sit?")* Can I …?

FRED: *(Giving up his chair.)* Oh, sure, sure.

LOGAN: *(Sort of to himself, while he looks over FRED's work.)*
           Okay. Looks like you've got your data columns *here*.
           Automatically breaks your students down into your
           three achievement groups — right, okay — low,
           medium, high — okay. It sorts the data —

FRED: "Data." Ha, ha. When I started, you know what we
           used to call "data"? "Grades." Ha, ha. "Grades." Those
           were the days.

LOGAN: Yeah, right? This all looks good so far …Wow.

FRED: What?

LOGAN: Every one of your students hit their goal. How'd you
           manage that?

FRED: Good teaching?

LOGAN: Every single *one*?

FRED: *Ex*cellent teaching? *(Silence. FRED gives LOGAN a
           look.)* Are you trying to ask me if they are real? It's
           okay. You can ask me. "Mr. Dryser, are these S.G.O.'s
           real?" No. They are not real. I made them up. The only
           way I could get the kids to score like that would be if I
           gave them the answers.

LOGAN: But what if somebody questions it?

FRED: I have hard copies. I'm not an idiot. I have something
           they wrote their own names on. Just in case push
           comes to shove, but.

LOGAN: I can't believe you're faking their scores.

FRED: When you say it like that, it sounds bad. Hey, listen,
           if *my* kid — my *own* child — has a teacher that is not
           intelligent enough to figure out how to do this, then
           maybe that's not a person I want teaching my kid. You
           know what I mean? Who is gonna be dumb enough
           to put in some student growth numbers that are not

	gonna one hundred percent guarantee them a Highly Effective rating?
LOGAN:	I'm just surprised, I guess.
FRED:	Smoke and mirrors, kid. Smoke and mirrors.
LOGAN:	But if I noticed it …
FRED:	You think our supervisors don't know? Believe me, they know. They *need* us to do good. *We* do good, *they* do good. *Their* scores are tied to *our* scores. It's like a sales structure. *You* make more if the guys *under* you make more. Except that in a sales structure, you want to *help* the guys under you, so they perform better. Not this observation, "I-didn't-see-*this*, you're-a-two, I-*did*-see-this, you're-a-four" bullshit.
LOGAN:	Were you a four last year?
FRED:	My point is — the guy who came up with this whole evaluation thing —Michaelson? — where's he from? California? — My point is, I'd respect this guy Michaelson if he was like, "Hey, that's not how my evaluation model is supposed to be used. It was supposed to help teachers improve, not as a tool for school districts to evaluate how well you do your job. You can't use it like that." Stand up for the working man — he was a teacher, stand *up* for teachers. Not, "you score *this, three* observations next year — you score *this, one* observation."
LOGAN:	He is a she.
FRED:	Huh?
LOGAN:	The observation paradigm you're talking about. The Michaelson Model. Michaelson is a woman.
FRED:	No shit? Figures. I guess *I'd* whore it out, too, if they paid me enough.
LOGAN:	I think it's actually a good model.
FRED:	You drank the Kool Aid, huh?

LOGAN: You can't turn this in. They're gonna catch you. A hundred per*cent* they're gonna catch you.

FRED: I'm not doing anything wrong. Not really.

LOGAN: I think they might disagree.

FRED: I wasn't looking for an ethics lecture. I just wanted you to check my numbers.

LOGAN: Why are you doing this to me?

FRED: *What* am I doing?

LOGAN: What is this? A test? Is this some kind of a test?

FRED: Relax a second, kid.

LOGAN: "Check your numbers?" The numbers stink.

FRED: All right. All right.

LOGAN: And why do you call me "kid" all the time? Why do you do that?

FRED: Hey, I'm just trying to give you some free advice. From somebody who has been around the block.

LOGAN: You called me "kid" in front of the whole school last week.

FRED: Did I?

LOGAN: At the faculty meeting. You said, "The kid's real good." You said that in front of everybody.

FRED: I was giving you a compliment.

LOGAN: What do you get out of putting me down?

FRED: "*Get* out of?"

LOGAN: You know the numbers give you away. You knew that before I walked in here. So you brought me in here to what? To show off? To show me how smart you are?

FRED: Maybe I'm trying to teach you a little something, kid. Huh? Maybe you should just shut up and take the compliment.

LOGAN: Just don't do anything you wouldn't want to see in the newspaper tomorrow.

FRED: I'm not raping little kids. I'm making my job a little easier.

LOGAN: Anytime something goes wrong in this country, people blame the schools. All I'm saying is, don't give them another reason.

FRED: Why? Are you gonna *tell* on me?

LOGAN: No.

FRED: What are we? Adults? Or are we children? Is this the school yard? You gonna tell the playground monitor?

LOGAN: I just said, "No."

FRED: Goddamn right, "No."

(LOGAN stands and tries to maneuver out from behind the desk. FRED corners him in.)

LOGAN: Get out of my way.

FRED: Sit down.

LOGAN: I'm asking you nicely.

FRED: Oh, "you're asking me nicely?"

LOGAN: What is this? "Meet me behind the football field after school"?

FRED: I said, "Sit down."

LOGAN: What's wrong with you?

FRED: I'm the guy who might just save your ass.

LOGAN: What the hell are you talking about?

FRED: "Loves New Wave Jazz music, especially trumpet. Binge watches *Scooby Doo*. But only the new episodes." *(LOGAN is surprised.)* "A passion for good quinoa with spinach." *(LOGAN becomes slowly mortified.)* Hey, relax kid. Your secret is safe with me. "Quinoa." What even is that?

LOGAN: It's a grain.

FRED: I know what it is.

LOGAN: Because not everybody knows.

FRED: "Quinoa?" Really? And *those* are just the *few* things
           that are fit to talk about in mixed company. Back in *my*
           day, the rest of those things were things we wouldn't
           talk about it public, much less post on the internet for
           the whole world to see.

LOGAN: What are you doing?

FRED: Wait a second. Did I say "secret"? Can something be
           "secret" if everybody knows about it?

LOGAN: Why did you look up my dating profile?

FRED: *Me*?! Jesus Christ. I can't even work a spreadsheet, you
           think I'm —? The *kids*! The *kids* looked it up. They
           found you.

LOGAN: Not possible.

FRED: Mister High Tech, Mister Computer, Mister Online
           Lessons, Mister Spreadsheet. So much smarter, so
           much savvier — what's it like? Dating a computer?
           Kids found your profile?

LOGAN: I'm telling you, kids did not find my profile. I have so
           many privacy settings, it's like Fort Knox. Like, *I* can
           barely find it.

FRED: That guy you're talking to? "Bryan" is it? With a
           "Y?" *(LOGAN — terror.)* Is one of the girls in my
           class. She's pretending to be him. Hey, it's all right. It
           happens to the best of us. You walk around here like
           your shit don't stink. Like you're cock of the walk. You
           think you're pretty smart. You went to State. Yeah, well
           guess who else went to State? Yeah, that's right. And
           look where we are now. Right in the same wing, right
           next door to each other.

LOGAN: I'm allowed to have a dating profile.

FRED: Oh sure. You're allowed to have a lot of things.

LOGAN: Who I am out there, and who I am in here, that's two different things.

FRED: Once you're a teacher, you're a teacher. And that person that lived out there? That was a human being? They are in the past.

(A long beat.)

LOGAN: They tell you not to eat in the teachers' lunchroom.

FRED: "They?"

LOGAN: "They," common wisdom. Because eventually we are going to meet somebody like you.

FRED: Good-looking, charming, full of snarky war stories?

LOGAN: A teacher whose goal in life is to bring the world down and *us with* it.

FRED: *(This stings. This misunderstanding is embarrassing.)* That's not what I'm doing.

LOGAN: Pushing kids to get my dating profile?

FRED: Hey, hey, hold on now.

LOGAN: There are plenty of other ways you could have said what you had to say.

FRED: All right. Maybe you're right. Look, I like you. You're a bright young man. I'm not trying to knock you down. I'm trying to open your eyes. Common Wisdom never taught in the American public school system. This isn't, "a mind is a terrible thing to waste" and "we are the world" and "go out and make a difference." This is get chewed up and spit out and wake up the next day and come in and do it all over again and keep your eye on the prize of retirement and the free luncheon the union throws for you at the end of a career full of disappointments.

LOGAN: I'm not looking to make a career full of disappointments.

FRED: Nobody *is*.

LOGAN: I'm looking to make successes.

FRED: The successes only stand out because of how many disappointments there are. Look, I'm trying to help you. *(Genuinely hurt, at being so misconstrued.)* Come on, Logan. Mr. Crane … *(Pause.)* You're angry at me. You're actually *angry* at me.

LOGAN: You *are* what the data *says* you are. You can't B.S. it your whole life.

FRED: It's just data. It's just numbers. Flip them this way, flip them that way. You can make them say whatever you want.

LOGAN: You can't fake data. Maybe you could, back in the day of the dinosaur. But not anymore.

FRED: You're angry because I'm right. And you *know* I'm right. *(Referring again to the dating profile.)* "Six foot one, a hundred eighty pounds." Oh, please.

LOGAN: That's not the same thing.

FRED: "Yale pre-med?" That's not the same thing? How can you say you were "Yale pre-med" if you weren't "Yale pre-med?"

LOGAN: Because that is a whole made up world, and everybody knows that. Everybody agrees. Out there is make-believe. But in here? In here, this is supposed to be the real world. This is supposed to be real preparation for what it's really gonna *be* like out there.

FRED: "You can be President of the United States. You can be an astronaut. You can be anything you want to be." That's *real* to you? Good luck in *this* profession.

LOGAN: Nobody has wanted to be an astronaut in twenty years, Fred. Who'd want to? I can make a bigger difference with my phone. I can *run* America from my phone. And make a hell of a lot of money doing it, too. And I don't need to be President or go to space to do it. If you stopped and looked at what was really going on in here, maybe you'd understand that.

FRED: *(FRED scoffs, shakes his head.)* You've got it all figured out, huh?

LOGAN: Don't take it too hard. You'll catch on eventually. *(LOGAN gathers his belongings. He stops at the door.)* I'll see you tomorrow morning, kid.

(LOGAN exits. FRED is left sitting behind his desk.)

END OF PLAY

WE JUMP BROOM

by Mildred Inez Lewis

CHARACTERS

NELL, (late teens, early 20s) African American

WINNY, (late teens, early 20s) African American

SETTING

A hidden clearing outside of an Alabama cotton plantation. It is close on midnight during Indian Summer. The clearing is lit by a Harvest Moon.

TIME

1830s.

NOTE

There are no grammatical errors. The characters' language is not broken. It is fashioned from the English they've been allowed and inflected with the grammatical patterns and rhythms of their native tongue, Fon, the language of the Dahomey tribe.

PRODUCTION HISTORY

We Jump Broom was a finalist in the Samuel French Off-Off Broadway, 2022. The production was directed by Adrienne D. Williams. The cast was as follows:

NELL: Siarra Donna

WINNY: Aja Montgomery

In Darkness. NELL and WINNY laugh and gasp with lovemaking pleasure then roll away from each other.

LIGHTS RISE. NELL is loose and relaxed. Draped in a scratchy horse blanket, she leans back and watches WINNY intently. WINNY buttons her blouse with her back to NELL and the audience. She looks oddly prim.

NELL: Turn round.

WINNY: *(teasing)* I done give you a lot of pleasure. Set with it and leave me 'lone.

NELL: Meet me again tonight.

WINNY: We can't meet up two nights in a row. You know that.

(NELL embraces WINNY. WINNY protects the place of a scar.)

WINNY: Gimme my breath back.

NELL: Naw. Everything about you belongs to me. All of me's yours.

(WINNY wiggles away, then peeks over her shoulder.)

WINNY: What 'cha lookin' at?

NELL: I like to watch.

WINNY: You as bad as a man.

NELL: Bet I do some things a man wouldn't.

(WINNY, now fully clothed, turns.)

WINNY: I could feel your eyes on me all day long. From ten rows away. You burning holes into my back past all that cotton.

NELL: Wishing them skirts off.

WINNY: Made me sweat so bad, I looked round to see if anybody else could feel your heat. I was scared John Henry 'spect something, but he scared of his own shadow since mister branded him.

NELL: You took yours without a whimper.

WINNY: It was so much pain, I wasn't sure I was still alive.

NELL: My poor chile.

WINNY: I crawl into your pallet that night in front of
          everybody. Didn't care what nobody was gon' say.
          They could 'splain it cause we from the same village
          or whatever all else. Had to be with you.

NELL: I got to hold you all night. The sun kissed me awake
          with you in my arms.

WINNY: You, me and all that pain.

NELL: You didn't cry one tear. I was proud of you.

WINNY: Why?

NELL: I —

WINNY: Why we got to be so strong? Who made it like that?

NELL: A time like that shows what someone's made of. You
          showed out. Got up and walked to them fields the
          next morning like nothing happened. John Henry was
          watching to see if you would break. You never give him
          that happiness. That means a lot.

WINNY: I wish I could be weak sometimes.

NELL: I'm not claiming weakness. *(teasing)* You want to
          flounce round, pretendin' like Missus do?

WINNY: Pretendin's right. She hurt you, then go cryin' to
          Mister so he can —

NELL: — turn round and get John Henry to beat you some
          more.

(They laugh. It's a little bitter.)

WINNY: Don't pay Missus no mind. She don't know no better
          than what she's been taught. The things they beat outta
          us, they beat into her. I'm talking about something

else. I guess I don't mean weak, but I wish we could be soft with each other.

(WINNY grows wistful.)

NELL: Hey.

(NELL draws WINNY into a clapping game.²)

WINNY: Thank you.

(WINNY starts to cry.)

NELL: Don't …

(WINNY forces her tears back.)

WINNY: If I let one go, we'll drown. I've got an ocean of tears locked up inside me.

NELL: Might be enough water to carry us over the sea back home.

WINNY: Don't go dreamin' like that. It dangerous.

NELL: More danger being dead inside.

WINNY: Some things got to stay buried deep. I'll go back first. You wait a spell.

(WINNY unconsciously touches the scar from the chest brand.)

NELL: Don't do that.

WINNY: Do what? Stop trying to stretch the time out. I done already told you. We gots to go.

NELL: You stubborn as a mule, gal. Why the goddess give me somebody as hard headed as you?

WINNY: *(half sings to the heavens)* Yemanja, Yemanja. Goddess of waters. You give us tears and the water to wash them away. Answer my beloved. Tell her why you made me like me and she like herself.

---

2 Reference: https://youtu.be/SqIWL70SdtQ]

(WINNY retrieves small bones from her pocket, rattles them, opens her eyes and reads them like tea leaves.)

NELL: *(a little awed)* What she say?

WINNY: If we don't get back, we gon' be in trouble.

(They laugh. WINNY covers her scar again.)

NELL: Stop hiding that scar from me. I ain't afraid of it. You got it cause of me.

WINNY: It's ugly.

NELL: You've never let me see it. I want to kiss it.

(NELL reaches for WINNY. WINNY eludes her.)

WINNY: They'll be missing us in quarters.

NELL: They might already know we gone.

WINNY: They do know. But they ain't gon *say* nothin', less we make it so they have to. We need to be back before first light. Even mister abide by that.

NELL: Mister don't abide by nothin'.

(The ferocity of NELL's words contrasts with her trembling.)

WINNY: You won't have to suffer him again. I fixed that. I'll always fix it.

NELL: He was like a stone crushing the life from my chest. The worst was after ...

(WINNY shakes her head. "Please stop.")

NELL: It eats me up keeping it locked up inside. I let you have your truth. Let me have mine.

WINNY: Tell Hetty or Topsie —

NELL: I don't tell them wide-hipped gals nothin'.

WINNY: We can trust them. They know 'bout us. Least they suspect, but they haven't said anything. Hetty got a way of listening. I talk to her sometimes.

NELL: They got they own troubles. We 'posed to be for each other. I don't want to tell nobody else.

WINNY: When something pains you, it hurts me a long time. When you put words to a thing, I can't stop seeing it in my mind. Sometimes it bears down so hard, I can't hardly move.

NELL: Please, Winny.

WINNY: Be quick about it. I can't let it sink into my spirit. And we got to get back.

NELL: After he done his business, he sat me on his lap. My insides were torn up.

WINNY: *(quietly)* Is that why you don't bleed right?

NELL: *(nods)* He was laughing, like it was funny. He shake me until he make me laugh with him. I laugh hard to make everything stop. But my laughs started turning into screams 'til they got so loud, his missus had to hear. I think he like that, cause that's when he let me go.

WINNY: I fixed him with these.

(WINNY shakes the bones hard.)

WINNY: The old ways can still work. He ain't ever gon' look your way again.

(NELL points to the scar.)

NELL: But …

WINNY: It was my turn to pay. In the end, we all gots to pay. You're done paying him.

(She touches her chest.)

WINNY: This pays it in full.

NELL: I'm afraid for our girl young'uns. Especially the ones don't have anybody looking out for 'em. We got to do something for 'em.

WINNY: Can't. We can't hardly do for ourselves.

NELL: We not gon' even try?

WINNY: My body can't take another brand.

NELL: I don't believe goddess give you that magic just for us two.

WINNY: You want me to get caught? There's danger all around us.

(NELL shakes her head in frustration.)

NELL: You just scared.

WINNY: Course I'm scared. You should be, too. There's a thing you got to understand. But you can't tell no one. We don't know who we can trust.

(NELL nods.)

WINNY: Promise me!

NELL: Yes'm.

WINNY: Mister's talking about selling. Auntie whispered it to me at supper awhile back. You tell it and they find out, he's not gon sell her. He'll kill her. She don't deserve that.

NELL: You didn't tell me.

WINNY: This time's the only snatch of sweetness we get. I ain't throwing it away for somethin' we already know. He do what he want. Auntie think he's planning on selling 15 or 20 of us.

NELL: Bucks or us?

WINNY: Both. I don't want you worrying on it.

NELL: How you expect me not to?

WINNY: You better find a way.

NELL: I know one thing.

WINNY: Gal, I done told you and told you —

NELL: I don't mean run away. Too many catchers out on them roads. I know that much.

WINNY: At least you still got some sense.

NELL: Marry me.

(NELL takes out a small whisk broom. Beat.)

WINNY: Don't you let nobody see you with that. What's wrong with you? It's against their law.

NELL: Their law, not ours. We're Dahomey. Our way says anybody that loves can marry.

WINNY: We're not Dahomey any more. Forget.

NELL: I don't care what they say. I belong to myself. I want us to belong to each other. In our way, the Dahomey way. Jump with me.

WINNY: You planned this.

NELL: Yes'm. Took me weeks. Hiding it every few days so wouldn't nobody find it.

WINNY: Nobody means me?

NELL: Sure do. Remember how the old women swept the dirt before weddings? Making patterns for a couple to grow into.

WINNY: We don't have witnesses.

NELL: The stars be our witness.

WINNY: What if mister sells me? He done threatened it. Me still walking and working is a 'buke to him.

(NELL gently sweeps the ground.)

NELL: I'd walk to the end of earth to find you.

WINNY: How you gon' do that?

NELL: We come from warriors.

(NELL points to Winny's scar.)

NELL: You found yo' strength when we most needed it.
I'd find mine.

WINNY: When you love hard, you don't need that.

(WINNY points to the broom.)

NELL: I do. When we become ancestors, I need our
descendants to have a legacy. That matters to me.

WINNY: *(tries to joke)* Who you planning for me to lay with to
gather these descendants?

NELL: I don't care. He wouldn't be with you. I would.
You think too much. This time let's just do.

WINNY: Don't be stupid. We gots to think all the time. Got to
plot out every move, then five, six steps past that if we
want to live.

NELL: We dying anyway. He killed my womb. When he
marked you, he broke somethin' in you. We got to do
this to keep the half-life we do have goin'.

*(The dawn begins breaking. WINNY looks up at it. NELL positions
the broom.)*

NELL: Jump now and we'll be back 'fore it's too late.

WINNY: I'm scared.

NELL: Throw the bones.

*(WINNY throws the bones. She looks at NELL and nods. The bones
said "yes.")*

WINNY: One more again? To be sure.

NELL: Throw.

(WINNY throws. Another "yes.")

NELL: See? Broom, broom, who gon' jump the broom?

WINNY
AND
NELL: Broom, broom, who gon' jump the broom?

WINNY: I, Winny …

NELL: No. Say your true name.

WINNY: Marnar. I, Marnar, a Dahomey woman …

NELL: I, Fugra. Dahomey woman. Goddess Yemanja! Before you, we take each other.

(The women hold their arms out to each other.)

WINNY
AND
NELL: Broom, broom. Who gon' jump the broom? We gon' jump the broom!

(The women jump over the broom, look behind them, kiss passionately, then exit running.)

END OF PLAY

A TRAGEDY OF OWLS

by John Mabey

CHARACTERS

LAU MAZIREL, woman, 30s, white, attorney and member of the Dutch resistance

WILLEM ARONDEUS, man, 40s, white, artist and member of the Dutch resistance

SETTING

A prison in The Netherlands

TIME

June 1943

NOTE

This play is a dramatic interpretation of real people and events. As Lau Mazirel visits Willem Arondeus in prison, the events, names, locations, and prison visit itself are true to history (as well as Willem's request of Lau at the end and his final words to her); however, the rest of the dialogue is a representation of their conversation.

In the few years before his death, Willem authored works including *The Owl House* (1938) and *The Tragedy of the Dream* (1939). The title of this play, *A Tragedy of Owls*, is in homage to these titles of his works and also holds special significance in this play.

PRODUCTION HISTORY

A Tragedy Of Owls was presented by Rainy Day Artistic Collective, WA, on March 19 & 20, 2022. The production was directed by Ruthie Stanley. The cast was as follows:

LAU MAZIREL: Jennifer Rashleigh

WILLEM ARONDEUS: Jim Haines

WILLEM is in restraints as LAU examines his wounded face.

LAU: Hold still.

WILLEM: Nothing gets done when we hold still.

LAU: Quiet.

WILLEM: Why? My fate is certain. And short.

LAU: I just prefer modesty.

(WILLEM laughs. He then grimaces in pain and pulls away from her.)

LAU: It hurts when you laugh?

WILLEM: And breathe.

LAU: Even your wounds have wounds. It's not right. In the trial —

WILLEM: Nothing is right anymore. Laws are a joke.

LAU: Laws are my life.

WILLEM: The law is what you do, what happened that night is who you are.

LAU: We are all many things.

WILLEM: And right now are you "friend" or "attorney?"

LAU: There's not much time and I need something.

WILLEM: As "friend" or "attorney?"

LAU: Everything's intertwined.

WILLEM: So you're not answering my question..

LAU: I just did. But you never listen, even when it's more than your life I'm trying to save.

(LAU tries to wash his face with her hand. WILLEM doesn't stop her.)

WILLEM: Shouldn't bother. The Nazis toss bruised fruit whether it's washed or not.

LAU: So much will be washed away in the end.

WILLEM: Unless we make it known.

(She studies his face.)

LAU: It's okay to be frightened.

WILLEM: None of this is coming from fear.

LAU: We don't have the luxury of lies today.

WILLEM: I'm only frightened for others.

LAU: Like Sjoerd?

(WILLEM reacts strongly, moving as far away from her as possible.)

WILLEM: I've never heard that name.

LAU: We're running out of time, and that's the second time
           you've lied today. Possibly third.

WILLEM: Leave.

LAU: They already know.

WILLEM: He was nowhere near the bombing.

LAU: Willem, they already know. Everything. The two
           of you.

(Her meaning washes over him.)

LAU: But there's a chance for him to live.

WILLEM: To "live" or to "have a life?"

LAU: They're the same.

WILLEM: Invisible cages are still cages.

LAU: If you and he could simply renounce any sort of
           intimate —

(WILLEM laughs again, grimacing in pain.)

LAU: Was it worth it?

WILLEM: Do you mean bombing the Nazi records? My
           relationship with Sjoerd? The laugh?

(LAU turns away, starting to leave, until he answers.)

WILLEM: Yes it was. All of it.

(She stops.)

WILLEM: And I need something, too.

LAU: From "friend" or "attorney?"

WILLEM: Sjoerd. Is he ...

(His voice trails off.)

LAU: Looking like you? Yes. But less combative.

WILLEM: He rarely speaks anyway.

LAU: And right now he can barely move his lips. They never heal quickly when split.

WILLEM: You need to deliver a message.

LAU: Make it short, I have no tools for writing. Even had to remove my hairpin before coming in your cell.

WILLEM: No small mercies.

LAU: What do you want him to know?

WILLEM: Not him ... it's for the court. I need you to confirm that yes, I am what they say.

LAU: Willem, you clearly don't mean —

WILLEM: A homosexual. And so is Sjoerd. And neither of us were cowards.

(Beat.)

(LAU laughs, but it's not a happy one.)

LAU: They beat you harder than I thought.

WILLEM: I don't expect you to understand.

LAU: But you expect me to be an accomplice to his death.

WILLEM: We're both already gone.

LAU: He doesn't need to be. The evidence is weaker.

WILLEM: The sooner you admit it's out of your hands —

LAU: *(Indicating her own hands)* You know better than anyone what these hands have done. What they can do. What they've already risked.

(Beat.)

WILLEM: Who was it?

LAU: No one betrayed you.

WILLEM: Then Sjoerd would be far, far away from here.

LAU: There was a notebook, discovered when they searched your apartment. One you tried to burn.

WILLEM: Tried?

LAU: Some things are very difficult to destroy.

WILLEM: I betrayed myself, then. All of us.

(LAU sees an opening and tries her plea again.)

LAU: If you truly believe that, help me now. Deny there was ever a relationship between you two ... of that sort.

WILLEM: When I first met him on the side of the road, Sjoerd was crouching in tears.

LAU: I already know this story.

WILLEM: Not the most important part.

LAU: Willem, the guards will return any —

WILLEM: I discovered this frail, tiny man holding another frail, tiny creature...cradled to his chest. Neither seemed to have long to live. Wings crushed, eyes wide. Outcasts.

LAU: Willem, focus.

WILLEM: This stranger, cradling a baby owl, as war raged all around. And I held my discovery as he held his. A tiny act of courage that sparked a love that lit a fuse that helped thousands to live.

LAU: The world doesn't want to know such things, Willem.

It never will.

WILLEM: Not as outcasts. But just imagine if we defined ourselves? That's what I'm asking.

LAU: You won't have to live with what you're asking. I will.

WILLEM: But I won't die knowing we'll just be erased.

(LAU doesn't reply. WILLEM sees this an opening and tries his plea again.)

WILLEM: I woke suddenly ... there was a sound outside our bedroom window. Someone moving in the darkness. I gripped the knife as Sjoerd and I went outside. Suddenly we saw it ... in the trees. Then another. I swear there was two, then three, then four, then ... so many. Surrounding us. I knew what it meant. We've already said our goodbyes.

LAU: It's rare to see so many owls. Perhaps it was all a dream.

WILLEM: The dream was everything that came before.

LAU: "Parliament." It's called a "parliament of owls."

WILLEM: Terrible name.

LAU: And yet.

WILLEM: I wonder what they'd call themselves if given the chance, too. *(Beat)* Help me, Lau.

LAU: 800,000 identity cards were destroyed that day, thousands of Jews escaped. But no one will ever celebrate that a homosexual ... even several ... did anything brave. Let alone believe it.

WILLEM: But you'll know.

LAU: I'm no one. Not even very good at my job, based on today.

WILLEM: We are all many things, remember?

LAU: I'm not sure I still believe that.

WILLEM: An act of courage anyway.

LAU: It's hard being courageous when you're frightened.
Terrified.

WILLEM: Maybe they actually look the same.

LAU: Since when?

WILLEM: Since you. *(Beat)* Let it be known.

(LAU examines his wounded face once again as in the beginning, but this time with a finality. Then the sound of heavy footsteps, a door opening. She exits.)

(The epilogue below may be presented in various ways, but the playwright requests that it be made available at the conclusion of the play.)

EPILOGUE

Willem Arondeus and Sjoerd Bakker were both executed a month later on July 1, 1943.

After the Netherlands was liberated in 1945, the Dutch government awarded the entire group of resistance fighters a posthumous medal. But due to homophobia, the contributions of Willem, Sjoerd, and the rest of its openly LGBT members were largely erased from public acknowledgment.

In the 1980s, these LGBT resistance fighters were finally given full recognition. They were posthumously awarded the Resistance Memorial Cross as well as recognized as Righteous Among the Nations by Yad Vashem (Israel's official memorial to Holocaust victims).

Lau Mazirel lived for another 30 years. She dedicated her career to resistance activities throughout WWII, even getting arrested herself in 1944 for rescuing Jewish children on deportation trains. After the war, she became a leader in the fight for LGBT rights.

END OF PLAY

THE WELCOME

by Jennifer Maisel

CHARACTERS

GRETA — 70, female, any ethnicity

JANA — 19, female, any ethnicity

SETTING

A bedroom in Greta's Los Angeles home. The guest room.
It doesn't have a lot of personality. It's nice though. Ready for
whoever needs to be there. Jana has a backpack with her things.

TIME

Now and in the future.

NOTE

This is a 21st century play in a 21st century world. Please cast
accordingly.

PRODUCTION HISTORY

THE WELCOME was presented by the Playwright's Union at
Atwater Village Theatre in Los Angeles, CA, May 19, 2023.

JANA:	This is so nice of you.
GRETA:	It's nothing.
JANA:	It's not nothing. Pretty room. Clean sheets. For a complete stranger.
GRETA:	Not complete.
JANA:	A phone call.
GRETA:	It was a good call —
JANA:	It wasn't special —
GRETA:	It connected us — and I don't know about you but I felt —
JANA:	What —
GRETA:	Like what we used to call, back in the day, my day, before your days, the phone line — the actual physical line — was like a tangible reflection of our connection —
JANA:	I have used a landline, you know.
GRETA:	Of course you have —
JANA:	I'm just saying —
GRETA:	I didn't mean —
JANA:	People, people my age, we're the last to have that memory, probably. To bridge that gap, consistently, between telephone wires and 5G.
GRETA:	I just meant —
JANA:	My mom still has a landline.
GRETA:	She does?
JANA:	It's unplugged. Because only spammers call it. She says it's for emergencies. For when the grid goes down. But she's a hoarder so I think it's that it's just another thing with only the slightest bit of possible use left in it she can't let go of.

GRETA: I just meant the difference between something you can grasp and something that's ... ether. And it felt like our voices grasped each other in that call.

JANA: Whatever you say.

GRETA: To me —

JANA: ...

GRETA: ...

JANA: ...

GRETA: The alarm is set for 6 since we have to be there — Bathroom is the second door on your right. I left you towels.

JANA: Thank you.

GRETA: ...

JANA: ...

GRETA: The fridge is stocked.

JANA: You didn't have to —

GRETA: You do have to eat.

JANA: I just mean —

GRETA: No animal products on the third shelf —

JANA: What?

GRETA: You said you were plant-based. I wanted to make sure you had an animal product free zone. Just ignore shelves one and two. Who knew they make cheese out of cashews? But they do.

JANA: ...

GRETA: Or if you like — I mean if you don't like the plant-based things to be near the animal-based things — I could have my neighbor Diana hold on to the prosciutto and the half and half.

JANA:	I said I was a plant-lover.
GRETA:	…
JANA:	Like I like plants.
GRETA:	Are you sure?
JANA:	And burgers. I like burgers. Meaty bloody burgers. Smothered in milky cheddar. Lots of moo.
GRETA:	Oh. The connection was —
JANA:	Static-y and ether-y. Not tangible.
GRETA:	Oh.
JANA:	You're not going to make me eat cheese made out of things that shouldn't make cheese, are you?
GRETA:	Oh, I'm going to tie you to the bed and force-feed you. Right down your throat.
JANA:	…
GRETA:	I'm not. I wouldn't —
JANA/ GRETA:	Should I go?/Don't go.
GRETA:	I'm not funny. Apparently.
JANA:	…
GRETA:	…
JANA:	Succulents. Mostly. Harder to kill.
GRETA:	I'm terrible at plants. I need something that tells me it's hungry. That reminds me it needs taking care of. Mice. Gerbils. Dogs. Kids. Kids I'm great at.
JANA:	I thought you didn't —
GRETA:	Other people's kids.
JANA:	…
GRETA:	…

(Jana spies a basket.)

JANA: Is that a —

GRETA: /It's nothing — /

JANA: /It is — it's a/ —

GRETA: I spend too much time on Pinterest. Retirement is a shitty tricky way of passing hours. I wanted you to feel —

JANA: You made a welcome basket.

GRETA: No … really … it's just a —

JANA: It says it.

(She reads the tag.)

JANA: Welcome Jana. Welcome Jana. It's very Miss Manners.

GRETA: I'm all about the etiquette.

JANA: Welcome me. Commence the tap dance and bestowing of the lei.

GRETA: Let me strike up the band.

JANA: Unfurl the big banner!

GRETA: Bring out the cake.

JANA: There actually is cake, isn't there? Plant-based cake.

GRETA: …

JANA: There is!

GRETA: I didn't really know —

JANA: God. If only everyone knew they get cake they'd be driving here in droves. Fuck the police — there's cake!

GRETA: There's not really much of a handbook. Actually, there's no handbook at all. They think —

JANA: They?

GRETA: You know —

JANA:	They —
GRETA:	The less of a paper trail, the better. No tangibles. Even if it's legal. Here. Oh, did you turn off —
JANA:	What?
GRETA:	Your location services?
JANA:	My —
GRETA:	The tracking.
JANA:	Really?
GRETA:	They say — Just in case — Your friends. Your mom.
JANA:	I don't think she — She wouldn't even know how to do that. *(regarding the basket)* Ginger chews? Essential oils? *(JANA sniffs a sachet)* Lavender? You made this, didn't you? It's got a J on it. You made this.
GRETA:	…
JANA:	Like a spa-day basket. Only without the spa.
GRETA:	I just thought — you might feel —
JANA:	…
GRETA:	Like you wanted to be welcomed.
JANA:	…
GRETA:	…
JANA:	My mom is not unwelcoming.
GRETA:	I didn't say —
JANA:	She just has her —
GRETA:	Jana —
JANA:	— own set of beliefs.
GRETA:	/It's not about her/ —
JANA:	/Which is not religious/ exactly. More like ingrained. Stuck somewhere deep inside her and just like all the

shit she can't get rid of in the house, she can't get rid of this in her head. And she, personally, would never have been able to willingly part with a being in her uterus because she has to hold on tight to everything.

GRETA: I meant your state wasn't welcoming. Of your ... state.

JANA: Oh —

GRETA: I don't know your mom. I wouldn't talk about someone I don't know like that.

JANA: I wouldn't know. I don't know you. This is ... this is still ether and I can't ... just can't have it becoming tangible.

GRETA: ...

JANA: This is —

GRETA: Scary?

JANA: Like an out-of-body experience. I thought I'd come to California for the palm trees and the stars on the walk-of-fame. Disneyland. Happiest place on earth.

GRETA: I've never been.

JANA: You live here.

GRETA: I always thought it would be strange to go without a kid and you know, parents want to be the one to have those theme park moments with their kid. I get it. I remember the out-of-body.

JANA: You do?

GRETA: We had to drive across state lines too, but with addresses on scraps of paper we were supposed to memorize. We had to knock hoping someone would be there. The right someone. I waited 18 hours in my car till he showed up. I never knew if I got the day wrong or if he did. He was angry I had parked too close — that people would figure it out. Maybe it was his anger that —

JANA: ...

GRETA: I had to call my mom from the payphone and lie and say my friend's car broke down and I was staying the night. I don't know whether she believed me or just opted to believe me rather than know whatever the truth was. She couldn't know. There was no way for her to know where I actually was. Even with the lines that took our voices from the phone booth to her kitchen. I could have been anywhere. Doing anything.

JANA: ...

GRETA: She was never very welcoming of the truth.

JANA: You had one.

GRETA: It's why I don't have kids.

JANA: ...

GRETA: He was angry. Worried about being exposed. He wasn't wrong to be worried. But he was angry. He rushed.

JANA: You haven't forgotten any of it, have you?

GRETA: Don't think that means I regret it.

JANA: I don't want to do this. I mean, I want to do this I just wish it wasn't a thing I had to deal with doing.

GRETA: I know.

JANA: ...

GRETA: I don't want it to be the way it was for me for you. For anyone. Which is why —

JANA: ...

GRETA: You can take that sachet home with you. If you want.

(JANA pulls a small, wrapped thing out of her backpack.)

JANA: My mom always says never show up empty-handed.
            (JANA holds it out to her.) She also always says gifts are
            given so the person will remember you every time they
            see it ...

            ...

            I kind of hope I don't remember you. Remember this.

(GRETA reaches over and takes the sachet. Puts it in her pocket.
The two of them. A beat.)

                        END OF PLAY

THAT MOMENT WHEN...

by Steven G. Martin

CHARACTERS

PAUL, male, any age, any background. A college student.

CON, male, any age, any background. A college student.

SETTING

A room in a college library. There are two empty desks on either side of the stage. A chair sits behind both desks.

TIME

One evening late the spring semester.

NOTE

Actors in *That Moment When …* are asked not only to physically perform the stage directions, but also narrate them with emotion. Even if stage directions have no observable physical action, there should still be emotion in the narration.

PAUL and CON can be any age, but the play works best if they are close in age.

A double slash symbol in the script (//) indicates where the next line of dialogue should begin. The goal is to create overlapping dialogue.

PRODUCTION HISTORY

That Moment When … was presented by MadLab Theatre in Columbus, OH, May 12–28, 2022. The production was directed by Will Macke. The cast was as follows:

PAUL: Lane Schlicher

CON: Corey Ragan

PAUL enters, carrying two thick books and wearing a backpack.

PAUL: Paul enters, carrying two thick books and wearing a backpack over his right shoulder. He walks slowly and steadily to the desk farthest from where he entered. He moves with purpose, but he does not rush.

He places his books on the desk with the covers facing up. He takes his backpack off his shoulder and places it next to the books. He pulls the chair away from the desk, sits, and moves back toward the desk.

He unzips the backpack and removes a pen, a notebook, and a highlighter. He opens his notebook to an empty page and carefully writes the date at the top, using his pen. He reaches for the book nearest to him and opens it more than three-quarters to the end. Unconsciously he puts the end of the pen in his mouth.

Paul places his index finger on the page and moves it as he reads. He does this with purpose, but he does not rush. He nods, unconsciously, as his eyes scan the text. He removes the cap from the highlighter and moves it across the page while simultaneously writing with the pen in the notebook. This takes more than a few moments. He turns the page.

(CON enters, harried. He carries a laptop computer, pen and paper, and a drink.)

CON: Con enters, harried. He carries a laptop computer, pen and paper, and a drink. He moves quickly, jarringly. He walks to the desk nearest to where he entered. Before he puts down the computer, pen and paper, he looks back to see if any of his belongings dropped to the floor. He confirms nothing fell and nods.

He carefully places his drink on the desk. He tosses everything else onto the desk. It makes a loud noise.

PAUL: Paul, startled, looks up, but quickly returns to the book.

CON: Con turns the chair at the desk around so it faces backward, and he sits. He opens the laptop and presses the power button. While it powers up, he picks up the drink and sips from it. He covers his mouth with his hand and burps softly. He unconsciously taps his fingers against the desk, waiting for the laptop to power up.

PAUL: Paul looks up again, annoyed.

CON: Con continues to tap, slightly bored.

PAUL: Paul looks around   CON: Con looks around
        the room.   the room.

PAUL: Paul sees Con. He stares, transfixed. His heartbeat speeds up. He takes a quick, deep breath.

CON: Con sees Paul. He smiles. It is a radiant smile. It is a heroic smile. His heartbeat speeds up.

PAUL: Paul looks away, resting his forehead against his upraised hand. He does not breathe.

CON: Con still smiles. He looks back to his laptop and types his username and password.

PAUL: Paul stares at the book. He does not read. He does not breathe.

CON: Con turns on a web browser and types an address into a search engine. He turns his head to look at Paul. He watches him. He smiles.

PAUL: Paul stares at the book. He does not read. He does not breathe.

CON: Con watches Paul. He smiles.

PAUL: Paul moves his pen against the notebook. He scribbles across the length a couple of times.

CON: Con looks back at his laptop. He types quickly but makes an error. He uses the mouse to highlight the error and then deletes it with a keystroke on the keyboard. He retypes the information and presses the enter button. He uses the mouse to scroll through the webpage.

He looks at Paul briefly. He returns his gaze to the webpage.

PAUL: Paul stops moving his pen. He exhales. He looks at Con.

CON: Con writes briefly on his notebook while staring at the computer screen. His eyebrows furrow, he shakes his head, and continues to use the mouse to scroll through the page.

PAUL: Paul watches Con. He tries to breathe normally.

CON: Con runs his hand over his head as he reads the webpage. He reaches for his drink and sips from it. He scrolls farther down the page, peering in closer to the screen, eyes squinting.

PAUL: Paul averts his eyes and looks at the pages in the book. He sighs. He does not read.

CON: Con puts down his drink, but instead it falls onto its side. Liquid pours out over the desk. Con exclaims.

| PAUL: | Paul looks over to Con and sees the spill. He pushes his chair, stands, and quickly exits the same direction he entered. | CON: | Con stands, and quickly moves his laptop away from the growing puddle of liquid. He puts his papers, pen and computer on the chair. |

(PAUL exits the same direction he entered.)

CON: Con reaches for the drink and stands it up. He moves the chair away from the desk. He uses the side of his hand to attempt to keep the spill from the edge of the desk. He pulls at the hem of his shirt and considers whether or not to use it to mop up the spill. He grimaces and —

(PAUL enters with a stack of paper towels.)

PAUL: Paul enters with a stack of paper towels and walks quickly to Con's desk. He places the stack on the desk, opens one of them, and places it on the spilt liquid.

CON: Con watches Paul, then opens two more paper towels and places them on the spill. He wipes the paper towels across the surface of the desk.

PAUL: Paul unfolds more towels and pats them on smaller puddles of liquid.

CON: Con unfolds more towels and again wipes them across the length of the desk.

PAUL: Paul gently touches the desk to check if it's clean.

CON: Con balls up the towels that he and Paul used. He turns to Paul, smiles, and extends his hand to shake Paul's.

PAUL: Paul extends his hand to shake Con's. It shakes a little.

PAUL
AND
CON: Their hands touch.

    They do not move.

    They look at one another.

    They do not move.

    Their hearts beat faster.

    They do not move.

    They breathe in unison.

    They do not move.

(A bell in the library's tower tolls.)

PAUL: Paul pulls // away his hand from Con's.

CON: Con steps backward.

(A bell in the library's tower tolls.)

PAUL: Paul exhales deeply, // trying to control his nerves.

CON: Con blinks. A lot.

(A bell in the library's tower tolls.)

PAUL: Paul turns away from Con. He walks to his desk.
          He holds his hand against his chest, rubbing it. He
          pulls out the chair at his desk and sits. He stares down
          at his book.

CON: He turns to face the exit.

PAUL: Paul lifts his head in Con's direction.

CON: Con walks slowly.

PAUL: Paul watches Con walk.

CON: Con exits.

(CON exits.)

PAUL: Paul watches.

          Paul watches.

          Paul watches.

          Paul watches. He sighs. He shakes his head.

          Paul turns back to his book. He does not read. He
          unconsciously puts the end of his pen in the mouth.
          He strums his fingers on top of the desk. He feels his
          heartbeat slow down. He feels his breathing become
          deeper. He puts his head on his book, facing away
          from the entrance.

(CON enters, holding two cans of pop.)

CON: Con enters, holding two cans of pop. He walks to
          Paul's desk. He moves with purpose, but he does not
          rush. He taps Paul's shoulder.

PAUL: Paul looks up, startled. He sees Con.

CON: Con hands Paul a can and places the other on the desk. He walks to the other desk and picks up the chair. He walks back to Paul's desk, puts the chair down, turns it around so it faces backward, and sits. He opens the tab on the can.

PAUL: Paul opens the tab on his can.

PAUL AND CON: He takes a sip from the can.

CON: Con extends his hand to Paul.

PAUL: Paul extends his hand to Paul. It shakes a little.

PAUL AND CON: Their hands touch.

They watch one another.

Their hands touch.

They watch one another.

CON: "Hi."

END OF PLAY

SAD LONELY PEOPLE

by Seth McNeill

CHARACTERS

HARRIET: 20s–30s, Female, any race

WADE: 20s–30s, Male, any race

SETTING

A party in a Manhattan penthouse facing Times Square on New Year's Eve.

NOTE

Line breaks without punctuation indicate that the character is interrupting themselves. There should be no pause between the cut-off line and the next one.

PRODUCTION HISTORY

Sad Lonely People was presented by Southeast Missouri State University at the Wendy Kurka Rust Flexible Theatre, October 27–29, 2022. The play was directed by Ben Streeter.

Disco lights on a guy and a girl looking forward through the window in a high rise penthouse, both of them holding plastic cups. It is New Year's Eve. He is dressed in what his mother probably thinks is fashionable. She is dressed as if she could not give less of a shit. An uncomfortable silence.

WADE: So do you um

            do you have like

            do you have New Year's resolutions?

HARRIET: I make weekly resolutions. Well, okay I guess tomorrow's a Sunday so technically I do have a New Year's resolution but it's really just my next weekly one.

WADE: ... Oh, okay. So what's the one for this week?

HARRIET: I don't like ... share them.

(Beat)

WADE: Making new friends.

HARRIET: Huh?

WADE: Sorry, I mean that's my resolution. Fresh blood and such, you know?

HARRIET: I'm fine with the old ones.

WADE: Oh, I didn't mean I was getting rid of ...

HARRIET: I was / just kidding.

WADE: The old ones they all moved away, like this mass exodus. Well not "mass," it was like three people and two of them were married to each other, but ...

HARRIET: Been there.

WADE: Friends moving away?

HARRIET: *(with quiet gravity)* No, I've been wherever they're going.

WADE: ... *(uncomprehending)* Yeah.

HARRIET: I have no idea what I meant by that. Seemed profound, but … I'm kind of drunk.

WADE: Me too. Oh, wait this is sparkling cider, I guess I'm just sleepy.

HARRIET: They don't break out bubbly until it's almost time.

WADE: It's like less than ten minutes.

HARRIET: You're right. You gonna watch the ball drop?

WADE: No.

(WADE giggles)

HARRIET: What?

WADE: It's just kind of funny. "Watch the ball drop." Hehe.

HARRIET: Huh?

WADE: Like puberty, or well I guess balls drop before that so whatever. And we're not facing in the right direction for that.

HARRIET: For what?

WADE: Ball dropping.

HARRIET: … Are you fucking serious?

WADE: *(Referring to window)* Yeah, the view is like maybe 30 degrees off.

HARRIET: Motherfucker! That was my …

WADE: That was your resolution?

HARRIET: I try to keep them attainable. *(Beat)* I need to find a cheap snog.

WADE: *(Wasn't thinking about that at all)* Oh yeah, I need to do that too.

HARRIET: Wait, were you thinking we would …?

WADE: No, I wasn't talking to you because you're a woman but just because you're a person.

HARRIET: I'm not really picking up sexual tension or anything here.

WADE: Me neither, I don't actually find you attractive. Sorry that was really rude.

HARRIET: ... *(Assessing him)* We could stand closer and see if something magical happens.

(They consider for a moment, then slowly stand closer. Nothing remotely magical happens for either of them.)

HARRIET: That does nothing for me. I was hoping that would work out so I could get this shit over with.

WADE: Maybe we should settle though.

HARRIET: No it's fine. Where did that even come from, the kissing thing? I hate that shit, like I'm —

Is that guy looking at me?

WADE: I think he's looking at me. Out of my league though

I mean I'm not gay but I just mean if I were he would be out of my league.

HARRIET: He's not checking you out, though. He's judging your outfit.

WADE: Really, why? *(Looking at his outfit)* I guess that's fair.

HARRIET: *(Makes eye contact with another person, but unsuccessful)* Nope, not buying what I'm selling. Whatever, you have a thick neck. *(Seeing a woman looking at WADE)* She's definitely looking at you. Like a hungry, inebriated little badger.

WADE: That was kind of harsh.

HARRIET: Is my comparison inaccurate? *(Looking again pointedly)* Nope! Pretty apt!

WADE: She is fairly short. If a girl is that short I'm always afraid they're going to strain their neck.

HARRIET: I dated a tall guy, eventually I couldn't do it anymore.

WADE: You dumped him because he was tall?

HARRIET: Well, no not really, he dumped me, but I think it was
          because I would only kiss him while he was bending at
          the waist. He had lower back problems.

WADE: Sorry to hear that.

HARRIET: It was his own fault, his posture was terrible.

WADE: I meant the breakup.

HARRIET: It's fine it was a couple years ago.

WADE: … I've never really had a girlfriend

            Sorry that's really personal I'm a bit *(Referring to cup)*
            oh wait no I'm not never mind.

(Awkward pause)

WADE: I think I'm uncomfortable with silence so I just
            say things.

(Silence)

HARRIET: Used to be I would look out a window like this over
          all these buildings and think, "there are so many stories
          happening just within these couple of city blocks, this
          is amazing." I would try to see in people's apartment
          windows.

          I know — voyeur. Like I would watch them do their
          laundry and the first thing I would think is, "I wonder
          what happened that made them need to wash their
          clothes at this particular moment."

          Okay the first thing I would think is, "Shit, they
          have their own washer/dryer in New York, those
          lucky fuckers!" But after that I would think, "What
          happened to them? Maybe they spilled coffee on their
          pants on the way home from work, or maybe they
          had really good sex and need to clean the sheets, or
          really *bad* sex and need to clean the sheets. Or maybe
          someone punched them in the face and they bled on
          their shirt." That's what I think if they used bleach.

I used to be so curious about people. This charge of energy by being around all the … happenings. But now I see all of the lights in the windows and I'm just like, "Go to sleep Millions of People, there is nothing you're doing that is more interesting than a soft mattress and a down comforter." Early twenties was a good time. Had my shit together just enough to live on my own terms, and just clueless enough to be excited about it. *(Giggles darkly, drunkly)* Happy New Year! *(Pause)* So no girlfriends ever, that's pretty bad.

WADE: I sort of wish I could just wake up one morning and find out I got married the day before. Then I could just make the best of it.

HARRIET: We should just resign ourselves to spinsterhood. Or in your case —

You know bachelorhood doesn't sound nearly as bad as spinsterhood, it sounds kind of relaxed and at worst slightly boring, but spinsterhood sounds like a life of quiet desperation ending in suicide by cats. *(Looking him over)* You look like my dad.

WADE: Really?

HARRIET: Yeah, that's why there's no *(Makes "chemistry" gesture)* between us. I've never understood girls who try to find someone like their dad. I love my dad and he's really great, but that's a fucking weird phenomenon.

WADE: My mom left my dad when I was five. Sorry, I should've segued … I mean the reason I say that is like I've never wanted to date someone like my mom. I want basically the opposite.

HARRIET: That seems like a bit of a hangup.

WADE: Probably.

HARRIET: Sorry about your mom, though.

WADE: My dad said she cheated on him. A lot actually. I mean he mentioned it a lot, and I don't even know if it's true, it just sort of sticks because it was something said by a parent.

HARRIET: I wonder if that's where the word "apparent" came from: Something that seems obviously true because it was said by A parent.

WADE: Actually, I think it comes from the root word —

HARRIET: Don't worry about it, man. *(Beat)* Our conversation has been on a pretty depressing track from the point you said you don't have any friends.

WADE: I didn't say I don't have *any* friends, I just —

HARRIET: Yeah, yeah, yeah, but still …

(The sound of commotion indicating the countdown)

WADE: I think we're about to …

(Both check their cups to find them empty, but raise them anyway)

BOTH: *(Rather unenthusiastically)* Ten, nine, eight, seven, six, five, four, three, two, one, happy new year.

(They look at each other, contemplating kissing, but again nothing magical happens. "Auld Lang Syne" is heard in the background and continues under the following dialogue.)

HARRIET: *(Sighing)* Fuck it.

WADE: Yeah it's fine. I didn't figure I would end up finding anyone anyway.

(Silence)

WADE: *(Staring out the window)* You know it's probably better if we don't know what's going to happen or not happen or probably happen … Or unless we knew something good were about to happen, but that's sort of not really the norm. Most of the time whatever you hope for probably won't happen or if it does happen it won't be quite fully realized or even if it is fully realized it won't bring you the same satisfaction as you thought it would. So then you hope for a different thing and it's this string of one thing after another that you grab onto and maybe at some point you've arrived

Although I doubt it

Although if I didn't hope for that I probably couldn't keep going and keeping going is better than just settling for something mediocre right?

(Beat)

HARRIET: You should be on medication.

WADE: I am, it doesn't work very well. I'm okay, I just had to get that out of my system. And we're friends right, so I've already achieved my resolution

Oh wait, it happened before the countdown, crap.

HARRIET: There's enough sad lonely people out there you could throw a rock in any direction

Boom! friend. Can't be picky of course.

WADE: Yeah they can't be either.

HARRIET: Jeez, man.

WADE: I'm just saying. My point is I'm not, like, better than most people.

HARRIET: You might be.

WADE: But probably not.

HARRIET: That's a pretty low bar, though. I'd say you're a bit better, based on our limited *(Gestures "acquaintance")*

WADE: ... Thanks. *(Beat)* You too.

HARRIET: Appreciate you saying that.

WADE: No problem.

(Silence as they look out the window)

END OF PLAY

SUGAR

by Jennifer O'Grady

CHARACTERS

JADEN, a woman of any age

LILIA, a woman of any age

SETTING

An apartment building hallway.

TIME

Now.

PRODUCTION HISTORY

Sugar was first produced as part of Lakeshore Players Theatre's 18th Annual 10-Minute Play Festival (White Bear Lake, MN) June 2–12, 2022. Produced by Franklin Heller. Directed by Kivan Kirk. The cast was as follows:

JADEN: Jenny Ramirez

LILIA: Kayla Hambek

Additional production as part of Little Fish Theatre's 21st annual "Pick of the Vine" (Los Angeles, CA) January 19–February 5, 2023. Artistic Directors Suzanne Dean & Stephanie A. Coltrin. Produced by Branda Lock. Directed by Margaret Schugt. The cast was as follows:

JADEN: Kirsten Hansen

LILIA: Geraldine Fuentes

JADEN stands in her apartment building hallway outside a closed apartment "door." She grips her cellphone. She listens a moment — she hears movement behind the door — then she knocks. Beat. She knocks again. Inside the apartment, LILIA hears the knocking. She goes to her side of the door and then listens.

JADEN: Hello? I'm your new neighbor. We haven't met, but I live right next door. Hello? I thought I heard you moving around inside. Are you home?

LILIA: *(Beat)* Sorry — I can't open up.

JADEN: Oh — hi!

LILIA: I'm sick. Sorry.

JADEN: Really sick?

LILIA: What?

JADEN: I mean is it an emergency, or … ?

LILIA: No. But I'm contagious.

JADEN: Sorry to hear that. I'm Jaden, by the way. I live right next door.

LILIA: You said.

JADEN: And your name is … ?

LILIA: *(Beat)* Lilia.

JADEN: Nice to meet you, Lilia. I don't usually do this sort of thing, but I had some free time so I thought I'd make sure everything's okay.

LILIA: Why wouldn't it be?

JADEN: No reason. I'm just checking on neighbors. You know, "being a good neighbor?" You were on my list.

(Beat.)

LILIA: You have a list?

JADEN: Apartment 2A, 2B, 2C — they're all fine. Now I'm here at your door and I'm right next door, so after this I think I'll quit for the night.

LILIA: What about all the other floors?

JADEN: I already did those. I'm working backwards.

(Beat.)

LILIA: Oh.

JADEN: I'll tell you the truth, I'm really doing it for me. I'm in advertising, endless hours. I'm hardly ever home. You definitely won't see me around here much.

LILIA: *(Beat)* Right.

JADEN: It's hard to meet new neighbors so I thought I'd meet everyone this way. I've already met some folks down the hall.

LILIA: I'm surprised they opened up for you.

JADEN: Well, some people spoke through their closed doors, like you're doing. Most didn't answer, but I could hear them moving around inside.

LILIA: Right.

JADEN: What's that?

LILIA: Nothing.

JADEN: So do you need anything?

LILIA: Why would I?

JADEN: You just said you were sick …

LILIA: Oh. Right. I'm good.

JADEN: I guess your husband helps with the shopping, huh?

LILIA: *(Beat)* What?

JADEN: Sorry. Maybe he's your boyfriend.

LILIA: He's … my boyfriend. What does it matter?

JADEN: I don't mean to pry. I saw him in the hall the other day. Seems like a, you know, strong guy. Just want to make sure there's nothing I can do for you.

LILIA: No thanks.

(Sound of an elevator opening. JADEN looks. Offstage, a woman we can't see gets off the elevator.)

JADEN: *(To offstage woman)* Hi there!

(The offstage woman ignores her and turns a corner.)

LILIA: Who's that?

JADEN: Middle-aged woman? Red hair. Not too friendly.

LILIA: Right.

JADEN: You know her?

LILIA: Like you said, she isn't friendly.

JADEN: What about the other folks on this floor?

LILIA: You said you rang their bells ...

JADEN: Most of them didn't answer.

LILIA: It's that type of floor.

JADEN: People don't want to get involved, huh?

LILIA: You could say that.

JADEN: I guess that's human nature. Not everybody wants to help. I mean if they know somebody's sick.

LILIA: Well, thanks for stopping by.

JADEN: If you'd like me to come in and clean, I could.

LILIA: No thanks.

JADEN: I could make you some tea, or ... ?

LILIA: No. Thank you.

JADEN: Nothing at all I can do for you?

LILIA: I appreciate it. Thanks for coming by.

JADEN: Actually, is there any way I could borrow a cup of sugar?

(A beat.)

LILIA: Sugar?

JADEN: I've been doing some baking and stupidly ran out. Any chance I could borrow some?

(LILIA doesn't answer.)

JADEN: I just need a little. Like a teaspoon? Or even less. Hell, I'll even take Sweet 'n Low. You don't have to open your door. I mean if you're worried about being contagious. I'll just slide an envelope under your door and if you could please put the sugar into that I would literally be in your debt forever.

LILIA: Fine.

(JADEN takes an envelope from her pocket and slides it quickly under LILIA's door. LILIA picks it up and sees a note inside. Beat. She takes it out and reads. A beat. They speak quietly.)

JADEN: Lilia?

(Beat.)

LILIA: I can't.

JADEN: Open your door.

LILIA: I can't!

JADEN: I know it's hard to trust, but you need to trust me.

LILIA: I don't know you!

JADEN: Do you need to? I can hear what's going on. Open up and I promise I will help.

LILIA: Nobody can help ...

JADEN: Please open your door. We don't have a lot of time.

LILIA: I can't! He's coming back soon.

JADEN: I know. A friend will text me when he's on the way.

LILIA: Who?

JADEN: Please just open the door now.

(LILIA hesitates then opens the door. They look at each other. Beat.)

JADEN: Now go and get your wallet.

LILIA: But …

JADEN: We don't have much time.

LILIA: I can't just leave!

JADEN: All you need to do is grab your wallet and get out.

(LILIA doesn't move.)

JADEN: Lilia, I'm gonna be blunt. If you stay here, you will die here. Is that what you want? Are you gonna let him do that to you? Please, go and get your wallet!

(Beat.)

LILIA: What about my other things?

JADEN: I'll bribe the super to let me in later.

LILIA: Where will I go?

JADEN: Don't worry. There's a van outside.

LILIA: What van?

JADEN: It's sent by a woman's shelter. You'll be fine and I will help you.

LILIA: Why, why are you doing this?

JADEN: Because I have to. Because I couldn't live with myself if I didn't. Because I hate his guts and I don't even know him. I want you to live. Now go and get your wallet!

(Beat. LILIA turns and goes for the wallet. JADEN dials her phone.)

JADEN: *(Into phone)* Hey, Mari. Call the driver and tell him to start the van, then call the shelter and tell them she's on her way. Thank you. I couldn't have done this without you. Here she comes.

(JADEN hangs up, as LILIA returns with her purse.)

JADEN: Come on. I'll walk you out.

LILIA: I don't understand why you're doing this for me.

JADEN: Because someone did it for me, which is the only reason I'm standing here now. Welcome to your new life, Lilia.

(A brief moment and then they exit.)

END OF PLAY

RUBATO

by Noah T. Parnes

CHARACTERS

JOSEPHINE, just turned 83, a piano teacher. JOSEPHINE is a woman of any race.

TREY, late 30s, a parent. TREY is a man of any race.

SETTING

JOSEPHINE'S living room, where she has taught piano lessons for the past 30 years or so.

TIME

Now or thereabouts.

NOTE

This play is dedicated to Josephine Caruso.

PRODUCTION HISTORY

Rubato was first performed in New York City for the Cherry Picking Festival at Wild Project on August 22, 2022. The production was directed by Clare Mottola. The cast was as follows:

JOSEPHINE: Carmen Marrin

TREY: Will Conard

Lights up on a living room with two pianos in it, side by side. One is much older than the other. In front of the poofiest couch anyone has ever seen, there is a small table topped with a container of little chocolates.

JOSEPHINE is seated in a rolling swivel chair — her domain is limited by the plastic covering that covers a small fraction of the full-floor carpet. She has trouble walking, but the chair can move to where she needs to be when teaching in this room.

TREY has just entered and has been standing rather awkwardly for few seconds.

TREY gestures toward the container of chocolates.

TREY: May I?

JOSEPHINE: Of course.

(TREY chooses a chocolate and pops it into his mouth.)

JOSEPHINE: Jasper chooses the same ones.

TREY: Does he?

JOSEPHINE: I take it you're here to tell me he's quitting.

TREY: Well.

JOSEPHINE: Many a parent has broken my heart on behalf of their child, I can take it.

TREY: He doesn't practice.

JOSEPHINE: I know that.

TREY: And he wanted you to know that he's starting baseball.

JOSEPHINE: A likely story.

TREY: He just doesn't want to play anymore.

JOSEPHINE: And you've told him he'll regret it?

TREY: First thing I tried.

JOSEPHINE: Well then I guess we have nothing else to discuss.
I'll check my book and give you a call.

TREY: Thank you, Josephine.

(TREY turns to go. JOSEPHINE rolls back to her piano.
TREY pauses. JOSEPHINE notices but doesn't turn around.)

JOSEPHINE: Yes, you may have another chocolate.

TREY: Do you wish I had kept playing?

(JOSEPHINE still has her back to TREY.)

JOSEPHINE: I find that wishing does not typically yield
tangible results.

TREY: But do you think I should have?

(No answer.)

TREY: How many kids have quit on you over the years?
I'm just curious.

JOSEPHINE: Children make their own decisions. I can't control
the attrition rate.

TREY: But you're doing all right?

JOSEPHINE: What do you mean?

TREY: Financially.

(JOSEPHINE turns.)

JOSEPHINE: I have two Steinway pianos.

TREY: But someone is taking care of you?

JOSEPHINE: Do I really seem that infirm?

TREY: I want to make sure that —

JOSEPHINE: Look at me. I know you feel guilty. Look at me.
Were you a prodigy? No. Were you a particularly
musical child? Maybe. The fact of the matter is that
your regret will not sway your child's compass, nor
will it heal my arthritis or bring back the skills. But
that was years ago! Decades! Let it go! I certainly

have. And back then I was young! *In comparison.*
A new teacher. I can't tell you how many students
have played, quit, returned, quit again, gone to
college, come back, had a kid and plopped him
down on that same bench. Not in the time since
I taught *you* anyway.

(A slight pause.)

TREY: *(almost to playfully spite her)* I still have some
          muscle memory.

(JOSEPHINE is surprised. She gestures to the piano.)

JOSEPHINE: Be my guest.

TREY: Oh I don't think I can just …

(JOSEPHINE looks at him.)

TREY: I can only play one thing. Not even, it's just
          the beginning.

JOSEPHINE: Don't surrender before you've even begun!

TREY: It's short, it's a little, simple — it's … like you said,
          it was decades ago.

JOSEPHINE: But your muscle memory has maintained it.
               Or so you say …

TREY: I'm nervous now!

JOSEPHINE: To play "Heart and Soul" for me??

TREY: It's not "Heart and Soul."

JOSEPHINE: Well. Not everyone is lucky enough to be in your
               position. Are you going to continue the charade or
               are you going to play?

*(TREY takes a second to consider his options. And then he goes and
sits at the piano. He gets himself comfortable.)*

JOSEPHINE: Would you like a pillow?

TREY: I can't believe I'm doing this.

(TREY rests his hands on the keys. He starts to play the very beginning of Clair de Lune, *by Debussy. It's pretty, definitely not particularly polished, but —)*

JOSEPHINE: Slow down.

(TREY shoots her an incredulous look.)

JOSEPHINE: Start again. Slow down.

(TREY takes a deep breath and starts again, slower. JOSEPHINE was, of course, correct.)

JOSEPHINE: Let the melody sing.

(TREY tries to do this, not sure if it's working. He makes a mistake. Wrong note. TREY looks to JOSEPHINE. She nods. What does this mean??? He starts again, maybe with a wrong note but he continues. It's not perfect, but it is pretty. And, abruptly, it's over.)

TREY: That's all I know.

JOSEPHINE: It's a beautiful piece. You should learn the rest.

TREY: The beginning is easy.

JOSEPHINE: The follow-through could be easier. You need to sink into the keys more. Don't just plunk it out.

TREY: I was trying not to.

(JOSEPHINE rolls her chair over and places one hand on TREY'S hand. She presses one of his fingers into a key on the piano. The sound rings.)

JOSEPHINE: Do you feel this?

(A moment.)

TREY: He says you yell at him.

JOSEPHINE: I do not.

(TREY looks at her. JOSEPHINE removes her hand.)

JOSEPHINE: I hold him to a standard to which I hold all of my students. I am firm, but I do not yell.

TREY: He's sensitive.

JOSEPHINE:	To his credit. I do not teach piano to hurt children's feelings.
TREY:	You have hurt his feelings.
JOSEPHINE:	Then bring him here and I will apologize.
TREY:	He doesn't practice.
JOSEPHINE:	I know this. It's all right, I want him to enjoy making music —
TREY:	He doesn't practice because even when he does it isn't good enough for you.
JOSEPHINE:	He could be great. He has an ear, he knows when he plays things wrong but he rushes through them, he's impatient. I won't ignore that; I would be doing him a disservice.
TREY:	What if he takes a break? A pause, a *rest*. He'll start baseball and …
JOSEPHINE:	Those never work. And lord knows children refuse to multitask.

(TREY stands up and moves out of JOSEPHINE'S rollie chair area.)

TREY:	Kids can do both.
JOSEPHINE:	I'm not debating whether they can or cannot. They won't.
TREY:	He just … he wants to be good at something.
JOSEPHINE:	Then by all means, let him quit! He will certainly get better at something else with that kind of attitude!
TREY:	That's not fair.
JOSEPHINE:	But we both know he'll regret it, and we agree that it's his burden to bear. To know he *could* have been … "good."
TREY:	But he wants to *feel* like he's —

JOSEPHINE: And what do you want? What do you want for your child? It is an obvious mistake to anyone who has lived more than eleven years but we *must* let the children make their own choices, let them decide to abandon their passions before they develop and choose to watch their skills disintegrate as their brains lose their plasticity, and yes, he will find something else, he will play *baseball*, but he won't be able to come crawling back and play me Clair de Lune when that disappointment crystalizes because I will be dead. He will just force his child into playing with a far less talented teacher, and the cycle will be doomed to repeat.

TREY: I don't want him to quit.

JOSEPHINE: Then you should make him tell me himself. He doesn't want to disappoint me. He doesn't want to see my wrinkles when he tells me he's done, that he doesn't want to improve, when he tells me he's scared of me and that I damage his self-esteem. I'm sure he thinks I'm a crone, that's why he sent you here to butter me up and soften the blow, he doesn't want to get close to me, he doesn't want to see that he's wrong.

TREY: I don't believe he thinks that.

JOSEPHINE: And you are *letting him*, coddling him, here to do his dirty work, and now of course *you're* wishing you had stuck it out a few more years, that you could remember the rest of that piece, wishing that I could teach it to you right now, but unfortunately wishing does not yield results. And I know it is almost tasteless for a piano teacher to say this, but only *practice* can do that.

So. I will take a look at my book and I will call you, and you will send me a check, and that will be that.

TREY: I would like to learn the rest of that piece.

JOSEPHINE: Are you available Mondays at four?

(A moment. TREY wishes he were. JOSEPHINE wishes he were.)

TREY: I remember when I started and my hands couldn't reach an octave. And you told me that I'd grow. And I did! I remember that. And I remember what an octave is. And I remember what *forte* means and that Schumann or Schubert or some composer somewhere broke their ring finger trying to strengthen it. And I remember playing in recitals and I remember making mistakes. And … he'll remember a lot. Even with less. I don't want him to quit. He doesn't want to quit. I'll have him come see you. Thank you for teaching him.

(JOSEPHINE nods. TREY turns to leave.)

JOSEPHINE: Before you go.

(TREY turns to JOSEPHINE. JOSEPHINE stands up for the first time in the play. It is difficult for her. She stands using a cane. She is an elderly woman, after all. TREY watches her the entire time.)

JOSEPHINE: Bring him a chocolate.

END OF PLAY

THE ERGONOMIC PERFECTION
OF THE ROTARY PHONE

by Brian James Polak

CHARACTERS

BREE (they/them): Always the favored child by their parents. A total fuck-up as a kid but received all the attention as the "baby." Never got along with CARY until becoming adults. As they fully age into adulthood, they have a lot of empathy for CARY, but completely unsure how to help them through their mental health crisis.

CARY (she/her): The older sibling. Highly educated. Working on a PhD prior to the mental illness overtaking her. No matter how hard she tried, could never earn the admiration and respect she wanted from her parents. When she sees people she knew prior to hospitalization, like BREE, she isn't sure they're real and thinks it's possible they've been replaced by imposters. This is a form of schizophrenia referred to as "imposter syndrome."

SETTING

An in-patient psychiatric health facility.

TIME

Present day.

NOTE

Although their specific ages are not mentioned in the script, it is important that both characters are adults.

PRODUCTION HISTORY

The world premiere of *The Ergonomic Perfection of the Rotary Phone* took place August 28–31, 2022, at The Den Theater in Chicago, IL. The play was produced by Broken Nose Theater as part of their 9th Annual Bechdel Festival. The production was directed by Lizzie Lovelady with Dramaturgy from David Weiss. The cast was as follows:

BREE: Michael-Ellen Walden

CARY: Kim Boller

An aged room. The furniture is worn. Walls were last painted a generation or more ago. Water stains the ceiling tiles from which florescent lights dangle. Wire cages protect the lights from flying objects. But it's day so what little light there is in the room streams in through the windows, partially covered by thick, torn, stained, fabric curtains. Everything has seen better days in this place. CARY stands facing a window. She is talking into the receiver of on an old rotary phone that rests on a nearby table. The curly cord stretches as CARY tries to talk as far from the door as possible. An unlit cigarette protrudes from her mouth.

CARY: I know what you're saying. I don't think you understand what *I'm* saying. That's all well and good, but this isn't my first rodeo. I know how you people conduct business. Have you even read any of the documentation I forwarded to you? It's all right there. What's it show? There's clear evidence of modern slavery. Do you even check your email? Who do I need to talk to then? The senator? I don't believe for a second that anybody in your office has the capacity to judge the veracity of that video let alone comprehend the magnitude of what it's documenting. Somebody needs to loop in the United Nations. And Congress. Because we're talking about Human Rights violations!

(CARY takes a drag of the unlit cig.)

CARY: I'm beginning to wonder if I can even trust you. It sounds to me like you're not even the same person. You used to be on my side. Then get me results! I have hours of video. The last thing I want to do is get the press involved, but I'll do what I have to.

(Just as a door to the room begins to open —)

CARY: I —'ll call you back —

(— CARY slams the receiver down ... as BREE half-enters with an uncertain gaze ... Their hand unwilling to let go of the doorknob ... Their feet unable to commit to entering the room.)

CARY: Who are you?

BREE: It's your ... It's ... Bree?

CARY: How do I know it's really you?

(BREE closes the door. They stand with their back practically pressed against it. CARY looks them up and down.)

BREE: Because I'm me. I know it's been a minute, but —

CARY: I've been fooled before.

BREE: Not by — I've never fooled you.

CARY: Sure you haven't.

BREE: Are you still giving me shit about the goldfish in the swimming pool? You know I'm not the one —

CARY: Do something Bree would never do.

BREE: What?

CARY: Prove you're Bree.

BREE: By doing something I wouldn't do?

CARY: Exactly.

BREE: Cary, come on.

CARY: Proof.

BREE: What wouldn't I do? I don't even —

CARY: You've got ten seconds before I call the cops.

(CARY picks up the handset to the rotary phone).

BREE: The COPS?! What have I —

CARY: You could be impersonating my sister. Seven seconds.

BREE: Oh god.

CARY: Four seconds. Two seconds.

(BREE lets out a huge burp).

CARY: Ew.

BREE: Excuse me.

CARY: Bree would never burp like that.

BREE: You said to do something I wouldn't do.

CARY: Yeah, but that was gross.

BREE: Sorry.

CARY: I shoulda known it was you. Nobody in their right mind would put that outfit together with those shoes.

BREE: I wanted to look nice.

CARY: You look colorblind.

BREE: Thanks.

CARY: Don't just stand there. Come in.

(CARY takes a drag on the unlit cigarette. BREE hesitantly approaches the rotary phone).

BREE: You're still smoking.

CARY: Smoking's not allowed.

(CARY takes a long, empty drag, stubs out the cigarette in an ashless ashtray. Pulls another from a box. Mimes lighting it. Takes another drag. BREE admiringly runs a hand over the phone).

BREE: I love these old phones. This reminds me of the one on Mom's desk. I'd sit there and play with the rotary. *Zing, zing, zing.* Pretending I was a banker making a deal.

CARY: Mom's was green. There was an old photo of baby you playing with that phone. Probably still on Mom's fridge.

BREE: That fridge is in a landfill somewhere. The buyers remodeled. Gutted everything.

CARY: She banned us from the office when you accidentally called her oncologist.

BREE: Oh my god, I forgot about that. The number was on a sticky note next to the phone. It was so damn tempting.

CARY: The doctor told Mom. I got a spanking.

BREE: I don't remember that.

CARY: I was supposed to be babysitting you so, of course it was my fault.

(BREE fiddles with the phone. They feel the weight of the receiver).

BREE: It's funny how Mom hung onto the analogue world right to the end.

(They put the receiver to their ear).

BREE: Too bad this doesn't work. *(They hang up the receiver).*

CARY: Why are you here?

BREE: This place seems …

CARY: Why are you here?

BREE: Wanted to say hey. See what you're up to.

CARY: That's a good one.

BREE: I missed you. *(BREE picks up the cigarettes).* Can I have one?

(CARY gives a thumbs up. BREE pulls a cig from the box).

CARY: Today of all days.

BREE: Like I said. I missed you —

CARY: You missed me *today*.

BREE: Exactly.

CARY: But not yesterday?

BREE: No. I've missed you every day… I always miss you.

CARY: Like I'm on vacation or something.

BREE: …

CARY: Why isn't Mom with you?

BREE: Is it always quiet like this?

CARY: They cleared the room for me.

BREE:	That's nice of them.
CARY:	They're all a bunch of plumbs. Where's Mom?
BREE:	You know where Mom is.
CARY:	Do I?
BREE:	What's it like on a normal day. Here, I mean. Like when they don't empty the room for you?
CARY:	I don't pay attention to what's going on. People come and go. I'm busy doing my research.
BREE:	Is there ... a library?
CARY:	Why are you here, Bree?
BREE:	I can't just visit you? Do you want me to leave?
CARY:	You said you *missed* me. It's funny how it took so long ... to miss me. Nobody else has visited. You're the first and only.
BREE:	You made it clear nobody is welcome. We aren't exactly advertising what's going on. Nobody except the family even knows you're here.
CARY:	Mom's never once called. Written a letter. Anything.
BREE:	... You don't remember her funeral?
CARY:	I've been meaning to talk to you about that. How do we know she really died?
BREE:	She was sick for years. We were both with her at the end.
CARY:	Did you ever see her body? In the casket?
BREE:	Yes! And you had the chance but were too skittish.
CARY:	The fact remains I never saw her dead body, so who knows?
BREE:	You think she faked her death?
CARY:	You don't know she didn't.

BREE: I hope that isn't true.

CARY: That's the work I've been doing these past few months.
           I'm on the phone every day trying to track her down.
           I'm *this* close to cracking the case. I just need the
           Secretary of State to admit to war crimes.

BREE: The Secretary of State ... of the country?

CARY: Exactly.

BREE: What war crimes? What *war*?

CARY: It's a war crime to hold a U.S. citizen against their will.
           And what I think happened was Mom learned some
           information they didn't want her to know. She was
           in that office all the time. Digging up information.
           You know it.

BREE: She was an accountant.

CARY: Sure she was, little sis. It's modern slavery. Look it up.
           It takes many forms and is a growing global problem.
           People don't realize it's right in front of them —
           exploitative situations that a person cannot refuse
           or leave because of abuse of power, threats, violence,
           coercion, deception —

BREE: Are you swallowing your meds?

(CARY looks at BREE).

CARY: You may think my mind is broken. The truth is what's
           in my head is simply beyond your comprehension.
           And my memory is crystal clear no matter how
           many pills I take. I know what you did. I remember
           everything.

BREE: What I did?

CARY: And I know why Alex doesn't visit with the kids.

BREE: I don't want to make excuses for anybody... you know
           Alex loves you... But the kids. They're too young to
           really understand ... this.

CARY: So am I.

(BREE takes a drag off an unlit cigarette).

BREE: God, I wish I could light this thing.

CARY: Believe me, it's better this way.

BREE: But they're not going to be too young forever. Soon they're gonna become aware. And wonder ... about where their mom is.

CARY: How do you even know those are my children? You go look in their eyes and tell me if you believe they are the same kids I birthed.

BREE: Your kids are your kids. Believe me. I've been with them every single day since you've ...

CARY: That must be nice for you.

BREE: I'm just worried about them. I want what is best ...

CARY: Then get me the hell out of here.

BREE: Alex thinks you've been pretending ... faking everything ... to avoid the divorce.

CARY: What do you think?

BREE: I don't think you're pretending anything.

CARY: Thanks.

BREE: Because you're not that good an actor.

CARY: Fuck Alex. And fuck you for even mentioning their name.

BREE: Sorry.

CARY: Why are you seeing them every day?

BREE: What?

CARY: You said you see the kids every day? How is that?

BREE: I babysit.

CARY: Every day?

BREE:	Yeah. Every day.
CARY:	Okay now I'm starting to see this clearly.
BREE:	Good!
CARY:	*That's* why I'm in this place. It's why you're here today, isn't it? You took my children because you can't have any of your own!
BREE:	That's rude. And not true. I'm trying to be — parental — because they need it.
CARY:	Parental?! That's a good one. You're a cold-hearted bitch just like Mom. Using me. *Always* using me to get what you want.
BREE:	Stop it, Cary.
CARY:	Admit the truth. You're all dried up inside, so my kids are the next best thing.
BREE:	God dammit, Cary. I've invested too much of my own life and emotional capital to be called names — and be accused of some ridiculous conspiratorial bullshit. I'm not listening to it anymore. It's your turn to listen to me, got it? You're here because of the batshit stuff you were pulling. Demanding documents from the mayor's office. Screaming at the judge — I've been saving your ass since all this started, but I won't do it again if you continue to accuse me of shit. I'm fucking done. You got that? D-O-N-E. I care for your little ones because I love them and I love you. But your ass will be trapped in this place for the rest of your life if you don't get your shit together. You got that? Huh? Look at me! Do you hear what I'm saying to you?

(CARY nods tentatively).

BREE:	I want us to go back to the way we used to be. Siblings. Friends.

(CARY pulls another cigarette from the box. Offers one to BREE. It's quiet for a moment as they pretend to puff away).

BREE: These suck without the smoke.

CARY: Bree ...

BREE: Yeah?

CARY: I never would have done this to you.

BREE: You have no idea how —

CARY: You just dumped me here.

BREE: Can't you see ... Cary ... you aren't ... healthy.

CARY: Maybe I went a little too far in court. I get that. I really
          do. But. But. Why did it have to come to this, Bree? I
          mean, wasn't there anything else that could have been
          done? You have no idea how awful it is here. It's just
          so lonely. And I'm scared that *this* is it. When the fog
          clears, and I look out that window, all I see is myself
          getting old and dying all by myself. In some dark
          corner of this room. Alone.

*(BREE wants to say something ... I'm with you. You aren't alone.
I love you. They can't say anything.)*

BREE: ...

CARY: But. But. But. But what I can't stop thinking about
          is how ... How you can look after my *children*, but...
          you can't look after *me*?

BREE: I'm sorry I yelled at you.

CARY: What am I supposed to do?

BREE: Take your meds.

CARY: It's just so hard.

BREE: I know it is.

(BREE doesn't know what else to say.)

BREE: Can I hug you?

(CARY nods. They embrace).

CARY: You're wearing Grandma's perfume.

BREE: You remember.

CARY: It's not my memory that's the problem.

(They separate. BREE looks at the cigarette they're holding).

BREE: I have a lighter in my car. What if we smoked these for real?

CARY: That would be amazing.

BREE: I'm gonna grab it and come right back. We can blow the smoke out the window.

CARY: Thank you.

BREE: BRB.

(BREE exits. CARY picks up the phone, notices its weight. Admires it for the briefest moment.

Then dials a number and begins talking).

CARY: She went to get a lighter.

(CARY looks back toward the exit …)

CARY: She doesn't realize they won't let her back in with it.

END OF PLAY

A BENEVOLENT ALLIANCE
OF MOURNERS

by Ken Preuss

CHARACTERS

ELLIE, Female. Around 20 years old. Disaffected a bit by years of singing at funerals. Perhaps wise beyond her age. Sarcastic but sincere. Any race or ethnicity.

ALEX, Any gender. Around 20 years old. Out of sorts from the loss of a friend. Using humor to hide the pain, avoiding the reality as much as possible. Any race or ethnicity.

SETTING

An outdoor area near a backdoor of a church

TIME

Modern day, winter

PRODUCTION HISTORY

A BENEVOLENT ALLIANCE OF MOURNERS was presented by The Sullivan County Dramatic Workshop at The Theatre Association of New York State Festival in Rome, New York on November 19, 2022. The production was directed by Gabriel Pinciotti. The cast was as follows:

ELLIE: Julia Kehrley

ALEX: Gabriel Pinciotti

At rise: ELLIE leans on a wall, looking at the sky. A guitar sits to one side. ALEX enters, looking back to make sure no one is watching. Thinking no one is there, ALEX pulls out a pack of cigarettes, turns, and comes face to face with ELLIE. ALEX screams and recovers.

ALEX: Christ. You scared me.

ELLIE: Sorry.

ALEX: *(Berating the word choice comically)* And I've used the Lord's name in vain in a church.

ELLIE: Technically, we're outside the church, so you're good.

ALEX: I'm sneaking out for a cigarette, so I'm not *that good.* *(Indicates the pack)* This has gotta be against the rules, right?

ELLIE: There's a list of ten inside. Didn't see a "Thou Shalt Not Smoke."

ALEX: *(Laughs a bit)* My mother would still disapprove, though. Says I'm killin' mys… *(Stops suddenly at the choice of words)* Shouldn't be laughing. Not here. Not now.

ELLIE: Beats crying all the time.

ALEX: It sure the hell does. *(Beat)* Can I say "hell?"

ELLIE: It's fine. They actually use that one inside sometimes.

ALEX: Not today, I hope. *(Gestures with the pack)* Want one?

ELLIE: No. Thank you. Just out here to warm up.

ALEX: It's 35 degrees.

ELLIE: Warm up, *vocally.* *(Points to guitar)* I'm singing at the end of the service.

ALEX: Oh. I'll put these away, so I don't mess up your voice. *(Beat)* You're not going for that smoky jazz singer thing, are you?

ELLIE: Probably the wrong vibe for the venue.

ALEX: Probably. *(Puts pack away and pulls out a folded paper)*
          I suppose you're listed in the program. I kinda avoided
          looking at it. Like seeing things in print is going to
          make this all real. *(Beat)* Program? That even the word?
          It's not like I'm at a freakin' musical.

ELLIE: Musicals are happier.

ALEX: Not all of them. *Cabaret. Les Mis. West Side Story. Little
          Shop of Horrors:* Stage version — not screen.

ELLIE: You know your stuff.

ALEX: Been to a lot of musicals.

ELLIE: *Program* is fine. Or brochure. Pamphlet. Order
          of Service.

ALEX: You know your stuff, too.

ELLIE: Been to a lot of funerals.

ALEX: Maybe you could mix in a birthday sometime.
          Birthdays are happier.

ELLIE: Not all of them. *(This thought seems to linger or hold a
          bit of weight.)*

ALEX: Right. Things'll be starting soon. I'll let you warm up.

ELLIE: I'm done, actually. You headed back in?

ALEX: I can wait.

ELLIE: I can, too. Unless you really need that cigarette?

ALEX: *(Shakes head, waving off the suggestion)* I'll survive.
          (Reacts to the word choice) It's actually nice to talk
          with someone new. I keep thinking I'm gonna say
          something stupid in there. I've got no experience with
          this kind of thing.

ELLIE: Some might consider *not being used to funerals* a *good*
          thing.

ALEX: *(A slight smile)* See? Messing up already.

ELLIE: Best to get that over with before you go inside.

ALEX:	*(Smiles again)* You're pretty funny for a funeral singer.
ELLIE:	Best to get that over with before *I go inside.*
ALEX:	I don't know. Everybody is so ... numb. They have a right to be, but they could use a few smiles. Eventually. *(Beat)* How do you know Jeremy?
ELLIE:	I don't. *Didn't.* I met his dad. After.
ALEX:	There a Craig's List for funeral performers or something?
ELLIE:	His neighbor's co-worker lost her mom. My number was shared. Kind of how it works.
ALEX:	A benevolent alliance of mourners. *(Beat as ELLIE nods)* That'd make a great name for a band.
ELLIE:	I'll keep it in mind in case I change career paths.
ALEX:	Is this your *actual career?* Singing for strangers on the saddest day possible?
ELLIE:	Wasn't the plan. And not really a story you want to hear.
ALEX:	I could use a *different story.* Not ready for this one to be true yet.
ELLIE:	Mine's no fairy tale either.
ALEX:	Fairy tales aren't even fairy tales. They wrote a whole musical about it.

(ALEX gestures, silently encouraging ELLIE to share, perhaps using the cigarettes as a playful threat. ELLIE obliges.)

ELLIE:	My sister, Grace, was the performer in the family. Sang everywhere. Talent shows ... coffee shops ... supermarket grand openings. Taught me everything I know.
ALEX:	Sounds nice.
ELLIE:	Was. For a long time. She went on the road after high school. Tried the music thing for real. Auditions. Demos. Agents. Didn't work out.

ALEX:	She gave up on music?
ELLIE:	Gave up on everything. Her twentieth birthday.
ALEX:	*(Realizes what she means)* Oh. Sorry. I didn't mean to make you talk about it.
ELLIE:	It's fine. Not like I wasn't thinking about her anyway. *(Crosses away a bit)* I warm up outside at these things, every time. As if she's up there, watching after me. Let her know I'm still moving forward, thinking about her, taking care of her guitar.
ALEX:	That how you started? Grace's funeral?
ELLIE:	*(Nods)* Almost five years ago. Bob Dylan. "Forever Young." *(Beat as she ponders the title)* True, too. Forever young. Coupla months, we'll be the same age.
ALEX:	You ever get over it? Losing someone this way?
ELLIE:	Over it? No. Not yet anyway. I understand it better, though, I think. 20's an odd age. Things you don't tell your friends. Things you won't tell your parents. Things you can't tell a 14-year-old. Everyone checked in on her, but none of us saw what was going on.
ALEX:	"The Blind Men and the Elephant."
ELLIE:	That another musical?
ALEX:	Parable. These blind travelers touch different parts of an elephant. Trunk. Ear. Leg. Tail. They each understand things from their own perspective, but no one gets the whole picture.
ELLIE:	Everyone needs that *whole picture* person.
ALEX:	I should've been that for Jeremy. Was. Through high school, anyway.
ELLIE:	People grow up.
ALEX:	We graduated last Spring. We didn't grow up. Just *apart*.

ELLIE: You go off to school. You get busy. You make new friends.

ALEX: Sometimes you don't.

ELLIE: That what happened? With Jeremy?

ALEX: I don't know. We were in touch. It was just different. You text. You post. You stay connected but there's … less of a connection.

ELLIE: People can lose themselves when they're on their own.

ALEX: *(Almost to self) Find* themselves, too. *(With growing intensity)* We'd've seen each other Thanksgiving break. I had stuff to tell him. Stuff I haven't told … *(Changes gears suddenly)* I'm so freaking selfish. I'm getting angry that he's not here for me when I should've been there for him.

ELLIE: We're all here for each other. Revealing pieces of ourselves. Trying to figure things out. Looking for our full-picture person.

ALEX: "The Blind Men and the Elephant."

ELLIE: Good parable. *(An attempt to lighten things)* Lousy name for a band, though.

ALEX: *(A small laugh, releasing some of the tension)* What are you singing, anyway?

ELLIE: "Three Little Birds."

ALEX: *(A beat of confusion)* What is that? A children's song?

ELLIE: *(Laughs)* No. It's Bob Marley. *(Recites a lyric)* "Every little thing gonna be all right."

ALEX: Bob Dylan. *Bob* Marley. Do you sing any songs by people with other first names?

ELLIE: Nope. "Stairway to Heaven" once. Led Zeppelin but written by Robert Plant who's just a Bob acting formal.

ALEX: Why "Three Little Birds?"

ELLIE: I offer a list of songs Grace used to sing. His dad picked it. Said something about the Red Sox. Whole crowd singing it right before a big home run. Said it always gives him hope.

ALEX: Hope sounds good. If Jeremy's up there watching, he'll be happy. He *loved* the Red Sox. Wore a hat everywhere. It's hard to picture him without it.

ELLIE: You have any? *Pictures?* I'd love to see one.

ALEX: *(Opens phone)* I'm sure I can find a few. *(Flips through some images, suddenly aware how many photos have been taken since last seeing Jeremy)* Been a while. *(Finally finds one)* End of summer. Red Sox hat as advertised. *(Beat)* This is actually the last time I saw him. If I'd known, I would've made sure it wasn't so blurry.

ELLIE: Blurry memories are better than none at all. *(A sad beat)* Any of the two of you together?

ALEX: I've got a great one he took. *(Opens an app and searches)* Oldie but goodie. I stole it and posted it way back. *(Finds the image, presents it with a flourish)*

ELLIE: *(A big smile)* Wow. Where are you?

ALEX: Ferris wheel. Town carnival. End of eighth grade.

ELLIE: *(Takes the phone and reads a quote on the image)* "All we see is sky for forever … Two friends on a perfect day." Great caption.

ALEX: *Evan Hansen. (In response to ELLIE's confused look)* It's a musical about …

(ALEX realizes a connection between the musical and the JEREMY'S fate and visibly reacts. ELLIE, not fully understanding, senses something and redirects the focus.)

ELLIE: *(Points to photo)* Are you two screaming here or laughing?

ALEX: We're stuck at the top. I'm hyperventilating. Jeremy's singing to calm me down.

ELLIE:	Like a lullaby?
ALEX:	Like the opposite. He sang so badly, I cracked up and forgot about being scared. *(Excitedly, remembers something)* Wait! He was singing "Three Little Birds!"
ELLIE:	No.
ALEX:	Yes! I mean, he only knew the "every little thing gonna be all right" part, but he kept repeating it every time it came around.
ELLIE:	They were playing it on the ride?
ALEX:	*(Points to photo)* There was this stage for entertainment. Marching bands. Dancers. Magicians. Someone was singing and Jeremy was joining in. Poorly. But with great enthusiasm.
ELLIE:	*(Looking closer at the phone)* Was this the 100-Year Celebration thing?
ALEX:	Probably. May have been *101 years* by the time we got down, though.
ELLIE:	I think you guys were listening to Grace. She sang at that carnival right before she left. I can actually see her on stage. It's distant and out of focus, but it's her.
ALEX:	I have a picture of Jeremy and Grace?
ELLIE:	When I text it to myself, we'll both have it. *(Steps away with the phone, revealing a slight smile)* I had zero photos of this show. Always wanted one.
ALEX:	Sorry it's blurry.
ELLIE:	Blurry's perfect. I can envision it different every time I look. Eyes wide as she sings. Closed as she solos. A smile. A snarl. I can even put myself in the audience.
ALEX:	*(Notices ELLIE swiping and typing)* What are you doing?
ELLIE:	Putting myself *in your phone.*

ALEX: Why?

ELLIE: We're keeping in touch. I volunteer to be your whole-picture person. Text me. Call me. Tell me stuff so somebody knows. I'll tell you stuff, too. If you want.

ALEX: *(Laughs)* How 'bout your name?

ELLIE: *(Looks up from the phone)* Ellie.

ALEX: I'm ...

ELLIE: Alex. I know. I snooped your Instagram. *(Quickly)* I can do that. We're friends. I mean, I'm *in* your favorite contacts.

ALEX: This is really happening, then?

ELLIE: We've dealt with stuff. We'll be good for each other. *(A smile as it comes to her)* A benevolent alliance of mourners. *(ELLIE hands back the phone. They share a look. A silent agreement)* I don't think it was an accident we met today.

ALEX: *(Beat)* I've heard it said that people come into our lives for a reason. We are led to those who help us most to grow, and we help them in return. That's *Wicked*.

ELLIE: Was gonna say *corny*, but I didn't want to ruin the moment.

ALEX: *(Laughs)* I mean *Wicked*. The musical. We'll help each other, but you've got some serious Broadway history to brush up on. You can teach me about the Bobs in return.

ELLIE: There are some really good ones. Bob Segar. Bob Geldof. Bobby Darin.

ALEX: Bobby Darin's the "Mack the Knife" guy.

ELLIE: So?

ALEX: "Mack the Knife" is from a musical. Well, a *play with music*, but it's a starting point.

ELLIE:	And a good place to stop. For now. Time to head in.
ALEX:	*(Takes a breath but holds in place)* What if I can't? What if I'm not ready?
ELLIE:	No one's ever ready. You've just got to move.
ALEX:	*(Finishing her thought)* Forward.
ELLIE:	Eventually, yes. *(A beat then quickly)* Right now, just to the side, so I can get my guitar.
ALEX:	Oh. Sorry. *(Grabs and hands her the guitar)* Break legs. Heal hearts.
ELLIE:	Lots of pressure. I'm just gonna sing. For the family. And *friends*. Remember the words you hear though. The words Grace and Jeremy sang for you the *last time* you were stuck.
ALEX:	"Every little thing gonna be all right."
ELLIE:	And if you don't believe me. *(Points up)* Look at the tree. Someone's watching over us.
ALEX:	*(Looks up)* Little birds. Only two, though. Three would've been perfect.
ELLIE:	I like it this way. Maybe these are ones we know.

(They look at the birds for a few beats. ALEX extends a hand, gesturing for ELLIE to proceed. As ELLIE starts away, ALEX takes a final look at the sky, then follows. They both exit ready to face what happens next.)

END OF PLAY

WATER DAMAGE

by Daniel Prillaman

CHARACTERS

RICH, 30s. Any ethnicity. Male. In unfamiliar territory.

VIOLET, 30s. Any ethnicity. Female. In familiar territory.

SETTING

RICH'S apartment in the East Village.

TIME

Afternoon.

NOTE

Content Warning: Domestic violence/abuse (auditory).

Development Note: This play was developed during Playdate Theatre's 2021 New Work Development Conference

PRODUCTION HISTORY

Water Damage was presented by Memoriam Development as a part of the 4th Annual Nightshade at Side Street Studio Arts in Elgin, IL September 30, October 1, 7, & 8, 2022. The production was directed by AJ Kepka. The cast was as follows:

RICH: Kyle Lemon

VIOLET: Amanda Davila

The interior of RICH'S apartment in the East Village.

It is nicely furnished and mostly clean, although perhaps a few open cardboard boxes are about or off to the sides.

Two closed doors stand opposite one another, flanking a cased opening to a bedroom. One of them leads to a bathroom, the other to the hallway of the building.

RICH sits on a couch.

He is not relaxed.

He seems anxious, waiting for something unknown to us.

Silence.

One long enough for his anxiety to spread to us.

Why is he just sitting there?

Something is wrong. What is it?

A knock at the apartment door startles him.

He collects himself and crosses to open it, revealing VIOLET, wearing a coat and pair of leather gloves.

VIOLET: Richard?

RICH: Yes. Uh, Rich is fine.

VIOLET: I'm Violet.

RICH: Yes. Thank you for coming. Chelsea said you really helped her when she was — dealing with ...

VIOLET: You seem hesitant.

RICH: It's not a skepticism. I don't think. I'm just ... I didn't think any of this stuff was real. You know? Just a movie thing.

VIOLET: Mmm. Believe me, sometimes I wish it wasn't.

(Beat.)

RICH: Uh, come in. Please. I'm sorry.

VIOLET: You're fine. Thank you.

(VIOLET enters the apartment. She looks around, but she does not touch anything. RICH watches her.)

VIOLET: *(Off seeing the boxes)* When did you move in?

RICH: About a month ago.

VIOLET: And when did you first experience activity?

RICH: Uh, the third night.

VIOLET: Mmm.

RICH: Is that significant?

VIOLET: Not necessarily. What happened?

RICH: Um. I was in the bathroom. Getting ready for bed. Brushing my teeth. Everything felt ... normal. And when I spit into the sink, I feel a drop of water. On the back of my neck. So I look up and I see this stain on the ceiling. It's water damage. It's not big, but it's not tiny either. It's like the size of a pancake. And it's dripping. And my first thought is, "Shit, I just moved in, you're telling me there's water damage?" I go to find a bucket or anything to put under it. I find my phone to call or leave a message for the landlord. And when I get back to the bathroom ... It's gone. No trace. Just disappeared.

VIOLET: Have you seen it since?

RICH: It feels like every other night. It's gotten bigger. Darker. Black, like ...

VIOLET: Blood?

RICH: I don't like going in there. I feel like I'm not alone. Like there's other people there with me. Not even watching me, just ... there. Which somehow feels worse.

VIOLET: Would you say most of your occurrences have been localized in that room?

RICH: Yes.

VIOLET: Any sounds? Knocking or rappings?

RICH: Sometimes? It's banging, usually. On the door.
          Other times just a thump. Like someone's dropped
          something. But it's soft.

VIOLET: What else?

RICH: I swear I'm starting to see people. Out of the corner
          of my eye. In the mirror. I'm having trouble keeping
          myself together. I'm not sleeping well, I — I can't
          move again, I can't — afford it.

VIOLET: What exactly did Chelsea tell you I do?

RICH: Honestly, she said you were magic.

(VIOLET laughs at that.)

RICH: But, uh, she said you help people. In situations like
          mine.

VIOLET: I do what I can. What I can do to help depends
          entirely on what it is you're dealing with.

RICH: And you can figure that out?

VIOLET: I can try.

RICH: What if it's something you can't help with?

VIOLET: Well, let's only worry about that if we need to, yes?
          (Starting to remove a glove) It's not magic. At least in
          the conventional sense. There are some people in the
          world who have been … gifted, let's say … with an
          extra sense of perception. It manifests differently for
          different people. For me, when I touch something,
          I see more of its history. Its meaning. Its intent.
          Whether I want to or not.

RICH: That sounds exhausting.

VIOLET: It made for a unique childhood at the least.

RICH: So you're going to go into my bathroom and figure out
          its intent?

VIOLET: I'm going to listen to whatever it tells me.

RICH: Right. Do I come with you? Or should I — ?

VIOLET: If you'd stay out here.

RICH: Right.

VIOLET: I'll just be a few minutes. *(Pointing to the bathroom door)* It's this?

RICH: Yes.

(VIOLET crosses to the bathroom door and collects herself. RICH watches. Anxious. VIOLET looks at him.)

VIOLET: Just breathe.

(VIOLET puts her hand on the doorknob, and after a moment, she opens the door and walks into the bathroom.)

(RICH waits. He doesn't really know what to do. So he elects to return to the couch.)

(He waits.)

(He waits. Perhaps he fiddles with his phone or adjusts something.)

(Suddenly, the bathroom door SLAMS shut. The doorknob jiggles ferociously and we hear banging from the other side, like someone's desperately trying to get out.)

(But RICH has not heard this.)

(Nor does he hear it. He continues to wait for VIOLET.)

(We begin to hear more sounds from inside the bathroom now: the wails of a woman in tears, mixed with the rage and screams of a man's abuse.)

(RICH does not hear this. He continues to wait.)

(The woman pleads. The man does not let up. The impacts, now, of fists or feet against a body.)

(RICH does not hear this. He continues to wait.)

(The sounds come to a climax. The woman pleads. The woman goes silent.)

(The soft thump of a body falling to the floor.)

(RICH does not hear this. He continues to wait.)

(Silence.)

(The bathroom door opens and VIOLET enters, traumatized by what she's seen and heard. RICH has heard her enter. He looks at her.)

RICH: Are you okay? Violet?

(VIOLET collects herself. As much as she can.)

VIOLET: Could you get me a glass of water, please?

RICH: Yes. Of course.

(RICH gets a glass of water for VIOLET while she continues to collect herself. As much as she can. RICH hands her the water.)

VIOLET: Thank you.

(She drinks. RICH waits.)

RICH: Did you hear anything? Or —

(Beat.)

VIOLET: Well. I will first say that I do not believe you are in any danger.

RICH: Well, that's … that's good.

VIOLET: Having said that. There is residual energy here.

RICH: Residual?

VIOLET: Something bad happened here, Rich.

RICH: You mean like … somebody died?

VIOLET: Yes. And they suffered.

(RICH takes this in.)

VIOLET: Sometimes when something bad … *(No, those aren't the right words)* Sometimes certain places remember things. Events happen in them, and they are large enough or happen often enough that they imprint themselves. On the place. Like a stain. Like water damage. The shade of it remains in the place long after the people involved. And every once in a while, it still drips. And those drips are that energy. Seeping through. The banging. The people you see out the corner of your eye.

It's important to understand that it is just a stain. It may shock you or scare you, but it doesn't have any awareness. And it doesn't mean you harm. You're just living in a wound that hasn't quite scarred over yet.

RICH: That's …

VIOLET: …

RICH: What do I do?

VIOLET: I wish I could say more than "you learn to live with it." As much as you can. It may fade over time. Often renovations or a change in the architecture can rustle these things loose. Sometimes they were there to begin with, long before we came into the picture. And they'll stay long after.

RICH: I don't know what to say.

VIOLET: That's okay. I don't, sometimes, either.

(Silence.)

(VIOLET goes to say something else but decides against it and procures a business card. She offers it to RICH.)

VIOLET: If you ever have more questions or need to talk. If you even just need someone else with you in the space … please call.

RICH: *(Taking the card)* Thank you.

(Beat.)

VIOLET: I know this isn't an easy answer. But you aren't alone. Everywhere is wounded. We just don't usually think about it unless the one we're in is louder than the others. I am sorry I couldn't be more helpful.

RICH: No. You have been. Really.

(RICH offers his hand. Then hesitates, remembering that hand-to-hand contact might not be her preferred method of affirmation.)

RICH: Oh, uh …

(VIOLET smiles. Decides. And extends her ungloved hand. RICH takes it.)

(A moment.)

VIOLET: Thank you for having me.

RICH: Thank you for coming.

(They break.)

(Beat.)

(VIOLET exits. RICH is alone. He doesn't really know what to do. He elects to return to the couch. He sits. He takes in the place.)

(Silence.)

(From inside the bathroom, the soft thump of a body falling to the floor.

RICH hears this and looks towards the room.)

(Beat.)

(He does not get up.)

(He turns his head away.)

(He breathes.)

(And he collects himself.)

(As much as he can.)

END OF PLAY

THE HUNT(S)

by Tori Rice

CHARACTERS

EMMA HUNT, a woman, 60s, recently widowed, superstitious, doesn't take crap from anyone, a believer. Any race or ethnicity.

SAM HUNT, EMMA's daughter, 40s, a paralegal, a skeptic. Any race or ethnicity.

SETTING

Deep in the woods behind EMMA's house in rural Indiana. "No Hunting" signs warn intruders to stay away.

TIME

Night — Early fall, present day

NOTE

A slash / indicates overlapping dialogue.

The word "shies" (pronounced with a long "i") refers to make-shift hunting lookouts.

PRODUCTION HISTORY

The Hunt(s) was presented on April 15, 2022, by Emporia State University Theatre as a part of the 2022 Festival of New Works. The production was directed by Eddie Lee. The cast was as follows:

EMMA HUNT:	Makayla Pearson
SAM HUNT:	Kaitlin Bartlett

EMMA sits with a shotgun across her lap. She wears "I believe" buttons. A flashlight, radio and cooler are within reach. Faint light from a camp lamp casts shadows. EMMA sings along to a song ala The Band's "The Weight." Her head slumps as she nods off. Startled, her head snaps up.

EMMA: NO!

(A loud rustling. EMMA pops up and points her shotgun in the direction of the noise. She cocks it with an audible click.)

EMMA: Who's there?

(SAM enters shining a flashlight in EMMA's face. She holds a sack.)

SAM: Jesus, Mom! Put the gun down /

EMMA: / Who's there? /

SAM: / Mom, seriously! /

EMMA: / You're blinding me!

SAM: I will lower mine if you lower yours.

(They do.)

SAM: What are you doing back here?

EMMA: I'm on vacation.

SAM: I'm serious.

EMMA: Taking in nature. How did you know I was out here?

SAM: Kathy called me.

EMMA: That cow. Why would she call you?

SAM: I was the emergency contact where you used to work.

EMMA: I got fired?

SAM: You haven't shown up in a month.

EMMA: I shouldn't have said anything to that fat bitch.

SAM: She was worried.

EMMA: Well, okay, "Emergency Contact," I'm fine.

SAM: *(Holding up the sack)* I brought you something to eat.

EMMA: *(Taking it)* Gee, thanks. Six weeks of no contact and now a peace offering sandwich. It must've been a big deal flying all the way back here to check up on lil' ole me. The last time I saw you, you were going on about /

SAM: / I tried to call you /

EMMA: / how you didn't have to put up with my crap anymore.

SAM: I thought we could put that behind us.

EMMA: You broke my brand-new stereo /

SAM: / I didn't break it on purpose! /

EMMA: / and then deserted me.

SAM: You were drinking!

EMMA: It was the last thing your father bought me.

SAM: It was an accident!

EMMA: He had just died.

SAM: You were out of control!

EMMA: It was my BIRTHDAY! /

SAM: / I DON'T GIVE A SHIT IF IT WAS YOUR BIRTHDAY! You were drinking and cursing! I had to put up with that as a kid, but I don't have to anymore! *(Beat.)* I'm sorry.

EMMA: Well, there you have it.

SAM: I didn't come here to rehash anything, Mom. I hated leaving things like that.

        It's getting cold. Let's go to the house.

EMMA: I can't. I'm waiting. I'm sure Kathy told you. Cow.

SAM: I wanted to talk to you myself. So … you are back here … taking in nature /

EMMA: / Oh, for crying out loud, quit pussyfooting around! I'm here for Bigfoot. Yeah, you heard me right — BIGFOOT. There have been sightings right here on my property. Your dad used to say he existed, that he had seen him. I thought it was the chemo and the painkillers, that his mind was shot. Well, that and your dad's good 'ole-fashioned brand of BS. He would tell everyone about Bigfoot — his doctor, the oil change guy, the cashier at Walmart. I thought he was just trying to make me laugh. But then he started taking these long walks here on the property, back when he could still walk. I would find him waiting. He got so weak at the end that he stopped going out. The night before he died, I woke up and your dad was gone. I ran into the woods and your dad was being carried off by this large, hairy beast. I screamed and the beast dropped your dad and took off. Your dad, he was light as a feather at that point. I picked him up and he grabbed my arm and smiled and said, "Emma, don't be scared. Bigfoot is here to help." *(Beat.)* You think I'm nuts.

SAM: It's only been two months.

EMMA: Your dad couldn't walk at the end. How do you explain that?

SAM: Someone came into the house while you were sleeping?

EMMA: Not someone. BIGFOOT. I know what I saw.

SAM: What you *think* you saw.

EMMA: Dammit! Go back to your cushy job and your perfect life and let me be!

SAM: I worked very hard to get where I am, Mom. A simple, "I'm proud of you, Sam" would be great.

EMMA: I AM NOT CRAZY.

SAM: I think you're —

EMMA: Oh, you think *this*, and you think *that*! Here's what I think. School screws people up. It makes you want to put things in a box, nice and neat. Life ain't like that, Sammy.

SAM: I'm trying to understand.

EMMA: Then don't think. Listen. Bigfoot is here. Right after your dad died, people started showing up. At first, they would just drive by real slow-like and stare, rubbernecking like an accident. I would come home and see the shies.

SAM: Hunters have been putting those up forever.

EMMA: They've got some damn nerve tacking those up in my trees to slaughter Bambi! I wanna yell, "Can't you read my 'No Hunting' signs, bastards?"

SAM: Dad was always taking those shies down.

EMMA: I finally caught one when I was coming home from work, and I took the shotgun out/

SAM: /oh my God /

EMMA: / and I cocked it, pointed it at this bearded asshole in camouflage, and I said, "Get your half-breed redneck ass off of my property."

SAM: *(laughing)* You did?

EMMA: And he said, "I wanna see him."

SAM: Who?

EMMA: Bigfoot.

SAM: He actually said Bigfoot?

EMMA: Yes, BIGFOOT! Go on the Google. The sightings are on there, and this is the new prime location. There's all kinds of weirdoes sneaking onto my property. I came out one morning and there were VAGINAS everywhere. Some pervert had been out here, I don't know, waiting for Bigfoot with 1970s porn I guess, and a dog had ripped up the magazine, and there were big, hairy vaginas all over my yard. No heads, no tits. Just VAGINAS. Like some sort of vagina minefield!

SAM: Can we go inside, Mom?

EMMA: I'm not leaving.

SAM: You don't look like you feel well.

EMMA: Now that is the first thing I will agree with.

SAM: I'd like to help you.

EMMA: I don't need that crappy job, I don't need Kathy, and I certainly don't need one more person telling me I'm crazy!

SAM: I never said you were crazy.

EMMA: Do you believe me?

SAM: Did you ... Were you drinking while Dad was sick?

EMMA: Goddammit!

SAM: Were you?

(EMMA points the gun at SAM.)

EMMA: Get off of my property! /

SAM: /Mom?! /

EMMA: /I haven't had a drink since the night you busted my stereo and left! /

SAM: /I'm just trying to help!

EMMA: Where were you during chemo and radiation, when your dad couldn't make it to the bathroom? Where were you then?

SAM: I came out! You wouldn't let me help! /

EMMA: / Bullshit! /

SAM: / I took off work, I flew out here /

EMMA: / Yes, whatever was convenient /

SAM: / I tried /

EMMA: / How BIG of you /

SAM: / FINE! If that's the way you want it, FINE! Dad was dying and there was this huge elephant in the room. It was like the two of you were pretending that some miracle would happen, and he would magically jump out of bed one day, healthy. You refused to call hospice, even though it was clear he was getting worse. You were so mean at the end, so spiteful, almost as if you thought Dad was dying on purpose! I couldn't stand to see it! And now it's like you are holding onto everything and never forgiving. But if you want to be left alone, FINE!

(SAM starts to leave.)

EMMA: *(Quietly)* I'm losing the house.

SAM: You're … Oh no … Oh, Mom …

EMMA: I can't make the payments.

SAM: But the life insurance …

EMMA: Right before your dad was diagnosed, he changed the policy. Never told me. Lots of secrets your dad had.

SAM: We'll figure something out, Mom.

EMMA: Your dad and me had this pact so we wouldn't be alone.

SAM: What pact?

EMMA: At first, I thought Bigfoot was here so I could, I don't know, market him or something, charge admission so I wouldn't lose the house. But then I realized it's something else. I don't need this house anymore. Your dad told me, "He's here to help."

SAM: *(Cautiously)* Please hand me the gun, Mom.

EMMA: Oh Sammy, the gun is for the others who would try to hurt him. I'm not going to let that happen.

SAM: Mom. Let's go back to the house.

(Loud rustling.)

SAM: Listen to me. Dad was the dreamer, not you.
You grounded this family. You made me feel safe.

EMMA: When Bigfoot comes, I am going with him.

SAM: Don't do this /

EMMA: / Shhhhh, you hear that? /

SAM: / I believe you, Mom, please /

EMMA: Hope, Samantha!

(EMMA hugs SAM, then runs into the darkness. SAM grabs the flashlight.)

SAM: MOM! No, wait! Mom? Where are you? MOM!
Mom?! *(Something catches her eye.)* Put her down!
(SAM shakes her head.) Wait! Where are you? Please
don't hurt my mom. Come out where I can see you! *(Is
she going crazy? What did she see?)* You said he's here to
help. But where did he take you? *(She fumbles for her
cell, dials 9-1-1 and then, choosing her words carefully:)*
I'd like to report a disappearance.

END OF PLAY

BURIED TREASURE

by George Sapio

CHARACTERS

CAROL — Female, 30s, highly frustrated
RANGER — Male, 60s, always has it covered

SETTING

A café somewhere.

TIME

Recent.

NOTES

Slashes "/" indicate where the next actor should start speaking.

PRODUCTION HISTORY

Buried Treasure was presented by the Actors Studio of
Newburyport, MA, October 21–22, 2022. The production
was directed by Marc Clopton. The cast was as follows:

CAROL: Jocelyn Duford

RANGER: Sandy Farrier

CAROL and RANGER at table in busy café. RANGER is looking at his phone. Next to RANGER is a large sack.

CAROL: Parole officer?

RANGER: My adoring fans.

(RANGER puts the phone down.)

CAROL: Did you at least get a costume?

RANGER: Look, love. I'm just not very comfortable with the whole pirate thing.

CAROL: It's for your grandson. Get over yourself.

RANGER: Yar.

CAROL: That's the spirit.

RANGER: What I don't like is the glorification of grand theft.

CAROL: Omigod. Seriously, Dad? Mister, "I have a suitcase full of stolen goods in the basement"?

RANGER: I still maintain I have no idea how that got there. Never saw it before in my life.

CAROL: Get. A. Costume. The party is in three days.

RANGER: I'm 64. I'm going to look a right twit.

CAROL: It's. For —

RANGER: My five-year-old grandson. Yes. I understand.

CAROL: He will be shattered if you don't show up.

RANGER: So you think that at the first meeting between myself and my five-year-old grandson …

CAROL: Who is named after you.

RANGER: Oh, so is "Jailbird" his middle name?

CAROL: His name is Trevor James Heath.

RANGER: He's going to get beat up a lot, you know.

CAROL: Dad.

(Phone buzzes, a text. RANGER almost answers, then ignores it.)

RANGER: It's what led me into a life of crime, that first name.
          It's why I've called myself "Ranger." Much better than
          "Trevor." "Trevor" sounds like he carries an umbrella
          on sunny days just in case and his mom puts an apple
          in his lunchbox every day.

CAROL: Bollocks, Dad. What led you down the path of crime
          and got you locked up is a naturally irresponsible
          mental state.

RANGER: So you think that the first meeting between me and
          my grandson will be augmented by me wearing a
          pirate costume?

CAROL: It's his birthday. And he likes pirates.

RANGER: Yeah, well, I hope he grows out of that fast.

CAROL: Dad, he's / five.

RANGER: Five. Yes, I get it. Does he know / where I've been?

CAROL: No. He's too young for that.

RANGER: When are you going to tell him?

CAROL: On his wedding day. I don't know! Dad, please.

RANGER: I should just stay away from him.

CAROL: No. He needs his grandpa.

(Phone buzzes. CAROL gives it a look. RANGER ignores it again.)

CAROL: Looking for more autographs, are they?

RANGER: He's done pretty well so far without his grandpa, so
          you must be doing okay. And I'll never be like a real
          grandpa, all warm and pipe-smoking and full of trite
          wisdom. And I do tend to move around a lot. You
          know that.

CAROL: He dreams about his grandfather the adventurer. Who
          travels the world over, seeking fame and fortune while

aiding the helpless and punishing the evil.

RANGER: You're bloody nuts, you are, telling him all that. How can anyone live up to that pack of nonsense?

CAROL: He's five! And because many of the other kids have grandparents and he felt left out. I had to compensate.

RANGER: Carol, my love. Think about this. You fill his head with insane stories of his adventurer hero grandfather and when he finds out his adventurer hero grandfather showed up at his fifth birthday party only three days after serving twelve years in prison for grand theft — with none of the allegedly stolen diamonds recovered, by the way, so how's that for due process — how's he going to feel?

CAROL: You are going to be there.

RANGER: I will do my grandfatherly duty and make his day. Look! *(Points to the big sack.)* I even got his present already!

CAROL: You are not giving him that flea-bitten bear! That thing needs to be trashed. I can't believe you made me drive six hours to some decrepit storage unit to get that. And who is Robert L. Parker, and does he know you just stole his mangy bear?

RANGER: Robert Leroy Parker was better known as Butch Cassidy.

CAROL: Oh lord. Really?

RANGER: He was a hero of mine way back when I was still young enough to be enamored of folk heroes. Besides, your little guy will love it. And you know why?

CAROL: Why, Butch?

RANGER: Because he's five! It's practically as big as he is! What child doesn't love a stuffed bear?

CAROL: You never got me a stuffed bear.

RANGER: You never asked for one. You can share / this one.

CAROL: I don't want one. I was / just being ...

RANGER: Look. I'm sorry.

CAROL: It's okay. It's just a toy.

RANGER: No. I mean I'm sorry for not being here for your last twelve years. Or for a lot of the previous twenty years. I'm sorry for being in jail and being a disgrace. I'm sorry for not being your dad when you needed one.

CAROL: You were there for a lot of my life. Well, some of it. A bit, anyway. I made up stories about where you were and what amazing, dangerous things you were doing.

RANGER: I was busy a lot. Looking out for my family.

CAROL: More like looking out so you could avoid your family.

RANGER: That's a little harsh.

CAROL: And now I have to serve as your legal residence.

RANGER: It's just a formality. For the parole board. They need an address. And I was there for you when it counted.

CAROL: For one of my marriages, anyway.

RANGER: How many times have you been married?

CAROL: There's a typical question from an attentive parent.

RANGER: I'm old. My memory isn't what it once was.

CAROL: Three marriages, Dad. Three.

RANGER: That reminds me. Mickey — he was number two, wasn't he? — says Hi.

CAROL: Really, Dad?

RANGER: He gets out in four. Did I mention he was a little ticked because you divorced him while he was in prison?

CAROL: He stole my car, emptied my pathetic bank account and left me broke, Dad. Mum had passed on and I had nowhere to go. I had to move back in with Ray.

RANGER: Remind me ...?

CAROL: Husband number one. And his wife, Sheryl, was none too pleased.

RANGER: Yeah, but it all worked out, didn't it? You're the best of friends with her, right?

CAROL: Right, Dad. Because all best friends thoughtfully leave their BFF's luggage next to the trash bins so it's easy to find when they come home from a double shift at the gas station.

RANGER: Oh, right. That Sheryl. I get confused.

(Phone buzzes again.)

CAROL: Are you going to read those texts?

RANGER: Nothing that can't wait.

CAROL: *(Suddenly suspicious)* Dad. You've been out only three days.

RANGER: I'm not doing anything wrong! Give me some credit, please!

CAROL: I will give you some credit when you show up at your grandson's fifth birthday party. Dressed like Blackbeard.

RANGER: What day is it again?

CAROL: Saturday.

RANGER: What time?

CAROL: Ten. A. M.

RANGER: I might have to leave a bit early.

CAROL: I should never have even asked.

RANGER: Or I could arrive a bit late.

CAROL: You shit.

RANGER: It's just bad timing!

(Phone buzzes. CAROL grabs for it, but RANGER is faster. He holds up a "wait" finger and looks at the texts.)

RANGER: Yeah. Saturday might be tricky.

CAROL: That's it.

(CAROL rises to exit.)

RANGER: Wait a minute, love.

CAROL: Why should I wait? What are those texts?

RANGER: Best I not divulge that information.

CAROL: You complete bastard.

RANGER: Sit down.

CAROL: I hate you.

RANGER: Do us a favor and sit.

CAROL: Do you a favor? Of all the unmitigated gall …

RANGER: If I give you a promise that I will be there on Saturday, dressed as you wish, will you sit down?

CAROL: Will you mean it?

RANGER: Carol. I promise that I will attend this Saturday's birthday party for my five-year-old grandson dressed as a pirate as you requested.

(CAROL looks at him, then sits.)

CAROL: Thank you.

RANGER: Now let me tell you a few things, my dear. You seem to have no end to your complaints against my performance as a dad. And to be fair, most of them are justified. I was not there to do my dadly duties when I should have been … on more than a few occasions. That's as may be, and I won't argue. An apology is nothing but words, and words are cheap; everyone can afford them. Actions are what counts. We are responsible for our own actions. No one else. Like the no one else sitting across from me who got herself thrown out on the street. Or the no one else took a dead-end job at a petrol station instead of going to vocational school and learning something useful. Or the no one else what got herself involved with drugs and spent two episodes in rehab. You spent way too much time feeling sorry for yourself.

CAROL: That's not fair.

RANGER: What's true is not always fair. You need to hold that thought close, because fair is not going to put steak in little Trevor's mouth.

CAROL: Steak. Yeah. Right.

RANGER: And I can't change my not being there for you. But I can promise that I will take care of your lad for years to come.

CAROL: What are you talking about?

RANGER: You have to make a choice, my girl. You're at a crossroads right here, right now. All you need to do is open that bag and look that bear in the face.

CAROL: I'm afraid to touch that thing!

RANGER: You need to look that bear in the face and tell him you do or don't want him. Because the rest of your life will go one of two ways. And it all depends on your ability to look a stuffed animal in the eyes.

CAROL: Dad, what is this? What will it prove?

RANGER: Do it. Show some spunk. Come on. It's only a bear. It's not a real person. I'm letting you off easy.

(CAROL decides, then opens the sack and removes a really mangy stuffed bear.)

CAROL: Omigod. This thing probably has cholera.

RANGER: In the eyes, Carol. Like someone with guts.

CAROL: I do not understand … *(Looks at bear. Beat.)* Dad?

RANGER: Yes?

CAROL: The eyes. What ... ?

(RANGER leans in.)

RANGER: And from here on we keep our voices real low, right?

CAROL: Are these ...Dad ... ?

RANGER: There are ten more of those beautiful little things stuffed up his bum. All recut. All untraceable. You take those, no more than one at a time, to any reputable dealer and say your dear old granny left it for you in her will. Never use the same dealer twice, and don't trade them in less than three years apart. That should make sure our little Trevor will have no worries in his future.

CAROL: Dad ...

(RANGER rises, kisses CAROL on top of her head.)

RANGER: Now remember what we talked about. I'm trusting you to make the right decisions from now on. Now tell the bear.

CAROL: What? Oh. Yes. *(Looking the bear in the eyes.)* I want you.

RANGER: See? That was easy. I'm off now. Business to attend to. And if I'm a bit late on Saturday, that'll be okay, won't it?

(RANGER exits, CAROL stares at the bear's eyes.)

END OF PLAY

ANCESTRY

by Connie Schindewolf

CHARACTERS

KIT, a 25-55 year-old woman. Any Race or ethnicity. Clever, sarcastic, exuberant.

MICKY, a 25-55 year-old man. Any Race or ethnicity. Intelligent, practical.

SETTING

The living room of KIT and MICKEY. There is a small couch or loveseat, and a table for drinks.

TIME

The Present

PRODUCTION HISTORY

Ancestry was presented by Theatre Odyssey in Sarasota, Florida, June 9–11, 2022, at the Asolo Cook Theatre. The production was directed by Leona Collesano. The cast was as follows:

KIT: Kathi Faulkner

MICKEY: Glenn Schudel

KIT and MICKEY'S living room. KIT is having a conversation on her phone with her best friend. She is holding two pieces of mail.

KIT: I can't believe it either, only three weeks. Some people have to wait three months. What? How would I know? Yes, I'm holding the envelope now. Yeah, he got his too. He really didn't want to do it at all, but I can be very persuasive you know. Just need a little spit I said, and you'll have all of your answers. Of course it's not as important to him since he's not adopted. I mean his parents have told him clues for years about his heritage, and he can see his family tree right in front of him at Thanksgiving dinner, right down to the bare roots of depravity if you consider his aunt Minnie. I'll tell you about her some other time. No, I'm not going to open his! You really think I could seal it back so he'd never know? No, no don't tempt me. I haven't even opened mine yet! Here goes. *(She opens the envelope and tries to figure out how to read it.)* Okay, Ancestry & Me, tell me who I am and where I'm from. Yeah, I will as soon as I can figure it out. Here it is, the percentages. We'll start with low to high. Are you ready to find out the scoop on your best friend? Let's see, I'm 1 percent Other. Well how vague can you get? Where exactly is "Other" geographically? 2 percent American Indian. Yeah, that's what it says. 9 percent German. Gee, you think I could have pulled off better than a D in High School German. 21 percent Northern European. Okay, turn the page and here comes the big one … 67 percent Egyptian Cat. What? That's what it says, Egyptian Cat! This is a joke! Mickey must be responsible for this. He's tricking me cuz he didn't want to do it. Forget I called. Bye.

(She looks at it again, and from here on out starts exhibiting the characteristics of a cat … hissing, grooming, batting at things in the air, rubbing up against things, purring, kneading. Nervous now, she starts grooming herself, licking her hand and slicking back her hair.)

She hears MICKEY coming, and she jumps on the back of the couch, holding the two envelopes. MICKEY enters and sets his briefcase down. KIT hisses but he doesn't hear her).

MICKEY: Hi, babe. Good day?

KIT: Oh, it was puurrrrfect!

MICKEY: Why the sarcasm?

KIT: How did you do it?

MICKEY: Do what?

KIT: You sly dog, you! Didn't want to take the DNA test so you're fooling with me and sent me a phony one!

MICKEY: I did no such thing. I'll let our spit be analyzed by the experts, but am I going to believe it? No.

KIT: *(Kneading on the couch out of nervousness)* You did not doctor my Ancestry & Me and say I was part cat, meow?

MICKEY: What?

KIT: *(Trying a new tactic now by going to him and rubbing up against him.)* Mickey, honey, didn't you send me a phony report, you know, making a joke, meow, trying to be funny?

MICKEY: No. What's wrong with you anyway? You're acting very strange. Are you PMSing?

KIT: *(Hisses)* Oh, that's right, turn everything into female problems. You know I've been fixed ... I mean, don't have that problem any more.

MICKEY: *(Making himself a drink)* I need a drink.

KIT: Got milk?

MICKEY: What?

KIT: Never mind.

(*MICKEY sits on the couch with his drink. KIT crouches down and licks out of his glass whenever he is not looking. Then she begins batting at something in the air.*)

MICKEY: Kit, come sit down with me. Let's figure this out, bring your report.

(*KIT gets the paper, drops it and then gets down on the floor and begins batting it around.*)

MICKEY: Kit! Stop. Bring it here.

(*KIT takes it to him and curls up by him on the couch like taking a nap.*)

MICKEY: Let's see what we have here. American Indian, that's interesting. Northern European, aren't we all? 67 percent Egyptian Cat? (*Laughing*) Oh, this is too good! Erin must know someone who could fake this. (*Waking her*) Kit, Erin must have done this!

KIT: No way! She was as surprised as I was. She wouldn't let me go on thinking I was part cat! (*Tries to cuddle up again, purring and rubbing up against him.*)

MICKEY: Who else could have pulled off this joke?

KIT: Don't know and I'm not sure if I care anymore.

MICKEY: You certainly don't believe you're part Egyptian cat, do you?

KIT: Of course not. That is so ridiculous! What would you like for dinner?

MICKEY: Don't care. Not really hungry now.

KIT: I was thinking maybe tuna …

(*MICKEY shakes his head "no" at each of the suggestions.*)

KIT: Salmon? … Halibut? … Flounder? … or … chicken livers!

MICKEY: Absolutely not! Disgusting. (*Looking at her paperwork again.*) Maybe it's a typographical error and they didn't mean "cat" but another word.

KIT:	Like what? Bat?
MICKEY:	No!
KIT:	Rat?
MICKEY:	Kit, that's ridiculous.
KIT:	*(Hissing.)* You just called me a rat.
MICKEY:	No. You misunderstood.

(KIT begins scratching on the furniture.)

MICKEY:	Honey, aren't you worried about hurting our furniture or … your manicure?
KIT:	I like my claws sharp.
MICKEY:	This has gone far enough. Now, I want you to think about what's going on here.
KIT:	*(Washing her face by licking her hands and then rubbing herself.)* What's going on here?
MICKEY:	Look at yourself. You're taking a bath with your paw, I mean hand.
KIT:	You always like to save water!
MICKEY:	Here's my take on it.
KIT:	On what?
MICKEY:	Your feline behavior.
KIT:	Don't know what you're talking about, meow. You don't even like cats.
MICKEY:	Just hear me out, please. *(Pause)* It's psychosomatic.
KIT:	*(Still taking a bath)* What?
MICKEY:	It means, what's on your mind is reflected physically. The mind, body connection. You read a report that said you were part cat, and your brain took over and started giving you those characteristics. *(He sneezes and coughs).*

KIT: Oh, I love it when you talk doctor talk. It makes you
          sound so intelligent. *(Rubbing up against him and
          purring)* My Dr. Freud! Come here, give me a kiss.

MICKEY: Later, honey, after we figure this out. *(Sneezes again.)*

(KIT arches her back and hisses.)

MICKEY: Listen to yourself. You're hissing at me!

KIT: That wasn't a hiss. You're the one with psychosomatic
          problems! I know you're allergic to cats, and you're
          sneezing so you must believe I'm a cat!

MICKEY: *(Blowing his nose)* I must be getting a cold.

KIT: You don't get a cold that fast! You're allergic to me.
          What a shame. That will make sex more challenging
          you know, meow.

MICKEY: This has got to stop! I will not be married to a cat,
          or even a woman who is 67 percent cat.

KIT: So you do believe it?

MICKEY: No. It's your brain, tricking you into believing what
          that stupid DNA test says. *(Sneezes).*

KIT: Speaking of which, meow, you haven't opened
          yours yet.

MICKEY: And I won't. The whole thing is ridiculous. Who cares
          about my ancestry? I care about the here and now.

KIT: You don't just find out your ancestry, but other things.

MICKEY: Like what?

KIT: You didn't read the whole report. Where is that paper?

*(KAT finds the paper, throws it up in the air, bats at it and paws it
around on the floor. MICKEY blows his nose.)*

MICKEY: I don't really want to hear any more.

KIT: Here it is. *(Reading)* Under genetic markers. I have no
          genetic variants for familial Feline Leukemia. Or Cat

Scratch fever. Whew! Thank God! That's a load off my mind. Aren't you happy for me?

MICKEY: No, I'm not happy you think you are a cat. I've about had ... *(he sneezes)* ... enough! If you stop this, I'll let you get a cat, a real cat, and I'll just take lots of antihistamines.

KIT: Let's look at yours. *(Pounces around the room until she finds it and hands it to him.)*

MICKEY: I will not. Don't want to know. I'm going to sue Ancestry & Me, don't think I won't. This has gone just too far.

KIT: *(Becoming amorous again)* Come on, my little, Mickey Dickey, let's see who you are. *(She purrs and rubs and really begins to make him sweat).* We can find out all about you and then maybe we can take a break and go to the bedroom. Please? I can even be a little rough, meow, cuz you're not going to get Cat Scratch fever from me! Huh? Come on!

MICKEY: I don't know.

KIT: Purrrty, purrrty please!

MICKEY: Well, I guess I could look at it. No harm in that.

KIT: Yah! *(She takes her paws and opens the envelope, puts it in her mouth, and hands it to him.)*

(MICKEY unfolds the letter gently).

KIT: *(Pouncing up and down).* What's it say? What's it say? Meow?

MICKEY: How do I read this?

KIT: Just skip over stuff and go to the percentages. Read from low to high. I can't stop purring I'm so nervous, and I'm shedding like crazy! *(KIT is kneading and purring like crazy. The purring stops once he starts reading.)*

MICKEY: Okay. Okay. It looks like I'm 1 percent Other.

KIT:	Me too, me too! See how much we have in common?
MICKEY:	3 percent South African.
KIT:	That's interesting. I never would have guessed.
MICKEY:	Me either.
KIT:	Go on, go on!
MICKEY:	5 percent Mongolian.
KIT:	Mongolian? I don't even know where that is.
MICKEY:	I think it's by China.
KIT:	Well, you do love to go to that Panda Buffet.
MICKEY:	37 percent Northern European, specifically the Scandinavian Countries.
KIT:	Well that makes sense, meow. You and your family always have to wear number fifty sunscreen. Go on, go on, what's the big one?
MICKEY:	*(Looking at paper again.)* And 54 percent …
KIT:	What? What? 54 percent what?
MICKEY:	Mid-European Mouse.
KIT:	Mouse?
MICKEY:	That's what it says!

(KIT arches her back and hisses. MICKEY lets out a mouse-like squeal, cowers and crouches, takes one look at KIT, and begins to run around the room. In cat-like fashion she chases him.)

END OF PLAY

CAPTAIN IMPERVIOUS

by Steve Shade

CHARACTERS

CARL, 18

JAMES, 19, his homey

SETTING

Carl's family basement rec room.

TIME

Present.

NOTE

The exchange between the two friends should be easygoing, playful, and fluid — rather than ponderous or constipated. It should move quickly, aside from the suggested beats: *Wayne's World* over Pinter.

PRODUCTION HISTORY

Captain Impervious was presented by The Blank Slate Project, Los Angeles, June 2022. The Blank Slate Project was instituted in 2013 as an Arts-in-Corrections program for creating theatre with/for incarcerated youth in the Gateway Program of the San Bernardino Juvenile Detention. Recently, it has expanded to probationary and community schools in the greater Los Angeles area.

CARL stands before a worn sofa. He speaks to us.

CARL: The Hindus have a common belief. On the day of your birth, God stamps the destiny of each child upon his or her forehead. It's fixed there. All that's left is a lifetime to follow the map set out for you. You can't change what is going to happen to you: good or bad. And you can't control what is going to happen to anybody else. You aren't responsible. You aren't God. But I'm not sure I swallow it. I like that it gets us off the hook for any mistakes. But it makes all our "aha" moments completely — well ... irrelevant.

(JAMES enters and sits on the sofa where CARL joins him.)

Here I am sitting in my room with C.I. And we are approaching one of those aha moments. Oh, His real name is James. He's been my homey since — well, we were in diapers together.

JAMES: We were never in diapers together. I'm almost a full year older than you.

CARL: Well, he's been my best since there even was a best. Captain Impervious I call him.

JAMES: *(To us)* It's stupid.

CARL: It's my own secret nickname for him.

JAMES: Not so secret now.

CARL: In sixth grade —

JAMES: Not this story again.

CARL: Sssh. In sixth grade, on the first day of class —

JAMES: It wasn't the first day of class.

CARL: Sssh. It doesn't matter. Would you let me establish the context here? *(Back to us)* Mr. Moreton, our English teacher, had us each stand up and introduce ourselves by answering the question, "What career do you hope to have when you grow up?"

JAMES: "What do you want to *be* when you grow up?" You're fucking with the setup.

CARL: "What do you want to be when you grow up?" *(To JAMES)* Okay?

JAMES: Did I say anything?

CARL: So after the usual responses: teacher, engineer, doctor, lawyer, he comes to James —

JAMES: You said you wanted to be a cocktail waitress.

CARL: I did not.

JAMES: *(Smiling; To us)* He did.

CARL: Anyway, he gets to James and James . . . "I'm James," and he just sits back down. And Moreton, of course, insists, "What do you want to be when you grow up?" And James stands up again, and without batting an eyelash says . . .

(CARL gestures to JAMES to finish.)

JAMES: "Impervious." It was an upcoming vocabulary word. I thought he'd be impressed.

CARL: He thought you were being an asshole.

JAMES: He always thought I was being an asshole. He never cut me a break.

CARL: Cause you made a bad first impression. You should have just said —

JAMES: The boring thing! I told the truth.

CARL: And he hit you with an NFA.

JAMES: *(To us)* That's Moreton code for "not following assignment."

CARL: James racked up a lot of NFAs that year.

JAMES: Says Mr. "OT."

CARL: *(To us)* That's Moreton code for "On Task."

JAMES:	You got away with everything. He rode me like a —
CARL:	Moreton took to calling him "Mr. Impervious" after that.
JAMES:	Stupid. The whole fuckin' year!
CARL:	But I upgraded him — to Captain Impervious.
JAMES:	Even stupider.
CARL:	I made him into a cartoon superhero. I even drew a picture to match.
JAMES:	I still have it.

(Feigning annoyance, JAMES holds up a sketch on a piece of lined paper.)

	Good thing, you didn't say you were going to be an artist.
CARL:	Well, it fit: Captain Impervious. When James dislocated his shoulder during 4th period gym class, he finished the entire basketball game before he told anyone.
JAMES:	Hey, we were winning!
CARL:	Nobody even knew he was in pain.
JAMES:	No paino, no gaino.
CARL:	On the morning James witnessed his Doberman being run over by a Hummer on his way to school, he made it to homeroom on time to accept his award as Top Salesman in the magazine subscription drive.
JAMES:	I told my mom not to name that fuckin' dog "Lucky."
CARL:	Captain Impervious.
JAMES:	All I won was a crummy Virgin Mary statue. And we are still getting those damn magazines!
CARL:	On the day that his family got the news that James' brother had gotten himself blown up in a military

maneuver in Iraq, James showed up for soccer practice. The coach tried to send him home. But he refused.

JAMES: I told him not to join the fuckin' army in the first place.

CARL: They sent him to the school counselor.

JAMES: Three days in a row!

CARL: But the school counselor finally cleared him.

JAMES: Like I told her Day One: I was fine.

CARL: I came to admire this incredible force field he possessed. That's why, when I drew Captain Impervious, I gave him a shield — a shield that could deflect any adversity coming his way. *(JAMES holds up the sketch to point out the shield.)*

CARL: Wounded shoulder —

JAMES: *(Shielding himself with the picture)* Deflect.

CARL: Scoring a first date with Evangeline Acuna.

JAMES: *(Dropping the "shield")* No deflect.

(JAMES continues to shield/un-shield himself as appropriate.)

CARL: Dog meets Hummer . . .

JAMES: Oh, Deflect.

CARL: Winning top salesman . . .

JAMES: Virgin Mary, come on down!

CARL: Brother blasted to smithereens . . .

JAMES: Double Deflect.

CARL: Placing out of Freshmen Algebra . . .

JAMES: Pardon me while I pass "Go."

CARL: Captain Impervious — became a benchmark to aspire to. I wasn't usually successful, but when faced with any setbacks, I would ask, "What would Captain Impervious do?" And like all superheroes, Captain

Impervious had a fantastic backstory: When James' mother was pregnant with him, she was sitting on the porch and was struck by a stray bullet. It pierced her abdomen. She thought it had killed her baby, but on closer inspection they found the bullet had merely grazed the baby's elbow.

(JAMES holds up his elbow.)

JAMES: I still have the scar.

CARL: Both baby and mother were fine incidentally.

JAMES: *(Pointing to his elbow)* Not incidentally.

CARL: Captain Impervious.

JAMES: Don't you'd think you better define "impervious" for those of them who don't know the word?

CARL: We're assuming an educated audience. They know what it means.

JAMES: Take it from a math whiz, there's always a lowest common denominator.

(JAMES produces a dictionary and hands it to CARL. He prompts CARL to read.)

CARL: According to Random House: "Not permitting penetration or passage."

JAMES: Whoa! That doesn't sound right.

CARL: "Incapable of being injured or impaired."

JAMES: That's better.

CARL: "Incapable of being influenced or affected."

JAMES: *(Smiling)* Yep. That sounds like me.

CARL: Did you need me to use it in a sentence? . . . Captain Impervious is . . . impervious.

JAMES: *(Taking the book)* Like I warned you, you can't get caught up in other people's losses.

CARL: Or even your own if you're Captain Impervious. I got tired of saying Captain Impervious all the time, so I shortened it to C.I.

JAMES: Ridiculous.

CARL: But sometimes — like now — he was plain James. Stop it, James. Because he was holding a glizzy to my head. *(JAMES points a finger at CARL's head.)* He always did shit like that. It was his weird sense of humor. *(To JAMES)* Guns have been known to go off.

JAMES: Relax, it's not even loaded.

CARL: That's what Alec Baldwin said. It still makes me nervous.

JAMES: Everything makes you nervous. You gotta work on that.

CARL: And who's that actor? — Bruce Lee's son — he was killed on the movie set of *The Crow*, screwing around with a blank gun.

JAMES: Who owns a blank gun? This is a Glock. A real gun with no bullets is less dangerous than a blank gun with bullets — that's all that proves.

CARL: What about Jesus' *(pronounced "Hey-zeus")* little brother? He found Jesus' metal. He thought it was empty — and pow — he popped his little sister playing.

JAMES: Jesus is an idiot, a fucking tecato. He was stupid for not hiding it better.

CARL: You blaming Jesus for killing his sister? That's harsh!

JAMES: You think I should blame the gun?

CARL: *(To us)* Then, he starts spinning the gun, like he's taking pot shots at the TV. *(To JAMES)* My dad just got us that TV, so you shoot it out, you better be prepared to travel. *(To us)* So he pointed the gun at me again. *(To JAMES)* I know you're upset. It's natural to be upset. But stop playing with the gun. Talk it out. Or just cry or something.

JAMES: When have you ever seen me cry?

CARL: Then maybe smoke a bowl and chill the fuck out.

JAMES: I never needed pharmaceuticals. Like some.

CARL: Maybe you could try prayer.

JAMES: Now you sound like my grandmother. *(CARL hands him a Bible.)* You're kidding me, right?

CARL: It works for Jake Peavey. It works for Tim Tebow. It works for a lot of people.

JAMES: I'd sooner try the pharmaceuticals.

CARL: Well, that works for a lot more people. Judging by the number of people crowding into the pot clinics and the liquor stores. There's a lot of pain out there. And there's a lot of people numbing it.

JAMES: Ooo, that's deep. Maybe you should be a psychiatrist "when you grow up?"

(JAMES points "the gun" at him again.)

CARL: *(To us)* I had considered it. After all, I had spent most of my seventeen years with him, trying to understand how his particular clock ticked. *(Beat. He pushes "the gun" away again.)* You know, you don't have to feel guilty.

JAMES: I don't feel guilty.

CARL: Good. Cause you shouldn't. *(Beat.)* So, you gonna go see her this afternoon?

JAMES: Negative.

CARL: You're not?

JAMES: Nah. I'm done.

CARL: Look, I know you're . . . Captain Impervious, but you should . . . go there. You should be there.

JAMES: Her mom's there.

CARL: Yeah, but she's *your* homegirl. She's your baby momma-to-be! ... Right?

JAMES: She won't even know I'm there.

CARL: But what if she comes out of the coma? What if she "wakes up?" She'd want you there. I mean you're the dad. Right?

JAMES: She looks ugly. All those tubes and shit.

CARL: They say when they might be able to remove the tubes?

JAMES: They did that this morning.

CARL: They did?! Well . . . When?

JAMES: This morning before I got there. Her Mom told them to.

CARL: But why would they ... ?

JAMES: They said there was no brain activity or something, so they took her off the life support.

(Long beat.)

CARL: But shouldn't you be there in case . . . in case she . . . she . . .

JAMES: Too late.

CARL: *(Looking hard at him)* Jesus! So . . .

(JAMES just continues to nod, not looking at CARL.)

Jesus! Well, why didn't you? . . . Jesus!

JAMES: Her mom told me to leave. She didn't want me there.

CARL: She can't blame you. You didn't even know she had those pills!

JAMES: She knew that Tatie kept texting and calling me that night. She looked through her phone.

CARL: Yeah, but Tatie was always texting you and calling you! A hundred times a day. You couldn't . . .

JAMES: She said I wasn't there for her when I should have been. So, I had no right — "no right!" — to be there now.

CARL: That's . . . harsh. That's just . . . her grief talking.

JAMES: She asked me why I never picked up, why I never responded. What else was I doing that was "so goddamn important?"

(Beat.)

CARL: What could you say?

JAMES: The truth. I told her I was with you. I was just hanging here with you.

(Beat. JAMES points "the gun" at CARL.)

CARL: *(To us)* Then, Captain Impervious did something completely unexpected. He found a solution. And it wasn't drugs. And it wasn't prayer. And I never saw it coming.

(JAMES turns "the gun" on himself and fires.)

          I just heard the impact. And then felt this . . . volcano spewing blood and bone.

(In slow-motion playback, JAMES reels from the gunshot. Beat. CARL wipes "the blood" from his face. JAMES looks at CARL, shrugs, then rises slowly and exits.

CARL comes forward to the position in which he began.)

          The "aha" moment was that James wasn't really Captain Impervious. And neither was I. And I would never ever be Captain . . . *that.* I cried for days. Drugs couldn't help. God couldn't help. *(Beat.)* But then I remembered the Hindus. How each child's destiny is stamped like a passport before the journey.

And I saw his map before me. And I saw mine . . . And I accepted it.

END OF PLAY

15 DEAD SOULS

by Leilani Squire

CHARACTERS

DORIS, female, 25, a World War II Army nurse of the European Theatre. She is the gatekeeper to the River; the one who leads the wounded soldiers home. She is gentle but firm, and a very wise soul. She taught first and second grade before the war. Any race or ethnicity.

JAMES, male, 71, a Vietnam combat veteran who has never returned home in the literal and metaphorical sense. He carries both the visible and invisible wounds of war. He played lead guitar in a rock band before he was drafted. Any race or ethnicity.

SETTING

The place between the mundane reality of everyday life and the realm where a soldier goes to heal the soul wounds of war.

TIME

Night. Present.

NOTE

During the Vietnam War, the United States G.I.s invented the phrase, "don't mean nothin'" to dismiss the unthinkable and the unbearable so they could keep moving on. The play is dedicated to those men and to the nurses of war who are still yet to be recognized.

PRODUCTION HISTORY

15 Dead Souls was presented by EST/LA in Los Angeles November 5–6, 2022. The production was directed by Leilani Squire. The cast was as follows:

DORIS: Hannah Marie Lloyd

JAMES: Patrick John Hurley

The stage is awash with rose and blue lighting. A vintage leather suitcase sits atop a vertically placed block upstage right; a smaller block flushed upstage of it. A longer block is horizontally placed upstage left. A military issued canteen and tin cup sit atop the smaller block.

A pool of white light illuminates DORIS downstage looking in the distance. She wears a World War II military issued nurse's uniform, the kind nurses wore in the field. Dog tags hang around her neck.

She finishes wrapping strips of a bloody bandage then moves to the blocks.

JAMES enters from the foyer and steps into DORIS' light. His torso is wrapped with a bloodied white bandage. He wears jungle fatigue pants and combat boots that look like they have traversed the world.

JAMES watches DORIS with caution.

During the dialogue: DORIS places the strips of bloody bandage inside the suitcase and removes a fresh wrapped white bandage. She puts the bandage in a pocket, closes the suitcase and places it by a block. She pours water from the canteen into the tin cup.

JAMES: Excuse me, Ma'am. Do you happen to know the way back to the highway?

DORIS: Can't say that I do.

JAMES: Must have taken the wrong turn.

DORIS: Happens a lot around here.

JAMES: You sure you don't know the way?

DORIS: Not to the highway ... You're hurt.

JAMES: Don't mean nothin'.

DORIS: *(Holding the tin cup out to him)* Here. Drink this.

JAMES: What is it?

DORIS: Water.

(He hesitates, then takes the tin cup and drinks.)

JAMES: So thirsty.

(She pours more water into the tin cup. He drinks.)

JAMES: Thank you, Ma'am. *(Holding the tin cup for her to take)*
           That's the sweetest water I've ever tasted.

DORIS: Keep it. You might need it.

JAMES: You sure do talk in riddles. Never understood the
           attraction, myself.

(He gives her the tin cup and crosses upstage left.)

JAMES: … Don't recognize the uniform.

DORIS: Army. Army Nurse Corps to be exact. Before your time.

(She takes the cup and the canteen back to the block.)

JAMES: Sure you don't know how to get back to the highway?

DORIS: James.

JAMES: *(Turning to her)* How do you know my name?

DORIS: You need to rest.

JAMES: It's been nice talking but I gotta get going.

DORIS: You're hurt.

JAMES: No offense, Captain, but this place gives me the creeps
           … There's gotta be a way back. Are you sure …

*(JAMES begins to slowly sink onto the upstage left block. DORIS
goes to him. He falls asleep as she quietly hums, and with a pair
of old military scissors cuts the bloody bandage wrapped around
his torso. He sleeps deeply as she sings and wraps the clean bandage
around his torso.)*

DORIS: *(Singing)*

           BODY PARTS AND TRACERS,

           STREAKING THROUGH THE SKY.

           WANDERING INTO THE CANYON,

           DON'T KNOW WHY.

BODY PARTS AND TRACERS,

LIGHTING UP THE NIGHT.

TREKKING THROUGH THE JUNGLE,

MAN, WHAT A SIGHT.

DREAMIN' OF HOME,
AND GOOD OL' APPLE PIE.

OH, MAN, WHAT A SIGHT.

DREAMIN' OF HOME,
AND GOOD OL' APPLE PIE.

JAMES: *(Waking up as if from a deep, deep sleep)* Where'd you hear that from?

DORIS: An old friend.

JAMES: Impossible.

DORIS: A lot of things may seem so. Look around.

JAMES: Haven't heard that song since the night before Terrell died. He wrote that crazy ass poem and put it to the most beautiful music. He had this certain sound like nobody else … like deep velvet. And man, could he blow that harp. His grandfather gave it to him when he could barely walk. Said his granddaddy's spirit was the one playing. But I knew better. It was Terrell's pouring into that music. The blues … black and blue we called it … Nothing scared him.

DORIS: Except his mamma.

JAMES: How do you know that?

DORIS: You're not the only one who carries the dead.

JAMES: Another riddle. Don't mean nothin'.

DORIS: Did to Terrell.

(Sound of the river in the distance fades up. Lighting shifts to sharper.)

JAMES: Do you hear that?

(JAMES stands and searches for the sound's source. Blocking his way to the river, DORIS holds out her hand.)

DORIS: Dance with me.

JAMES: No, thank you, Captain. Gotta get back.

(He walks to the front edge of the stage.)

DORIS: You know that's not the way.

(This stops him. The sound of the river fades.)

JAMES: That was the last night I knew what innocence meant. When Terrell sang that song. Sang all night long. Like he knew ... My first kill was at daybreak.

DORIS: I lost twenty-nine.

JAMES: You're a nurse. Not the same.

DORIS: Guilt weighs the same.

JAMES: Not when you're the survivor. Don't mean nothin'.

DORIS: We had so many casualties. Couldn't save them all. I still carry Freddie and Philip and Anton ... all ... the rest.

JAMES: Fifteen ... Fifteen dead souls.

(She strokes his heart area. Gently. Slowly.)

JAMES: Those fifteen followed me back. I've looked into their eyes every minute of every second since they took their last breath. Still smell the rain. The jungle. Their breath. Our sweat. Fifteen without names but with identities. And each one of them took a piece of me.

DORIS: The last one, was it by a river?

JAMES: Yes.

(She removes a stone from her pocket.)

DORIS: There is a river near here ... I found this stone for you.

JAMES:	I promised myself that I would never go near another damn river as long as I lived.
DORIS:	This one's different.
JAMES:	They're nothin' but a trap.
DORIS:	They know, you know.
JAMES:	What are you saying?
DORIS:	They are waiting for you.

(DORIS gives him the stone. He studies the stone.)

JAMES:	My grandmother was a nurse. Maybe you knew her.
DORIS:	Maybe. I knew a few. They were good people. The best.
JAMES:	She'd come visit us every summer. Take the train from Wichita and stay in the back room. She did the dishes every night after dinner. And then sit in the rocking chair and knit. Always knitting. That's what I remember the most about her. And this funky-ass bag she kept her stuff in. I'd sit on the floor by her feet and hold the yarn around my hands so she could wrap the yarn into a ball around and around. She smelled like roses.
DORIS:	That's a good memory.
JAMES:	Every Christmas she'd send me something she knitted that summer. Socks or a goofy sweater. I tossed them in the bottom drawer, too embarrassed to wear them.
DORIS:	*(She taps his heart area)* The fifteen … living inside here … time to let them go.
JAMES:	I'm about done with you and your crazy way of looking at things. I'm outta here, lady.

(He pushes past her and walks upstage left.)

DORIS:	If you leave you will always carry them … and sorrow … anger … guilt … and most of all … sadness.

JAMES: Let's not forget shame.

DORIS: That, too.

(He turns and faces her.)

JAMES: Am I dead?

DORIS: No, James, you are not dead.

JAMES: Feels like it.

DORIS: Do I look like I'm dead?

JAMES: You look like my grandmother.

DORIS: Everyone says that.

JAMES: Another riddle. I'm beginning to hate your fuckin' riddles.

(He pushes past her again and walks to the upstage right block and sits on it.)

DORIS: You used to enjoy riddles.

JAMES: That was a long time ago. Before … Before …

DORIS: You went to war.

JAMES: Sure you don't know the way to the highway?

DORIS: *(Sitting on the upstage left block)* I only know the way to the river.

JAMES: Thought the strangest thing, walking through the canyon … It's too heavy. These fifteen … So heavy … Label a human being the enemy it's much easier to destroy the enemy. Kill the identity it's easier to kill the person. Doesn't matter if it's a grandmother minding her own business or a kid not much older than you trying to kill you … Or a kid from Mississippi.

DORIS: It's time to take their souls to the river. You've carried them long enough.

JAMES: I don't know who I am without them.

DORIS: It's okay, James, to take off that old armor and put on new.

(Sounds of the river fade up. It's closer now. JAMES listens. DORIS listens, too. A song similar to Comin' Back to Me[3] *by Jefferson Airplane begins faintly beneath the River.)*

DORIS: It's the river.

JAMES: Dance with me.

(The general lighting and river sound fade. The song and a special center stage come up. They dance beneath the special. Slowly. Intimately. They stop. The music and light fade.)

(JAMES grabs the dog tags around DORIS' neck.)

JAMES: *(Reading)* James McDevitt. 4891865826 … I've been looking for these. You sneaky little devil.

DORIS: *(Enjoying the moment)* I've been called worse.

(DORIS slips the dog tags over his head. Then she pulls a locket from a pocket and hands it to JAMES.)

JAMES: My grandfather gave this locket to my grandmother so she wouldn't forget. She never took it off.

(He smells it as if the locket were perfume on the wind.)

JAMES: Roses … Guess I've been waiting for you just as much as you have been waiting for me.

(JAMES slips the locket over his head and puts the stone in a pocket. DORIS walks upstage.)

DORIS: There's the path right there. Take it down to the river.

JAMES: You know I don't like rivers.

DORIS: They're waiting for you.

JAMES: Who?

---

3 You must get copyright permission to use this song or any other music for a production.

DORIS: Come on, James, you know who. Sing them into the River. Let the water carry their souls back to the place of their birth. Then cross the River. The highway is just on the other side.

JAMES: This is another one of your riddles?

DORIS: You'll recognize some places, others you won't. You've changed too much. But that's okay, just keep going along the highway. Keep putting one foot in front of the other and you'll know the way.

JAMES: That's the way back home?

(He walks to her. They face each other. He slowly salutes. She returns the somber salute.)

DORIS: Go on, Soldier. They're waiting.

(One last look.)

(DORIS watches JAMES exit upstage.)

(DORIS pulls another pair of dog tags from inside her blouse, reads the name, and quickly glances toward the place JAMES entered. She grabs the bloodied bandage and goes toward the suitcase as lights fade.)

END OF PLAY

SCARY FACES HAPPY FACES

by Danny Tejera

CHARACTERS

MARIA, F, 70s.

ALEYSHA, F, late teens, her granddaughter.

NOTES

A "/" indicates the start of the next line of dialogue.

HOW TO PLAY IT

As a general rule: dry and matter of fact. The language is already language-y, so it's best not to lean into that. Less is more.

PRODUCTION HISTORY

Scary Faces Happy Faces was presented at the 47th Annual Samuel French Off Off Broadway Short Play Festival in New York City on August 17, 2022. The production was directed by Hanna Novak. The cast was as follows:

MARIA:	Rosemary Quinn
ALEYSHA:	Maria Perez
STAGE DIRECTIONS:	Dan Caffrey

A room with a bed. By the bed, a stool. In the bed, MARIA, 70s.
In the stool, her granddaughter ALEYSHA, late teens.

MARIA: Please don't scare me today.
           You scare me. Your face. You make scary faces.

ALEYSHA: I don't do it on purpose. You know that.
           My face twists into scary shapes and I can't control it.

MARIA: Well please try to control it, today, when you're with
           me, where we are. A hospital. You shouldn't make scary
           faces in hospitals.
           Especially in front of your grandma.

ALEYSHA: I'll try not to.

MARIA: Thanks dear. How's school?

ALEYSHA: Boring.

MARIA: That's not good.

ALEYSHA: I hate it.

MARIA: … Well, you shouldn't *hate* it. You should feel
           indifferent about it and find something more
           important to hate.

(ALEYSHA shrugs.)

MARIA: It's time for my pudding.

ALEYSHA: Where is it?

MARIA: On the counter. Can you feed me?

ALEYSHA: How?

MARIA: Remove the plastic cover. Stick a spoon in it. Put it in
           my mouth.

*(ALEYSHA opens a pudding, sticks a spoon in, and offers it to
her grandma.)*

MARIA: Closer. Closer. I can't move my neck!

(*ALEYSHA sticks the pudding in MARIA'S mouth. MARIA chews.*)

MARIA: Wipe the drip from my chin.

ALEYSHA: With what?

MARIA: A napkin!

ALEYSHA: I DON'T HAVE A NAPKIN.

MARIA: DON'T YELL AT YOUR GRANDMOTHER.

(*Beat.*)

ALEYSHA: ... I feel a scary face coming. (*They wait.*)
         ... Never mind. False alarm.

MARIA: Finish feeding me please.

(*ALEYSHA offers her another spoonful. MARIA doesn't take it.*)

MARIA: That's enough.

(*ALEYSHA puts the pudding back into the container, leaves container on the counter.*)

MARIA: Do you have a boyfriend?

ALEYSHA: No.

MARIA: And why is that?

ALEYSHA: I don't like boys.

MARIA: Do you like girls?

ALEYSHA: I don't like anyone.

MARIA: ... You'll grow out of that.

ALEYSHA: Can I smoke in here?

MARIA: No. When I met your grandfather, I didn't like him. He was in the army. He wore an army hat and had a gun. I *hated* him for that. But then we got married.

ALEYSHA: You've told me this / before.

MARIA: After we got married your grandfather said to me,
           "Maria, now that you're married to me, will you stop
           hating me?" And I said, "No."

           Five years went by, and I had your mother and her
           sisters. And your grandfather said, "Maria, now that
           you've had three daughters with me, will you stop
           hating me?"

           And I said, "No. I still hate you."

(MARIA broods. ALEYSHA lights a cigarette.)

ALEYSHA: Is that the whole story?

MARIA: More pudding please.

ALEYSHA: I can't. The doctors said you shouldn't have too much.

(MARIA broods.)

ALEYSHA: Do you want to see my dance routine?

MARIA: Yes.

ALEYSHA: Actually, I can't show it to you, because it still needs
           practice. But I can tell you how it goes:

           I walk to the middle of the stage. I wear a pink dress.
           I walk to the front. I look over the audience. Turn
           upstage. Turn downstage. Hold head. Rub temples.
           Neck up. Smile. Serious. Smile. Music. Drums. Voice.
           "We are the stars that sing. We are the birds who fly
           over the sky." Arms up. Bird motion. Bird sounds.
           "KOO! KOO!" Sad face. Walk to the wall. Fall against
           It. Collapse on the floor. Stand up. Walk to chair. Kick
           over chair. "We are like the wind. We are like a road,
           where the spirits pass over."

MARIA: Stop.

ALEYSHA: The beat drops. I thrust. I thrust. Head back. Look at
           the sky. I thrust for the earth. I thrust for the earth —

MARIA: STOP. YOU'RE SCARING ME.

(Beat. ALEYSHA smokes.)

ALEYSHA: What do you like to do here, Grandma? In the hospital. For fun. Do you ever have fun?

MARIA: I have lots of fun.

ALEYSHA: Oh yeah? Like how?

MARIA: I talk to people. Ask them about their grandchildren. Ask them about their maladies. I talk about what I'm reading. I talk about your grandfather.

ALEYSHA: He's dead.

MARIA: … I know that, dear. *(A beat.)*

It's really nice of you to come visit your grandmother today, Aleysha.

ALEYSHA: My mom made me.

MARIA: Well, that's nice of your mom to make you. It's nice when family makes you do things. One day you'll be old and you'll have a granddaughter too.

ALEYSHA: I'm never gonna be old.

MARIA: You think you're special?

ALEYSHA: Yeah. I do. Because of my scary faces.
Uh-oh. I definitely feel one coming this time.
Please look away, Grandma.

(MARIA quickly covers her eyes with her hands. ALEYSHA'S face contorts into a very scary shape. Stays that way. Stays that way. Then relaxes.)

(A moment. MARIA uncovers her eyes.)

MARIA: So. What are you going to be when you grow up?

ALEYSHA: A dancer.

MARIA: I was a dancer once.

ALEYSHA: What kind of dancer?

MARIA: … Well, we didn't have the same names for things that you do.

ALEYSHA: What did you call things?

MARIA: *(ignoring her.)* Can you massage my legs?

ALEYSHA: … What part of your legs?

MARIA: My calves, please.

(ALEYSHA is grossed out. She removes the hospital blanket from MARIA'S legs. Then rolls up a pantleg and starts to softly massage her calf.)

MARIA: *(she sighs.)* Oh boy. I'm tired.

ALEYSHA: Do you want a coffee?

MARIA: No. *(re: massage.)* That's enough.

(ALEYSHA stops massaging.)

MARIA: Do you know what you want for the holiday this year, honey?

ALEYSHA: Money.

MARIA: Money isn't everything, dear.

ALEYSHA: I'd like money please.

MARIA: Well. Okay then. *(She thinks about this. Then:)*
           We should pray.

ALEYSHA: Why?

MARIA: Because. That's what families do together.

(MARIA clasps her hands and closes her eyes. ALEYSHA reluctantly does the same.)

MARIA: I pray for the health and happiness of my loved ones, and for the health and happiness of the community at large.

ALEYSHA: I pray … also for the health and happiness of my loved ones, and for the health and happiness of the community at large.

*(They open their eyes and separate their hands. MARIA smiles.
ALEYSHA is frustrated.)*

ALEYSHA: How much longer…?

MARIA: *("How much longer what, dear?")* What, dear?

ALEYSHA: Do I have to *be* here?

MARIA: … I'd appreciate it if you stayed at least a few more minutes.

(MARIA starts to cry.)

MARIA: *(crying)* You never visit me. You never visit me. That's why today is so important. Today you're visiting me.

(ALEYSHA stares at her, unmoved. MARIA cries.)

ALEYSHA: Grandma.

(MARIA cries.)

ALEYSHA: Grandma, do you want me to make a happy face?

(MARIA stops crying.)

MARIA: No.

(A beat.)

MARIA: Where's the nurse? I'm hungry.

ALEYSHA: I don't know.

MARIA: Go check.

(ALEYSHA gets up and walks offstage. Then returns.)

ALEYSHA: She's on her dinner break.

MARIA: Oo. Can I have more pudding?

ALEYSHA: Sorry. There's none left. I accidentally threw it out when you had your eyes closed.

*(The pudding on the counter is indeed no longer there.
MARIA broods.)*

MARIA: Scratch my arm, please. *(ALEYSHA does.)* Higher.
             There. Thank you.

ALEYSHA: How do you go to the bathroom?

MARIA: Same way as you, dear. Do you have a boyfriend?

ALEYSHA: Stop asking me if I have a *boyfriend*, Grandma!
             It's so gross!

(MARIA loses her temper.)

MARIA: Do you care about anything?!

ALEYSHA: Yeah…

MARIA: Oh yeah?! Like what?!

ALEYSHA: *(suddenly furious.)* Ugh. I don't have to tell you the
             things that I care about!

MARIA: But I *want* to hear about them …

ALEYSHA: No! You don't! You only want to hear about certain
             things!

MARIA: Well, I don't know how to ask you about the other
             things that I don't know about!

ALEYSHA: Exactly. That's *exactly* what I mean, Grandma.

(A long, painful pause. MARIA is hurt.)

ALEYSHA: I have to go.

MARIA: Okay.

(Silence. ALEYSHA doesn't move.)

ALEYSHA: Yeah. I have to go. Do you want me to see if the nurse
             is back so you can have your dinner?

MARIA: I'm not hungry anymore.

*(ALEYSHA stands up, awkwardly hugs her grandma on the bed.
MARIA hugs her back.)*

MARIA: Thanks for visiting me, sweetie.

ALEYSHA: Thanks for seeing me, Grandma.

MARIA: I love you.

ALEYSHA: I love you too.

(ALEYSHA walks to the door. She turns around, looks at her grandma, then leaves.)

(A moment. Then MARIA addresses the audience directly.)

MARIA: Before she left, she made another scary face.
But she didn't warn me.

            She made the face right at me. And I looked at it.
And it was terrifying.

            It was the scariest face I'd ever seen.

            It looked exactly like this:

(MARIA makes a scary face at the audience. She continues talking normally throughout the following but her face remains in the scary shape.)

MARIA: And she left. She left the room and then the hospital.
But the face didn't leave.
It stayed here with me. Looking at me.
And eventually it became my face.
My permanent face.

            And when I watched a TV show at night,
this was my face.

            And when I read the newspaper in the morning,
this was my face.

            And I stopped remembering what it was like to not have a scary face.

            And in my mind, I said the word face so much that it stopped meaning the word face.

            Face started meaning other things.

Cherry.

Piñata.

Piranha.

Fanaticism.

Aquarius.

Adobe houses.

It was all face.

It was all face.

And when I died and went to heaven. I still had my face. My scary, scary face.

And when God told me the secrets of the universe all God said was face.

Face face face face

Face face face face

Face face face face face face face face face face face.

END OF PLAY

PLAYS
★FOR THREE OR★
MORE ACTORS

TREE HUGS

by Evan Baughfman

CHARACTERS

* PINEY THE ELDER, a pine tree, almost 300 years old. Any race or ethnicity.

* KRIS PINE, another pine tree, only 200 years old. Any race or ethnicity.

DAVIS, not a pine tree, 31 years old. Any race or ethnicity.

SETTING

At a small campsite, in the middle of the woods

TIME

Night

NOTE

* indicates that these roles can be played by actors of any gender; pronouns may be changed in the script to address production needs

PRODUCTION HISTORY

Tree Hugs was presented by the Barrow Group in NYC, June 17, 2022. The production was directed by Tim Abou-Nasr. The cast was as follows:

PINEY THE ELDER: Jonathan Lipnick

KRIS PINE: Amory Walsh

DAVIS: Gregg Blake

A sleeping bag is rolled out beside a makeshift fire pit. A backpack lies near the sleeping bag. A little fire glows in the pit.

A few feet away, a man, DAVIS, 31, in vibrantly colored shoes, hugs a pine tree, tightly. DAVIS embraces the tree as if it's a long-lost loved one.

Though, the tree, PINEY THE ELDER, with pinecones shaking in its branches, seems to be less than pleased with the human contact.

PINEY THE
ELDER: Uh … sir? Sir, can you please let go of me?

(Across the way, another tree, KRIS PINE, chuckles.)

KRIS PINE: All the trees out here, and this guy chooses to get close to you!

PINEY THE
ELDER: Not funny! Sir, can you … can you stop with the hugging? N … Now, sir. Anytime would be great. Really.

(But DAVIS hugs PINEY even tighter. He presses his cheek against PINEY'S trunk and smiles wide.)

DAVIS: God, you feel good.

PINEY THE
ELDER: Uhhhh. You're making me very uncomfortable, sir!

(KRIS PINE finds all of this to be rather hilarious. Can't stop chuckling.)

KRIS PINE: *(to DAVIS)* Hey, pal! My buddy over there's got some boundary issues. Won't even let a squirrel scurry around him. Me, on the other hand … I think I might be just the tree you're looking for.

(DAVIS runs his fingers lovingly over PINEY'S trunk. Caresses gently.)

DAVIS: Bark. Why is it called "bark?" You think whoever first came up with the term asked his dog for suggestions? *(As DAVIS runs his fingers over the tree trunk, PINEY reluctantly giggles.)*

It's like I can feel you breathing. Are you breathing?

PINEY THE
ELDER: Y…Yes! That … That tickles. S … Stop it!

KRIS PINE: Hey, pal! Come over here! I'm not ticklish!

(DAVIS looks at the bark in wide-eyed wonder.)

DAVIS: Your bark. Your skin. Your texture. Never felt anything quite like this before, have I? I mean, I have, but I don't think I ever really paid attention before now.

Tonight … Tonight is different.

(DAVIS continues caressing PINEY with his fingers.)

PINEY THE
ELDER: *(still ticklish, giggling)* S … Sir, if y … you don't stop … I … I'll h … have to d … drop p … pinecones on you!

KRIS PINE: Hey, pal, I said over here! And I won't concuss you with my seed pods.

PINEY THE
ELDER: I … I SAID, S … STOP!

(DAVIS won't stop touching PINEY, so PINEY drops a pinecone onto him. DAVIS doesn't really seem to notice.)

DAVIS: Can't believe I found you … after all this time … *(PINEY drops a second pinecone onto DAVIS. He looks up.)* Ow. *(A third pinecone hits him.)*

Ow! Hey!

(DAVIS rubs his head, right where the pinecone hit. He steps away from PINEY, confused.)

PINEY THE
ELDER: That's what you get! I warned you!

KRIS PINE:	I know I've said it before, but you've got a real knack for that.
PINEY THE ELDER:	Yeah, well, this idiot's a much easier target than a moving squirrel, that's for sure.

(PINEY throws a fourth pinecone. DAVIS dodges the attack.)

DAVIS:	What the hell!
PINEY THE ELDER:	BACK OFF, JERK!

(DAVIS staggers back a step or two, mouth agape.)

DAVIS:	I ... I knew it! You *are* breathing! You ... You *are* alive!
KRIS PINE:	Well, yeah. Does this guy not know how trees work?
PINEY THE ELDER:	Wait a second. I think he can ... Sir, do you understand the words that are coming out of my knothole?
DAVIS:	Yes! Yes, I understand you! The shrooms have kicked in, fully! I'm finally peaking!
PINEY THE ELDER:	"Shrooms?"
KRIS PINE:	I think he means those toadstools he stuffed into his face about an hour-and-a-half ago.
PINEY THE ELDER:	Oh. *Mush*rooms.
KRIS PINE:	Yeah.
PINEY THE ELDER:	Remember that little patch of *shrooms* that sprouted here back in the sixties? The odd stuff they always wanted to talk about?
KRIS PINE:	Little freaks.

PINEY THE ELDER:	Weird, little freaks.
KRIS PINE:	Fun guys, though.
PINEY THE ELDER:	Yeah. Fun guys. Really made you laugh and look at the world differently, didn't they?

(DAVIS giggles to himself.)

KRIS PINE:	Our pal here started acting strange not too long after eating what was in his little bag over there.
DAVIS:	Yes! Yes! Exactly! *(DAVIS claps his hands together.)* Sentience! Amazing! I *knew* it! I knew it! I mean, I hoped. *Really* hoped. But, deep down, I knew. Or now I know. But I always had a feeling. Just needed to open up my mind a little further to the possibility of hearing you. Just like Dad always said, you know?
KRIS PINE:	Totally.
DAVIS:	Communicating with trees! Wow!
PINEY THE ELDER:	Communicating with a person. Why?
DAVIS:	Why ... ?
PINEY THE ELDER:	Why, sir, are you here?
DAVIS:	Well, I'm camping, as you can see. To be one with nature. To be a part of the real world again, away from the city. To put some distance between myself and work ... and smog ... and, well, other people, too, if I'm being honest ... You know, to really get back to my roots.
KRIS PINE:	You have roots? Where?
PINEY THE ELDER:	He doesn't have roots. He has legs.

KRIS PINE: And big, colorful paws.

(DAVIS *looks down at his feet.*)

DAVIS: Paws … ? You mean, *shoes?*

PINEY THE
ELDER: Sure. Call them whatever you like.

KRIS PINE: I like how they look. Shoes.

DAVIS: Thank you.

KRIS PINE: I like how you move on top of them. Is it easy?

DAVIS: Moving?

KRIS PINE: Moving on your shoes.

DAVIS: Well, that's what they're for. To make my movements easier. More comfortable.

KRIS PINE: You can go wherever you want? One place to another? On your shoes?

DAVIS: Yes.

KRIS PINE: I don't move. Haven't moved in two hundred years.

PINEY THE
ELDER: Close to three hundred for me.

KRIS PINE: Our roots keep us here, unmoving. *Trap* us here.

PINEY THE
ELDER: It's not that bad.

KRIS PINE: Personally, I want more than this … this *standing around* all the time. I'd like a change of scenery. Someone different to talk to, for once. And squirrels don't count. All they talk about are their nuts!

PINEY THE
ELDER: Here we go again. *You're* nuts.

KRIS PINE: I want freedom.

PINEY THE
ELDER: We're trees.

KRIS PINE: *(to DAVIS)* I want to escape — *break free of* — my roots. And you want to get back to yours ... ? I don't understand.

DAVIS: They're ... metaphorical roots. All I meant was, I wanted to get back to ... happier times. Experience a bit of what I had in the past. Revisit memories of my youth, the things that made me *me*. Like camping. I used to do it a lot, with my dad.

KRIS PINE: You'd come out to the woods? With your father? When you were small?

DAVIS: Yeah. During the summer. We'd hike. Sit under the stars. Roast marshmallows. I'd listen to Dad's stories. A lot of the same ones ... the good ones ... over and over again.

PINEY THE ELDER: You visited these woods in particular?

DAVIS: Yes. And, once, we even stayed here. At this exact spot.

PINEY THE ELDER: You were here? When?

DAVIS: About twenty years ago.

KRIS PINE: You had that same color fur on top of your head back then? When you were small?

(DAVIS runs his fingers through his hair.)

DAVIS: I've always had this color. Well, except for a semester back in college when I tried blue.

KRIS PINE: Blue fur on *that* head?

DAVIS: I was going through a phase.

KRIS PINE: What I wouldn't give for a little extra color up in my branches! It's always the same, old boring thing around here.

(PINEY throws another pinecone at DAVIS ... but misses.)

DAVIS:	What's that for!
PINEY THE ELDER:	You ... We remember you!
DAVIS:	You do?
KRIS PINE:	We don't exactly get a lot of your kind out this way.
PINEY THE ELDER:	You ... You hurt me! You carved me up with your little claw!
DAVIS:	I'm sorry. That ... That was a long time ago, and —
KRIS PINE:	He got so upset that all his pine needles fell off.
DAVIS:	Really?
KRIS PINE:	Since then, he hasn't liked anybody touching him. No one but the wind.
PINEY THE ELDER:	What gave you the right to touch me the way you did?
DAVIS:	I was a kid. Just a dumb kid.
PINEY THE ELDER:	Excuse me, sir? *That's* your excuse?
DAVIS:	Dad left behind his pocketknife. He went off to get firewood. I got bored, so I ... I...
PINEY THE ELDER:	So you left your mark.
DAVIS:	My name, yes. And his. "*Davis + Dad = Forever.*"

(*DAVIS hangs his head. Falls silent.*)

KRIS PINE:	You dug into my buddy pretty deep. The scars are there. You can see still them, all this time later.

(*PINEY glares at DAVIS.*)

PINEY THE ELDER:	Thank you, sir. Thank you for that.

(*After a while ... *)

DAVIS:	I'm sorry.
PINEY THE ELDER:	I'm a living thing.
DAVIS:	I know.
KRIS PINE:	A thing that can't move. Can't hide. Can't run away.
DAVIS:	I know!
PINEY THE ELDER:	Why'd you return here? Is there something you'd like to add to my flesh?
DAVIS:	I've been coming to these woods every weekend the past few weeks, looking ... looking for you. And I finally find you.
PINEY THE ELDER:	To do more damage.
KRIS PINE:	To apologize, right?
DAVIS:	*(to PINEY)* I never should've carved anything into you. Dad let me know that as soon as he came back to camp.
KRIS PINE:	We remember.
DAVIS:	But I'm kind of glad I did it. Because, without those words on your trunk, I never would've found this spot again. I would've walked right past it.
PINEY THE ELDER:	Why. Are. You. Here?
DAVIS:	So I can plant my father next to you. *(DAVIS goes to his backpack, unzips it. He removes a beige container and walks back to the trees.)*
	Dad died months ago. He wanted to be cremated, for his ashes to be spread out in the forest where he spent so much of his free time.
KRIS PINE:	What's that thing you're holding?

DAVIS:	This is Dad. There's also a pine tree seed in here and some special soil. This urn ... this box ... is biodegradable. I had it all put together by a company I found online.
KRIS PINE:	We have no idea what any of that means.
DAVIS:	It means, I'm not going to just randomly spread my dad around these woods. I'm going to bury him here ... plant him into the earth beside you. Over time, he's going to grow into a tree, like you, and be one with nature, as he always liked to be.
PINEY THE ELDER:	So ... you're giving us a new friend?
KRIS PINE:	Someone else to finally talk to? *Really?*
DAVIS:	He'll have plenty of stories to share with both of you. Great stories. You'll enjoy hearing them again and again.

(DAVIS kneels down with the urn. Begins to dig into the ground with his hands. He pauses to play with the dirt a little, watching it sift through his fingers. Remember, he's as high as a kite.)

The last place we ever camped together, Dad. It's the perfect spot, don't you think?

(DAVIS turns back to the trees.)

He and Mom got divorced pretty soon after that trip. I moved away cross-country, didn't get to see Dad very much anymore. When I got older, he'd invite me on camping trips with him. But I always made excuses about why I couldn't ever join in. I was too busy with work. Too busy with friends. Too busy for Dad.

(DAVIS places the urn into the hole he's dug. He covers it with dirt, pats the earth.)

No more excuses, Dad. I'm going to camp with you as often as I can now. We're going to have those talks again. Just like old times.

(DAVIS *stands. Looks over to* PINEY.)

I could really use a hug right now. What do you say? Are we cool?

PINEY THE
ELDER: Sorry, sir. I'm not ready yet. But ... someday ... maybe.

KRIS PINE: I'll take a hug!

DAVIS: Okay. Yeah. All right.

(DAVIS *envelops* KRIS PINE *in a big ol' hug.*)

KRIS PINE: So much better than a squirrel!

(DAVIS *removes his shoes. Ties their laces together.*)

DAVIS: Here. Some color for you. And it'll make it easier to find you guys the next time I'm around.

(*He hangs the shoes from* KRIS PINE'S *branches.*)

Don't worry. I packed another pair.

KRIS PINE: *(giddy)* Shoes! SHOES!

PINEY THE
ELDER: Don't you go anywhere, now.

KRIS PINE: Ha! Not so sure I would leave anymore, even if I could.

(DAVIS *sits and leans back against* KRIS PINE'S *trunk. Relaxes.* KRIS PINE *seems to welcome the human connection.*)

DAVIS: Why go anyplace else? I don't think there's anywhere better to be.

END OF PLAY

CHAMP AT THE BORDER

by Lesley Becker

CHARACTERS

CHAMP   Female, plesiosaur.

VIKKI   Female, Canadian Border Guard.

GUS   Vermont Director of Tourism, male or female

SETTING

The office of the Canadian Border Service near Lake Champlain.

TIME

The present

NOTE

CHAMP is the famous lake monster in Lake Champlain at the Vermont-Canadian border.

PRODUCTION HISTORY

Champ at the Border was performed on December 13, 2022, in Burlington, Vermont at Hunt Middle School, directed by Lesley Becker. The cast was as follows:

CHAMP: Moya Thayer

VIKKI: Olivia Paulino

GUS: Winn Mount

A Canadian Border Crossing Office.

VIKKI, dressed in uniform with a red scarf, is behind the counter. CHAMP enters, dressed in simple but hip clothing, a red band around her neck, and a tail.

VIKKI: You, c'mon. You're next. In here.

(CHAMP enters, her flippers are in handcuffs.)

CHAMP: Please help me, I've got to get back to my family. They're waiting for me, and they don't know where they're going.

(VIKKI takes the handcuffs off CHAMP.)

VIKKI: You were arrested swimming across the border?

CHAMP: The border? An imaginary line in the lake? Borders are something people made up.

VIKKI: Name?

CHAMP: People call me Champ.

VIKKI: Champ is something Americans made up.

CHAMP: You can call me Gitaskogak, like the people before the Americans.

VIKKI: Champ, aka Gitaskogak.

CHAMP: Did you see the Champ photo Sandra Mansi took on exhibit at the Echo Center? It was verified by experts.

VIKKI: No. I did not. Date of birth?

CHAMP: March twelve, seventeen twenty-two.

VIKKI: You can't be three hundred years old.

CHAMP: *(preening)* Thanks. I get that a lot.

VIKKI: Address?

CHAMP: Don't have one. I'm in the process of moving. Previously Bitaw-bagok.

VIKKI:	How do you spell that?
CHAMP:	Okay, what the Americans call Lake Champlain.
VIKKI:	All right. I have heard of Champ. My son wants to be a cryptozoologist.
CHAMP:	A what?
VIKKI:	Cryptozoology is the study of unclassified and possibly unreal creatures. My son loves to watch the videos of Champ sightings around Charlotte.
CHAMP:	Personally, I like to play up around St. Albans.
VIKKI:	*(dryly)* Where Sandra Mansi took your picture with a Kodak Instamatic?
CHAMP:	*(coyly)* Maybe.
VIKKI:	You're indigent?
CHAMP:	No! Plesiosaur.
VIKKI:	I see. Are you homeless?
CHAMP:	No. Heading up to Missisquoi Bay. The lake waters have warmed up so much, salmon and trout moved up there. Salmon and trout is all we can eat. Plesiosaurs have had the same diet for centuries.
VIKKI:	You said, because the lake water is warmer?
CHAMP:	Climate change?
VIKKI:	Oh, right. *(realizing)* I mean, it's too bad.
CHAMP:	It's monstrous!
VIKKI:	So, you're a climate refugee? Canadian Immigration Service doesn't give visas for climate migration. Family or business are the proper reasons for immigration.
CHAMP:	I'm bringing the family! They missed the turn at North Hero, and now they're headed up to Rouses Point. Damn your paperwork! My kids are swimming around lost in a foreign country! Let me out of here!

VIKKI: Calm down. I have a child myself. I understand your concern for your family. However, by swimming across the border, you've entered Canada illegally. Let's finish this. A few more questions.

(GUS, a U.S. Director of Tourism enters.)

GUS: Champ!

CHAMP: Not you again!

GUS: Champ, what are you doing? Don't leave! We need you!

VIKKI: Who are you?

GUS: Gus Burns, Vermont Director of Tourism. *(pointing to Champ)* You don't know who you've got here! What's your name?

VIKKI: Vikki. And you're a crazy American who believes in lake monsters?

GUS: I'm taking her back.

VIKKI: It's a her?

GUS: Didn't you see the Mansi photograph? Verified by experts.

VIKKI: Your best scientific evidence is a photo taken with a Kodak Instamatic? Champ here is charged with illegal entry.

GUS: I'm taking her back to the U.S.

CHAMP: NO!

VIKKI: I'm going to have to get some backup here.

(VIKKI sends a text.)

GUS: There's plenty of food, more white perch than you could eat in a century!

CHAMP: White perch? That would be convenient for you, let the lake monsters eat the invasive species! No! We eat salmon and trout.

GUS: All right! We'll stock the lake with trout!

CHAMP: All year?

GUS: In the summer. Summer is the best time for a
              Champ sighting.

CHAMP: You can be sure there will never be another Champ
              sighting in Vermont if you don't help me get out of
              here now!

GUS: Don't do that! Vermont needs the excitement of the
              occasional lake monster sighting, to keep Champ swag
              relevant! And to float our tourism economy, which is
              worth billions! I'll help you! You matter to us, Champ!

VIKKI: You Americans have made yourselves quite the cottage
              industry around Champ.

GUS: Vermonters love our lake monsters.

VIKKI: You're a monster?

CHAMP: *(Showing her wounded feelings)* Right?

GUS: People love you! You're the mascot for our
              baseball team!

CHAMP: They made me into a cartoon character and put that
              on mugs, tote bags, ping-pong paddles and t-shirts!

*(GUS starts to show off his Champ tee shirt proudly, then thinks
better of it and covers it.)*

CHAMP: And the stuffed animals! They sell this nonsense up
              and down the lake!

GUS: We're overdue for a Champ sighting! Come on back,
              you'll see there's plenty of fish food.

CHAMP: Fish food!!! I don't live in an aquarium, though I'm
              sure an aquarium would pay a tidy sum for one of us,
              dead or alive.

GUS: How many of you are there?

CHAMP: Thirty in our pod, who are busy getting lost at the moment! I've got to go find them!

GUS: Customs told me they only saw one! There's thirty of you? Why hasn't anyone seen you in years?

CHAMP: Because we've been muddying the waters for centuries, whenever we see people. Any kind of debris and plants, we kick up murky clouds and then dive deep into the lake.

GUS: So you're all shy and don't like to be seen?

CHAMP: So we're all smart and don't want to get caught! We haven't felt safe since P.T. Barnum offered a reward of fifty thousand dollars for *our hide*!

GUS: That was the 1870s! Almost a hundred and fifty years ago.

CHAMP: We'd still be up on the surface, lounging in the sun, if we thought we were safe, like in the old days. Not that I'm that old myself. But my family was here with the dinosaurs.

VIKKI: Aren't you a dinosaur?

CHAMP: *(insulted)* Do I look like a dinosaur?

VIKKI: Well, for your ethnicity, I chose "other" and wrote in "dinosaur." Everyone needs a classification, you know.

GUS: She hasn't got one.

CHAMP: Researchers can't wait to get their hands on a dead one of us and figure it out.

VIKKI: My son wants a Champ costume for his birthday, and look, I'm making him a dinosaur costume. You must be related to dinosaurs, don't you have relatives in common?

CHAMP: Let me ask you this. How would you feel if you were classified as a fish? You do have relatives in common.

GUS: Dinosaur works for me.

CHAMP: If you read Scientific American, you would know scientists are certain that plesiosaurs are not dinosaurs.

VIKKI: What do scientists think you might be?

CHAMP: As I mentioned, they don't know!

(Beat)

CHAMP: Get me out of here, Vikki, and I'll show up at your son's birthday party!

VIKKI: You would!!

CHAMP: If you don't get me out of here, I will probably die! Then some zoologist can take me apart, bit by bit, in order to learn how I'm put together! That would be big news, and a real killer for tourism.

GUS: Oh, no!

VIKKI: My son would never forgive me, we can't let *that* happen!

GUS: Agreed.

CHAMP: If you're the one that "captures" me, the scientist that works me over will name my species after you — *Gracilus Vikkorai*! Then your son could never forget that you killed a lake monster!

VIKKI: Oh no! Border Service is coming! They're going to take you to a Holding Center.

CHAMP: Wait! A holding center?

GUS: Not the holding center!

CHAMP: With handcuffs and shackles?

GUS: For how long?

VIKKI: Hard to say. Your paperwork is incomplete, it could drag out!

CHAMP: People go in and don't know when they'll come out?

GUS: That's cruel and ... *inhumane*!

CHAMP: It's monstrous!!

VIKKI: You have to prove you aren't a security threat!

CHAMP: No, no, no! My babies will waste away at Rouse's Point while I'm in a holding cell! And I'll starve to death!

GUS: There must be another option!

VIKKI: Yes, yes, the manual says we have to consider alternatives to imprisonment!

GUS: What could it be?

VIKKI: The biodome?

GUS: The aquarium section!

CHAMP: No, no, no!

VIKKI: I don't think that will work.

GUS: Champ, do you promise, would you swear on a stack of Scientific American magazines, that you'll come back to Vermont?

CHAMP: In the summer!

GUS: That's worth millions! I'll get you out of here!

CHAMP: How?

GUS: Vikki, what is the description of Champ in the arrest report?

VIKKI: The red band around the neck. And of course, the tail. Like this dinosaur costume I'm making.

GUS: Here, Champ, put on my jacket. And my hat, pull it down over the star.

VIKKI: Take my scarf. And my son's costume! A tail, and the cape!

GUS: Champ, take my passport.

VIKKI: Put it over your shoulders, let it drop down over your back.

GUS: How does it look?

CHAMP: It looks awful.

(Beat)

CHAMP: I mean, thank you. Can I go now?

VIKKI: Come behind my counter, down the stairs to the parking garage and out to the road. There's a stream there that goes to the Richelieu River! You can get back to the lake that way! Take my security tag! Hurry!

GUS: Wait! Pull the cape over your tail! Okay. Get going!

VIKKI: My son's birthday is next Wednesday!

CHAMP: Bring him to Alburg Springs at three o'clock! No cameras!!

GUS: I'll look for you next summer! I should be out of the detention center by then.

CHAMP: Terrific!

VIKKI: Bye, Champ.

CHAMP: Good luck, Gus. By the way, that *was* me the day Sandra Mansi was up around St. Albans.

(CHAMP EXITS. GUS and VIKKI watch her leave.)

GUS: I knew that Mansi photo was the real thing!

VIKKI: Gus, they're coming. Ready?

(VIKKI put the handcuffs on GUS.)

GUS: Do I look like a lake monster?

VIKKI: Absolutely.

END OF PLAY

BY THE NEON LIGHTS
OF THE TACO BELL SIGN

by Monica Cross

CHARACTERS

CHRISSY, a woman, 21, college student. Any race or ethnicity.

GINNA, a woman, 21, college student. Any race or ethnicity.

TRINITY, any gender, any age, either someone really high or maybe some sort of guardian angel. Any race or ethnicity.

SETTING

Outside a Taco Bell.

TIME

A chilly autumn night.

PRODUCTION HISTORY

By the Neon Lights of the Taco Bell Sign was presented by Ixion Theatre Ensemble as part of "Let's Eat!: A Collection of Tasty Plays" by Ixion Theatre Ensemble in Lansing, MI, May 13–21, 2022. The Production was directed by Nick Lemmer. The cast was as follows:

CHRISSY: Storm Kopitsch

GINNA: Jillian Tosolt

TRINITY: Sarah Lynn

Broke college students, CHRISSY and GINNA stand in the parking lot of a Taco Bell on a chilly autumn night. The light of the Taco Bell sign casts a halo of neon light around them. They are both wearing layers, but neither looks particularly warm. The chill adds a stiffness to their demeanor. They both dig in their pockets — pants pockets, jacket pockets, sweatshirt pockets — checking each and every one, until they each have a fist full of change. They count the coins on their palms.

CHRISSY: I have 2.67.

GINNA: And 3 nickels. I think I have 3.95. Double check for me.

(They each simultaneously dump their change into the other person's free hand. And each begins sifting through the other's change.)

CHRISSY: 3.50. 3 dimes, and yeah. 3.95.

GINNA: Nope. This won't work. This one is a Canadian penny.

(GINNA picks it out and hands it to CHRISSY.)

CHRISSY: Really? I thought it was one of those new pennies with the shield on the back.

(CHRISSY takes it as looks at it carefully.)

GINNA: It's a maple leaf.

CHRISSY: Is that the only one?

GINNA: Yeah. So that puts this at 2.66, and a Canadian penny.

CHRISSY: Bringing our total to … ?

GINNA: 3.95 plus 5 brings us up to 4.

CHRISSY: … with the other two, that's 6.

GINNA: … and 66 now subtract the 5 we already added earlier … is .61.

CHRISSY: Woah. Look. We are like a nickel short of 6.66.

GINNA: Ah, yeah. The devil's change.

CHRISSY: I wonder if I have another nickel in my cup holder.

(*CHRISSY heads off towards her car.*)

GINNA: It's not worth it. Not unless you need exactly 6.66 to get us some burritos.

CHRISSY: But it's so cool though. Like the idea of having exactly 6.66 worth of change.

GINNA: Just go inside and order already. I'm starving.

CHRISSY: All right.

GINNA: And no bean burritos this time.

CHRISSY: Okay.

GINNA: I've eaten so many, I'm sick of them.

CHRISSY: I said, okay.

GINNA: Get the cheesy bean and rice burrito. It's cheaper and more filling.

CHRISSY: Do you want me to go in and order? Or do you want to stand around telling me what to order until six in the morning?

GINNA: Go.

(*CHRISSY goes into the Taco Bell. GINNA pulls a pack of cigarettes out of her pocket and begins to light one. Out of nowhere appears TRINITY.*)

TRINITY: Can I bum a smoke?

(*GINNA sizes up TRINITY and looks to see how many cigarette's she has left. It's just a few, but enough to share.*)

GINNA: Sure.

(*GINNA holds out a cigarette to TRINITY, who takes it. Then she holds out the lighter, TRINITY takes that too.*)

TRINITY: I appreciate ya.

GINNA: You kinda startled me. I didn't see you pull up.

TRINITY: Nah, I just came from over there.

(TRINITY doesn't indicate where.)

GINNA: Huh.

TRINITY: You've got stress radiating off of you like you just chugged a cup full of diablo sauce.

GINNA: I ... um ... excuse me?

TRINITY: There's a tension in your shoulders.

GINNA: Well, ya know. It's cold out here.

TRINITY: Sure, it is, but that looks different. Here, do you mind?

(TRINITY gestures to GINNA indicating TRINITY wants to touch her shoulders. GINNA pulls away.)

GINNA: What?

TRINITY: I can show you, but I would need to lay a hand on your back.

GINNA: I don't know ...

TRINITY: If you don't want to, that's fine.

GINNA: I'm not against it, I just don't know you.

TRINITY: You just shared with me one of the most important things in life.

GINNA: It's just a cigarette.

TRINITY: It's a bond.

(GINNA thinks about it.)

GINNA: And you're just going to touch my back?

TRINITY: Yes.

GINNA: All right, I guess.

(TRINITY touches GINNA's shoulders. GINNA tenses at the touch.)

TRINITY: Breathe into my hands.

GINNA: Into?

TRINITY: Just breathe.

(GINNA releases a breath and melts into TRINITY's hands.)

TRINITY: Let the tension melt away like molten nacho cheese.

GINNA: Isn't the nacho cheese hard as a rock?

TRINITY: Only if you let it just sit there. If you get it warm and gooey, it'll drip right through your fingers.

(TRINITY changes the subject.)

TRINITY: You having problems in school?

GINNA: Yea, I guess. I mean, it's more than that.

TRINITY: What is it then?

(TRINITY adjusts the placement of the hands on GINNA's back to a new source of tension.)

TRINITY: Breathe for me again. Like you just took a big bite of a quesadilla that is way too hot.

(GINNA breathes and releases a little bit.)

GINNA: It's just everything. There is so much going on in life, with my parents, at school, with my friends.

TRINITY: Like the friend who went inside?

GINNA: Nay, she's cool. I can be myself around her. It's the only down time I get.

TRINITY: Lean into that like she's your crunch wrap supreme.

GINNA: Yeah.

(TRINITY lets go of GINNA's back and goes back to smoking the cigarette.)

TRINITY: Feel the difference?

GINNA: Oh my god. I feel so light.

TRINITY: Like a thin drizzle of sour cream.

GINNA: Thank you so much.

TRINITY: No need to thank me. Just lean into your crunch wrap supreme.

(TRINITY walks off. GINNA looks after her and takes a long drag of her cigarette. CHRISSY enters, with a taco bell takeout bag.)

CHRISSY: We've got everything. There are nachos; there are burritos, quesadillas, and of course: cinnamon twists. I mean, we have so much food. This is like double the amount of food I've had so far today! I mean, we are going to go to bed with full bellies tonight!

GINNA: Did you see … ?

CHRISSY: Come on. Let's get out of here!

GINNA: I was talking to …

CHRISSY: You look like you've seen a ghost.

GINNA: Nah. But there was this really weird chick.

CHRISSY: Yeah?

GINNA: She bummed a cigarette off of me.

CHRISSY: I didn't see anyone.

GINNA: Yeah, she was talking about nacho cheese and diablo sauce.

CHRISSY: Sounds like a spicy combination.

GINNA: Yeah. She was just here.

CHRISSY: Ya know, you look a lot less stressed than when I went in there.

GINNA: It's probably my crunch wrap supreme.

CHRISSY: Aw man! I didn't get you a crunch wrap. Is that what you wanted?

GINNA: No. I've got what I need.

CHRISSY: Does that mean we can get out of the cold?

GINNA: Totally!

CHRISSY: Cool. Let's eat. *(CHRISSY heads off to her car. GINNA hesitates for a moment, takes one last drag of her cigarette.)*

GINNA: *(Muttering under her breath)* My crunch wrap supreme.

(Then, GINNA follows CHRISSY and the food.)

END OF PLAY

A TALE OF
AN UNEXPECTED GATHERING
AND ROMANCE
MADE ABSURD IN THE TELLING

by Rob Dames

CHARACTERS

NOT-HERE, a man, age and ethnicity are open

JUSTUS, a man, age and ethnicity are open

MAN, a Man, age and ethnicity are open

WOMAN, a woman?, age and ethnicity are open

SETTING

Somewhere unknown, deserted and vacant.

TIME

Now or perhaps then

PRODUCTION HISTORY

A TALE OF AN UNEXPECTED GATHERING AND ROMANCE MADE ABSURD IN THE TELLING was first produced by the FUSION Theatre Company (https://www.fusionnm.org/) as a winning entry in their 16th annual original short works festival, THE SEVEN, June 16th–19th, 2022 in Albuquerque, New Mexico. Festival Producer: Dennis Gromelski. Festival Curator: Jen Grigg. Directed by Jacqueline Reid. Lighting and Scenic Design by Richard K. Hogle. Sound Design by Chad Scheer. Properties Design by Robyn Phillips. Production Stage Manager: Victoria Ujczo.

NOT-HERE: William Sterchi

JUSTUS: Douglas Stewart

MAN: David Sinkus

WOMAN: Wendy Scot

A man, NOT-HERE, sits cross-legged in front of a stack of small branches stacked to make a fire. There is nothing else on the stage. He looks at the firewood stack, disassembles it, dusts off the place where the wood was, then carefully re-stacks it. A man, JUSTUS, enters riding an invisible horse. He has a little trouble controlling the horse. It dances around a bit nervously as he attempts to rein it in. Then it bucks but he maintains his seat.

NOT-HERE: You don't have a horse.

JUSTUS: I have wishes.

(JUSTUS dismounts and slaps the horse on the rump.)

JUSTUS: Off with you.

(He watches as it runs off.)

NOT-HERE: You'll never see him again.

JUSTUS: I can't see him now. Do you want to hear the story?

NOT-HERE: I don't speak with strangers.

JUSTUS: Am I a stranger?

NOT-HERE: I don't know you.

JUSTUS: Nor I you. May I ask your name and where you are from?

NOT-HERE: Not-here.

JUSTUS: If not here, then where?

NOT-HERE: It's my name.

JUSTUS: Not here?

NOT-HERE: Yes. But I prefer that you don't use it.

JUSTUS: What shall I call you?

NOT-HERE: There is no need to call. I'm here.

JUSTUS: True. My name is Just-us.

NOT-HERE: I didn't ask.

JUSTUS:	I volunteered. And ironically, it is just us. Now you want to hear the story?
NOT-HERE:	I'm preparing my supper.
JUSTUS:	You have no fire.
NOT-HERE:	I have no food. I choose not to waste fire when I have yet to find food.
JUSTUS:	Very wise. We must not squander our resources. Do you want to hear the story?
NOT-HERE:	Is it true?
JUSTUS:	It's a story.
NOT-HERE:	Can there not be true stories?
JUSTUS:	If it were true, I would consider it an account rather than a story. Do you want to hear the story?
NOT-HERE:	Perhaps after supper.
JUSTUS:	Very well.
NOT-HERE:	But I would prefer to hear an account. Something true. I don't like lies.
JUSTUS:	Is a story a lie? Perhaps it is an allegory which then would make it an ally of an account.
NOT-HERE:	First supper.
JUSTUS:	Very well. What shall we eat?
NOT-HERE:	I didn't expect you. I don't have enough for two.
JUSTUS:	You don't have enough for one.
NOT-HERE:	But I will. Now I will go in search of my dinner.

(NOT-HERE rises and wanders off.)

JUSTUS:	The story begins in a most peculiar way. Stories that begin in a normal way rarely lead to anything interesting.

(NOT-HERE returns. He carries a rabbit already skinned and impaled on a spit.)

JUSTUS: I was practicing the story for after supper. I see you found some supper.

NOT-HERE: Yes.

JUSTUS: It seems that you caught, killed, skinned and spitted that rabbit in rapid time.

NOT-HERE: I found him in this condition. He provides.

JUSTUS: Do you know Him?

NOT-HERE: Only by the stories.

JUSTUS: Are they stories or accounts?

NOT-HERE: More like fables.

(NOT-HERE suspends the rabbit over the firewood.)

JUSTUS: Are you going to light a fire?

NOT-HERE: No.

JUSTUS: Not being a culinary expert, I am uncertain as to your plan regarding cooking the spitted rabbit.

NOT-HERE: I have no plan.

JUSTUS: But you are hungry.

NOT-HERE: Yes.

JUSTUS: Then I can only surmise that you are not cooking the rabbit for your supper because once cooked and eaten, you would have to hear the story. Am I correct?

NOT-HERE: No.

JUSTUS: So, you wish to hear the story?

NOT-HERE: After supper.

JUSTUS: But with no fire, there will be no supper, ergo no story. Is that correct?

NOT-HERE: No.

JUSTUS: Very well then. Clearly my company is not wanted therefore, I shall leave.

(JUSTUS whistles shrilly. After a moment, he crosses to the invisible horse and mounts.)

JUSTUS: I bid you farewell.

NOT-HERE: Ta ...

(JUSTUS rides off. After a moment, a fire springs to life under the wood. JUSTUS races back in and quickly dismounts.)

JUSTUS: Ha!

NOT-HERE: Ha?

JUSTUS: Ha! I am a man who speaks his mind with no equivocation so I shall state loudly and clearly — You are a wizard! Correct?

NOT-HERE: No.

JUSTUS: All right. I am at my wit's end. I'll sit here silently and hungrily while you eat your rabbit.

NOT-HERE: Tell me the story.

JUSTUS: You haven't eaten.

NOT-HERE: I've lost my appetite.

JUSTUS: Very well ... This story begins in a peculiar way.

NOT-HERE: "Most."

JUSTUS: I'm sorry. What?

NOT-HERE: When you were practicing, you said a "most peculiar way." Start again.

JUSTUS: This story begins in a most peculiar way ...

(NOT-HERE removes the rabbit from the fire.)

JUSTUS: Do you want to hear the story?

NOT-HERE: First, I want to return this rabbit to his burrow since I'm not going to be eating it.

JUSTUS: The rabbit is dead. What value is a dead rabbit in
            a burrow?

NOT-HERE: The same as dead love in a marriage.

*(NOT-HERE exits with the rabbit. The fire goes out. A MAN
wearing a bathrobe, sunglasses, flip flops and carrying a beach chair
and an umbrella enters. He is accompanied by a WOMAN, dressed
in a robe, sunglasses, a large hat and carrying a beach umbrella and
a cooler. They take their places several paces away from JUSTUS. No
greetings are exchanged. JUSTUS watches them curiously. The MAN
plants the umbrella and opens it.)*

MAN: Good?

WOMAN: Good.

*(They place their respective chairs then remove their robes. They wear
some version of swimwear but not not at all contemporary)*

JUSTUS: You've come to the wrong place. There is no beach here.

MAN: The seas are rising. By my calculations, the ocean
            should be lapping at these shores in several years.
            When that occurs this beach will be overrun with
            beach-goers. There won't be a vacant spot on the
            sand. You might say that we have planned for that
            moment and have chosen to beat the crowd.

(JUSTUS rises and begins to move towards them.)

JUSTUS: If I might, your plan seems preposterous. Several
            days I understand, but several years …

MAN: Stop!

*(JUSTUS stops abruptly. MAN removes a roll of yellow tape
(like police tape). He rolls the tape out describing a line between
them and JUSTUS.)*

MAN: No deniers on this side of the line.

JUSTUS: This is a public space. Anyone can go anywhere.
            You are welcome to your beliefs. I have no interest
            in disputing them. But I am welcome to mine
            which include the right to cross this yellow line.

MAN:	This is private property.
JUSTUS:	How so?
MAN:	The law clearly describes that planting a flag or in its absence a beach umbrella qualifies as a valid claim.
JUSTUS:	In that case, I apologize. I am not a man who has read at law. I am an adventurer with a story to tell. Would you like to hear it?
WOMAN:	No.
JUSTUS:	It's a quite peculiar story ...

(NOT-HERE re-enters. He carries a large ice cream sundae.)

NOT-HERE:	"Most." Not quite.
JUSTUS:	I'm speaking with madam. *(To WOMAN)* It's a ... *most* peculiar story.
WOMAN:	No.
JUSTUS:	If I may ...
MAN:	Never, ever make her say "no" three times or a curse will fall upon you the likes of which even the Bible has never imagined.
JUSTUS:	I shall heed your advice. Where did you find an ice cream sundae?
NOT-HERE:	Where I looked. In my experience, one never finds something in a place he is not looking.
WOMAN:	I'm not his wife.
JUSTUS:	I didn't ask nor is it any of my concern but thank you for the update.
NOT-HERE:	She's not a woman.
JUSTUS:	Is that true? You are not a woman.
WOMAN:	I'm not his wife.
JUSTUS:	Ah, so I am to deduce that the reason you are not his wife is that you are not a woman.

MAN:	It is advisable that you keep your "deducing" to yourself. She makes claim to not being my wife but has made no claim on gender.
JUSTUS:	But in your estimation, she is not a woman.
NOT-HERE:	It is not an estimate. It is fact derived from knowledge.
WOMAN:	I'm his wife.
JUSTUS:	Ah ha, so you have isolated yourself in the wilderness escaping a marriage of conflicted sexual identity but into this hermitage comes your estranged wife and her paramour thus creating tension and perhaps turmoil.
MAN:	Tell us the story.
JUSTUS:	That won't be necessary. You are creating the story before my very eyes.
MAN:	This is your story?
NOT-HERE:	It did begin in a "most peculiar way."
MAN:	Do you know how it ends?
JUSTUS:	Yes.
NOT-HERE:	Will you tell us?
JUSTUS:	No.
MAN:	Why not?
JUSTUS:	No time, we are limited to ten minutes.

(JUSTUS whistles. His invisible horse returns. He mounts and begins to ride off.)

NOT-HERE: The sunset is over there.

(JUSTUS reverses direction and exits.)

END OF PLAY

SHE'S BLOWN AWAY

by Vince Gatton

CHARACTERS

IZZY, teen boy, any ethnicity, deep in the throes of love

RUPE, teen boy, any ethnicity, his eager sidekick

MIKA, Asian-American teen girl, their cool-headed friend

SETTING

A hidden-away nook on the outside of a high school — a back stairway no one uses, a loading dock, bleachers on a field where no one plays, something like that. Wherever there can be some open space on the ground, with a place to sit perched higher up.

TIME

Now, or soon.

PRODUCTION HISTORY

She's Blown Away was presented by Theater Resources Unlimited at their *TRUSpeak … Hear Our Voices!* Gala on March 20th, 2022, and streamed online through March 24th. It was produced by Claudia Zahn and directed by Robert Cuccioli, with technologist Brian Lawton. The cast was as follows:

IZZY: Jacob Henrie-Naffaa

RUPE: Patrick John O'Dea

MIKA: Jessica Luu Pelletier

A hidden-away nook on the outside of a high school — a back stairway no one uses, a loading dock, bleachers on a field where no one plays, something like that. It's just after the last class of the day, but just before activities start. MIKA and RUPE sit perched above as IZZY, buzzing with adrenaline, holds forth on the ground below. He is having fun.

IZZY: I know, I know! Two dozen red roses, waiting for her on her desk in Physics!

RUPE: Oooo, that's good.

IZZY: How much is two dozen roses?

MIKA: Um … two dozen?

IZZY: No, ha ha, but like, how much?

(RUPE does an arm gesture, around what he thinks the girth of two dozen roses would be.)

RUPE: Like this?

IZZY: Is that enough? It should be a lot.

MIKA: Do you even know how much two dozen roses cost?

IZZY: No.

MIKA: You can't afford *one* dozen. Try again.

RUPE: Well, then, like, a single rose, but with a stuffed teddy bear?

MIKA: Well, let's think, Rupe is Lina damaged in some way, mentally? Then no.

IZZY: You're right, it's not big enough anyway. Oh, crap, I've got Hi-Q in like five minutes.

RUPE: I have soccer in ten.

IZZY: Come on, you guys, think! It needs to be BIG.

MIKA: It does not. Need to be big.

IZZY: Oh, but it does.

MIKA: Oh, but it does not.

IZZY: Mika, you don't understand! It's *got* to be! It has to be big enough to show, to capture, to express the sheer overwhelming magnitude of my love for her.

MIKA: You don't even know her.

IZZY: But I do!

MIKA: You don't. You have Physics together.

IZZY: And Chemistry!

RUPE: What, no, you have Chemistry third period, she has it —

IZZY: I meant metaphorically, Rupe! Help me out here!

RUPE: OK ... well, what are her interests?

IZZY: Ah! Yes! Research! Luckily, her Insta isn't private.

(IZZY starts scrolling through Lina's Instagram on his phone.)

IZZY: She really likes puppies.

MIKA: OK, but are there any people on Instagram who don't like puppies?

IZZY: No, no, this is a thing! She's really into dogs!

RUPE: Does she have an actual dog?

IZZY: ... yes, YES, it looks like she has this one old dog! YES. That's the way in!

RUPE: OK, so you get her a present for her dog, like a toy or something.

MIKA: That is the least terrible idea so far.

IZZY: You guys. So disappointing. It's right under your noses. Big, remember! I need to get her ... an actual puppy!

RUPE: Go big or go home, I guess ...

MIKA: No.

IZZY:	Come on, as gestures go, that is big, and it's lovable! Big and Lovable.
MIKA:	Besides the … the myriad, the host, the veritable cornucopia … of other reasons that's a terrible idea, do you even know how much a puppy costs?
IZZY:	No, actually, how much?
MIKA:	More than roses, you goon! You can do a small gesture, you know.
IZZY:	Small gesture? No way. Won't cut it.
MIKA:	It's better, I'm telling you. Like, something to show her you've noticed her, and lets her start to notice you. Just pique her interest, dingus, don't hit her over the head. You're trying to use a chainsaw on a job that needs a scalpel.
RUPE:	Yikes.
MIKA:	I just mean, maybe you can try subtlety. Ya big dorks from North Dorkistan. You're supposed to be so smart, Mr. Hi-Q, you should be able to use your vast reading comprehension skills to interpret human nuance, for god's sake. Just … show her a little bit of who you are. The real you, not some … display. A small gesture says a lot, I'm telling you. If she likes you back, it'll *feel* huge.
IZZY:	It won't *feel* huge, it won't *feel* anything. She can't like me back yet, she barely knows I exist.
MIKA:	So let her know. Just start simple. Small gesture now, big gesture later.
IZZY:	I hear you, I do, but trust me on this, she has other guys after her. This has to be big.
RUPE:	I mean, maybe not though. Maybe starting small could be the right way to go …
IZZY:	Come on, Rupe! You're only saying that because the one big gesture you ever tried was a big total flop.

MIKA:	Oh?
IZZY:	Oh, yeah! Floppo! Did you never tell her about that?
RUPE:	No, what, oh god —
MIKA:	I don't think so.
IZZY:	Oh! Brutal! It was in 7th grade. Apparently there was this girl he liked and he gave her this elaborate 3-D pop-up valentine he made himself. Super elaborate. Had it sitting open on her desk when she came to class. She took one look at it, and what did she do? What do you think she did?
MIKA:	I can't wait to hear.
IZZY:	She threw it in the trash can in front of the whole class without saying a word.
MIKA:	Ouch.
IZZY:	I'm getting this right, right? That's what she did?

(RUPE doesn't answer.)

MIKA:	Pretty cold.
IZZY:	Right?
MIKA:	OK, but also — You know what every 7th grade girl's worst fear is? EVERYONE LOOKING AT HER. You're like 12 years old, the worst thing you can imagine is people watching you, waiting for a certain reaction and not knowing what the right one would be but knowing 100 percent that whatever reaction you have it will be the wrong one. No. Sorry, but I get it.
IZZY:	You have no romance in you, Mika. None. Your heart is a cold, dead place, barren of joy.
MIKA:	You got me, Iz. You figured me out.
IZZY:	Oh my god, OH MY GOD that's it: A SCAVENGER HUNT.
RUPE:	What?

IZZY: A scavenger hunt! That's it! It's totally it! I'll leave her a note, a mysterious note, a clue she needs to figure out, and that'll lead her to another clue, and then a whole string of clues, and they'll take her to all her favorite places and lead to all her favorite things, and it'll be this whole adventure which ends with like, me, with a single rose at like, her favorite restaurant — or no, no, wait even better, Homecoming!!! This is perfect! Now, that's big! I just have to figure out what all her favorite places and favorite things are, but that's the easy part.

MIKA: No, no, you're making her do all this work, when she doesn't know who or why? Why would she? Plus, it's super-stalkery.

IZZY: It's research.

MIKA: It's creepy.

IZZY: It's romantic!

MIKA: It is *not romantic*, it's *terrifying!* No, no, I mean this, listen to me, this is not funny, it's not fun, and you have to stop. Stop it. You will make her hate you, you're making *me* hate you. This is creepy stalker stuff and you need to believe me and stop it RIGHT NOW.

IZZY: OK, no, that's just not —

MIKA: RIGHT NOW RIGHT NOW RIGHT NOW, IZZY. RIGHT. NOW.

(A beat.)

IZZY: Mika. What? Wow. I'm not ... I'm not some kind of creep. I'm not.

MIKA: Well, stop acting like one.

IZZY: I ... I think it's a good idea.

MIKA: It's not, it's terrible. Please listen to me: it's terrible.

IZZY: I ... I ... OK, jeez. I'll keep thinking. Jeez. I have to get to Hi-Q. Rupe, meet me after?

(RUPE nods.)

IZZY: Dang, Mika. That hurt … For real. Dang.

(IZZY leaves. RUPE and MIKA sit in silence for a moment.)

MIKA: I didn't mean to be mean.

RUPE: Oh, he'll get over it, he doesn't retain anything.

MIKA: No, I know, not him. I mean when I threw out the valentine.

(A beat.)

RUPE: Oh, man. I had kinda hoped we could go our whole lives without ever having to talk about that valentine.

MIKA: It was a big gesture.

RUPE: Well … throwing it in the garbage was a pretty big gesture, too …

MIKA: OK, yeah, but that wasn't —

          A guy where my Aunt Haruka worked once started giving her presents and asking her out and making more and more of a stink when she said no. When I think about it now there was probably some fetishizing or Orientalism or whatever going on there, too, is what I think. Anyway, she tried being nice; she tried being tough; then she talked to HR and they finally fired the guy and she didn't have to see him anymore. Until one day he came back with a buttload of guns and he shot my Aunt Haruka, nine times. And a whole bunch of other people, too.

RUPE: Holy crap.

MIKA: Yeah.

RUPE: Holy crap. Did they get the guy?

MIKA: The cops didn't. Some of the people in the office rushed him. One of them had a machete or something. But my aunt was already dead.

RUPE: Oh, wow.

MIKA: Mad respect, though, to the lady with a machete in her desk.

RUPE: Wait, was this the one like four years ago? Like eight people died? So, when we were —

MIKA: Seventh grade, yeah.

RUPE: Oh, crap.

MIKA: Bingo.

RUPE: Holy crap.

         I'm sorry. I'm so, so sorry. I had no idea. I never would have. Done that. If I knew.

MIKA: Here's the thing, though, Rupe: even if it hadn't happened, I still would have hated that valentine. I just wouldn't have thrown it out. I would have wished for the earth to open up and swallow me whole and then tried to say something nice and made a joke or something and then I would have never been able to look at you again as long as I lived. But in that moment, I just thought, no. I didn't ask for this. No. I just ... didn't have it in me to make the priority some boy's feelings.

         So, yeah. Sorry not sorry, I guess.

RUPE: I guess, then ... I guess I'm glad you threw it out. At least this way you talked to me again.

MIKA: Yeah.

RUPE: Yeah. I'm supposed to be at soccer. Do you ... should I blow it off?

MIKA: No, what, no, I'm fine. Go to soccer. I'm fine.

RUPE: OK. You're sure? OK, then. I'll talk Izzy down, I promise. I'll handle it.

(RUPE gives a dumb little wave and starts to go, but then stops.)

I'm really sorry this happened to you. I'm sorry it happened to her. I bet she was really cool.

MIKA: She was, thanks.

(He turns to go again.)

MIKA: Hey, Rupe?

Nobody knows about my Aunt Haruka. I mean, a couple of people know she died, and how; but they don't know the why part. That she was who he was after. I can't stand the thought of anyone thinking it was her fault somehow, that all those people died. I couldn't stand it. Nobody knows that part but you, so …

RUPE: Got it. Safe with me. I promise.

(He starts to go again.)

MIKA: Hey. Rupe?

RUPE: Yeah?

MIKA: Just, um … FYI: telling somebody something nobody else knows? That counts. As a small gesture.

… Just FYI.

RUPE: *(after a moment)* … Oh! Huh. You were right. That … felt … huge.

(She nods. He nods back. They sort of smile at each other for an awkward beat or two. He gives his dumb little wave again, then goes.)

(She sits alone with her thoughts for a long moment as the lights fade.)

END OF PLAY

SUMMER SOLSTICE

by Matt Henderson

CHARACTERS

NERD 1, any age, race, or gender

NERD 2, any age, race, or gender

MALEDICTION, an evil hellspawn just looking for some kicks

SETTING

A park in the summer. A bench and a garbage can are nearby.

TIME

Present day.

PRODUCTION HISTORY

Summer Solstice was presented by the New Renaissance Theatre Company in Pittsburgh, PA, October 26, 2022. The production was directed by Joanna Getting. The cast was as follows:

NERD 1:	C. Adaeze Obiekezie
NERD 2:	Kalee George
MALEDICTION:	Joanna Getting

A park in the summer. NERD 1 and NERD 2 enter. It doesn't really matter what gender either of them is, or what race. They have a very hard time making eye contact with each other. They keep looking at each other's hands, pondering whether the hands ought to be touching. They just don't know. So they enthusiastically speak at each other's shoulders.

NERD 1:   Um.

NERD 2:   Um.

(Awkward pause.)

NERD 1:   *(Sudden forced enthusiasm)* WOW!!!!

NERD 2:   *(Confused and scared but trying to mirror the enthusiasm)* WOW!!!!

(Awkward pause.)

NERD 1:   THAT WAS SOME MOVIE, WASN'T IT?!

NERD 2:   Oh! Yeah, how about that?

NERD 1:   Yes.

NERD 2:   I think they did a GREAT job of sticking to the source material!

NERD 1:   The source material?

NERD 2:   Um.

NERD 1:   Um.

NERD 2:   Um, yes. The comic book. On which it was based.

NERD 1:   Ohhhh, on which it was based. Ohhhh. *(Takes a deep breath and forces excitement again)* YES!

NERD 2:   Uh, YES!

NERD 1:   SO GOOD!

NERD 2:   SO GOOD!

NERD 1:	BADASS!
NERD 2:	SO BADASS.
NERD 1:	Yes.
NERD 2:	… So.
NERD 1:	… How about that ending?! Does the world end in the comic book version too?
NERD 2:	*(About to eagerly explain what happens in the comic book)* Oh, you haven't read the comics? I thought you had. Well —
NERD 1:	*(Embarrassed)* Oh, yes! Yes, I've read it! It's one of my favorite comic books. Sorry, I forgot which one we were talking about for a second.
NERD 2:	*(Missed opportunity)* Oh.
NERD 1:	Yeah. It's my favorite.
NERD 2:	*(Brightening)* Mine too! Are you reading the new limited series?
NERD 1:	Oh my God! Yes! Um! I mean, I ordered it! But it's not here yet! It's on the way! It'll probably be there when I get home! I can't believe it's taken so long! Stupid mailman!
NERD 2:	… Yeah.
NERD 1:	Yeah. So the world ends, huh?
NERD 2:	Well, yeah. I mean, for the time being. I mean, you know.
NERD 1:	Oh, that's right, I know. Yeah. For the time being.
NERD 2:	Then it comes back.
NERD 1:	Ha! It always does!
NERD 2:	Sure does! Hahaha!

(They stare at each other's hands.)

NERD 1:	So, who was that guy in that scene at the end of the credits? I mean, I know who he is. I'm just testing you.
NERD 2:	Malediction, Destroyer of Light.
NERD 1:	CORRECT! VERY GOOD!
NERD 2:	Ha!
NERD 1:	You are so smart!
NERD 2:	*(Staring at the ground)* Oh. Thank you.
NERD 1:	*(Staring at the ground)* You're welcome.

(NERD 1 looks at NERD 2's hand sadly. They are silent a long time. NERD 1 slowly moves over and painfully tries to find a way to just sort of stand next to NERD 2 and lightly brush hands together. NERD 2 is wrapped up in the compliment that was just given and pays no attention to this attempt. NERD 1 is embarrassed and walks away from NERD 2 as if no attempt at intimacy was made.)

NERD 1:	So, I guess Malapropism comes back in the next movie!
NERD 2:	Malediction.
NERD 1:	Ohhh! Right? How could I have been so stupid? Malediction.
NERD 2:	That's okay. It's kind of good you messed up his name, in a way. If you say it three times, he appears and destroys all the hope and innocence in the world.
NERD 1:	Ohhhh, then I won't say it. Malediction, huh?
NERD 2:	*(Giggles)* You've said it twice, now.

(NERD 2 unthinkingly meets eyes with NERD 1. It's really nice.)

NERD 1:	*(Overwhelmed)* Oh. Sorry. I'm such a dork.
NERD 2:	It's okay. *(Long pause.)* I like dorks.

(NERD 2's never made such a brazen attempt at emotional intimacy before. NERD 1 doesn't know what to do. NERD 1 doesn't know

how to stop the smile that's forming on their face.)

NERD 1:	*(Forcing self to keep the emotional intimacy going)* I love summer comic book movies.
NERD 2:	Me too.
NERD 1:	And hot dogs. And lemonade.
NERD 2:	Yeah.
NERD 1:	And corn on the cob.
NERD 2:	Me too.
NERD 1:	I think summer's my favorite season!! I like how it's so sunny all the time!! There's just so much hope for the future!! Anything can happen!!

(This is too much personal revelation for NERD 2. NERD 2 looks down at the ground in order to regroup. There is a long silence. NERD 1 is embarrassed. NERD 1 is devastated. NERD 1 tries to come up with a joke.)

NERD 1:	So, uhhh … Malediction, huh? HAHA! OOPS, SAID IT A THIRD TIME!

(NERD 2 forces a laugh. Then MALEDICTION crawls out of the depths of hell and pops up from behind a park bench.)

MALEDICTION:	I am Malediction, Destroyer of Light. Devourer of Hope. Champion of Fear. I have been summoned from the depths, and all shall know me and despair.
NERD 1:	Oh, uh, hi.
NERD 2:	Oh my God.
MALEDICTION:	You two shall be the first to taste my wrath.
NERD 1:	Uh, this is awkward.
NERD 2:	I can't believe this is happening.
MALEDICTION:	I shall feed upon your hopes and dreams, your every wish for the future, everything

	you hope to achieve for yourself in your personal life, all attempts to step outside your comfort zone and make a connection, all of it will be destroyed! HAHAHAHAHAHAHAHAHAHA!
NERD 1:	*(Shyly protesting)* Um, that's not cool.
MALEDICTION:	TOO BAD!
NERD 1:	*(To NERD 2)* Is there a way to get him to go away once you summon him?
NERD 2:	*(To NERD 1)* Yeah, but I'd need the Magic Crystal of the Sun King. It possesses the overpowering light of confidence and joy. I have a plastic replica of it, but I left it back at my apartment.
MALEDICTION:	Oooooo, I love it!! So much hope and aspiration going on with you two! Such a tender sense of possibility in the air! *(Sucks the air)* It's delicious! Time to feast!
NERD 2:	Wait, what are you talking about?
MALEDICTION:	You two are going on a first date, are you not? First dates are my favorite thing to suck the hope out of.
NERD 1:	Um.
NERD 2:	Um.
NERD 1:	*(Looking at NERD 2's elbow)* I mean, that's not necessarily what this is, is it? I mean, I don't know if, I just, I kind of, I was thinking of seeing the movie anyway and you mentioned you were interested in seeing it, so I thought we might as well —
NERD 2:	Yeah, I mean, I'm a big fan of this comic book, been reading it for years —
NERD 1:	Me too —

NERD 2:	I just, I figured might as well go together, since we're going anyway —
MALEDICTION:	Oh stop already, let me suck your pure virginal souls.
NERD 1:	Uh, hey now —
NERD 2:	Not that it's any of your business, but I am totally not a virgin, at least depending on how you define "virginity," I mean I've done different stuff —
NERD 1:	Oh yeah, me too, I've done, you know, things —

(NERDS 1 and 2 glance at each other's elbows and stare at the ground uncomfortably.)

MALEDICTION:	Good, that's it, stop talking, now I can concentrate. *(Starts sucking the air)* Mmmm, so inexperienced, so awkward, so sensitive … Yes! This is exactly what I need to begin my campaign of terror! The purity of this first date is so strong! So sweet, so succulent! I shall gain more power than I ever dreamed!
NERD 2:	BUT IT'S NOT EVEN A DATE!
MALEDICTION:	What?
NERD 1:	Um.
NERD 2:	*(To NERD 1)* I'm sorry.
NERD 1:	No, it's all right, just um …
NERD 2:	I don't, I'm sorry, I'm just confused.
NERD 1:	No, it's all right, I asked you …
NERD 2:	But I wanted to go.
NERD 1:	Yes.
NERD 2:	I didn't know if you were thinking of it that way.

NERD 1:	I didn't make it clear.
NERD 2:	Neither did I.
MALEDICTION:	Well, make up your minds already! I have a lot I want to get done today.
NERD 1:	I'm sorry, I —
NERD 2:	No, it's okay —
NERD 1:	I didn't mean to make you think —
NERD 2:	It's okay —
NERD 1:	I haven't even actually read the comic book, I'd been meaning to, I really have, it's so lame to want to see the movie first —
NERD 2:	It's okay, don't apologize —
NERD 1:	And now I think, I mean you said, I mean I didn't say, and now we're not sure, it's just, I'm sorry —
NERD 2:	DON'T BE SORRY.
NERD 1:	Okay.

(Long pause. NERD 1 and NERD 2 stare at the ground. MALEDICTION feels awkward now.)

MALEDICTION:	Ohhh … you guys looked so hopeful. Well, uh, I mean if this isn't an actual date, then, uh …

(The silence makes MALEDICTION uncomfortable and he stares at the ground as well. All three keep their eyes down and tap their feet uncomfortably. Finally NERD 2 looks up a little bit. NERD 2 looks at MALEDICTION and NERD 1. NERD 2 makes a life-altering decision. NERD 2 inches almost imperceptibly closer to NERD 1. NERD 2 stares at NERD 1's hand. NERD 2's spent an entire life in the shadows. NERD 2 wants the light. NERD 2 takes NERD 1's hand quickly and decisively. NERD 1's eyes go wide. NERD 1 can hardly look at NERD 2. NERD 1 looks at NERD 2. MALEDICTION looks at the NERDS.)

MALEDICTION: What? You so didn't just do that.

(NERD 2 ever so cautiously smiles at NERD 1. NERD 1 smiles back, with so much less difficulty than usual. The light is blinding. MALEDICTION clutches at his body.)

MALEDICTION: I'm in such pain! What's happening?! You don't have the Magic Crystal of the Sun King on ya, do you?

(The hand-holding continues. This is totally a date. MALEDICTION frantically tries to suck the air.)

MALEDICTION: I don't understand! *(Sucks)* Where did all the purity go? *(Sucks)* The tentative hopefulness? *(Sucks)* It's almost as if it's turned into … *(Sucks, has a bad taste in his mouth)* strength! *(Sucks, even worse taste)* Bravery!

(The NERDS are beaming at each other.)

MALEDICTION: The dreams are gone! They're becoming reality! Oh God, I'm gonna be sick. *(Vomits behind a trash can)* I have to go. This is so gross. You people disgust me. *(Staggers away, coughing and retching)* Whatever. I'm totally coming back in the sequel! Just you wait! Oh God, I hate summer.

(MALEDICTION exits. NERD 2 looks at NERD 1 warmly.)

NERD 2:   I have every issue at my apartment. The comics are really good. I can lend you some, just to get you started on the basics. There's a lot to catch up on.

NERD 1:   Yay.

(They exit, holding hands awkwardly but warmly.)

END OF PLAY

EDDY & EDNA

by Donald Loftus

CHARACTERS

EDDY, EDNA's husband. 60+ A frail man. Any race or ethnicity.

EDNA, EDDY's wife. 60+. A loving and caring wife. Any race or ethnicity.

DANNY, EDDY & EDNA's son. 30+. A caring and concerned son. Any race or ethnicity.

SETTING

The modest kitchen in the Midwestern suburban home of EDDY & EDNA.

TIME

A summer morning.

PRODUCTION HISTORY

Eddy & Edna was presented by the New American Theatre in Los Angeles, California, November 12–20, 2022. The production was directed by Jeannine Wisnosky Stehlin.

The cast was as follows:

EDDY: Jordan Lund

EDNA: April Adams

DANNY: Floyd Lewis

EDNA is preparing breakfast. EDDY sits at the kitchen table, silently staring into space. EDNA brings the coffee pot to the table. She pauses and stares at EDDY'S trance-like expression.

EDNA: More coffee, dear?

(HE still doesn't respond, so SHE gets louder)

EDNA: Eddy? EDDY!!!

EDDY: WHAT!?!?

EDNA: I said do you want some more coffee?

EDDY: Jesus Christ, Edna!

EDNA: What!?!

EDDY: You scared the shit out of me! You've got to stop doing that!

EDNA: What are you talking about? Exactly how did I scare the …

EDDY: Just then! When you screamed my name like a God-damned, wild-assed banshee!!

EDNA: Oh, please. I barely raised my voice.

EDDY: No, really! My heart is pounding like a son of a bitch!

EDNA: Nonsense.

EDDY: No, really! Feel my heart. Go on. Feel it!

EDNA: Do you want more coffee or not?

EDDY: Yes. I'd like some more. But I can get it. I'm not helpless.

(HE starts to rise)

EDDY: You don't have to wait on me hand and foot.

EDNA: Sit. I'm up already.

(SHE pours the coffee and then sits across from him)

EDNA:	Are you okay, Eddy?
EDDY:	I'm fine. What do you mean?
EDNA:	I don't know. You just seem kind of …
EDDY:	Kind of what?
EDNA:	Just … kind of … out of sorts.
EDDY:	Out of sorts? What the hell does that even mean? Out of sorts?
EDNA:	I don't know …
EDDY:	Well, if you don't know, why do you keep asking me that?
EDNA:	Have I asked you that before?
EDDY:	Yes, every day. Every day it's the same thing. *(Imitating her)* "Are you okay, Eddy? Is everything all right? Are you feeling up to snuff, darling?"
EDNA:	I have never used the word "snuff" in my life!
EDDY:	But you never let up!
EDNA:	Well, I worry, that's all. You should be happy you've got someone who worries about you. Who cares enough to worry.
EDDY:	I am. But you worry too much. I'm fine.
EDNA:	You do know … I mean, I hope you do realize … that if something isn't right, you shouldn't keep that to yourself. *(SHE looks for a reaction that doesn't come)*
EDNA:	I'm just saying … it would be really stupid not to address a problem … *(Again, SHE looks for a reaction that doesn't come)* Eddy? EDDY!
EDDY:	What!?!
EDNA:	If there is something wrong …
EDDY:	I'm fine. Really. I'm fine.

EDNA: Okay, dear. Did you want some toast?

EDDY: No, no. I'm good. *(After a beat)* So, about this thing … how I'm not myself. Well, I must admit, there is something that is bothering me.

EDNA: There is? I knew it! What is it, Eddy?

EDDY: I feel like I am getting a little forgetful as of late.

EDNA: Yes? As of late?

EDDY: Yes. I mean, I don't know exactly when it started, but it's been going on for a few weeks, I think … at least for a few weeks. Have you noticed?

EDNA: Yes, Eddy … I have noticed. But it's not been a few weeks. It's been going on for over two years now …

EDDY: Two years!!!

EDNA: And I have tried to get you to see someone. A specialist in this sort of thing.

EDDY: A specialist in what sort of thing?

EDNA: You need help, Eddy.

EDDY: Help? Do you think I'm sick in the head? Do you think I'm crazy?

EDNA: No! And please don't go getting yourself all worked up again.

EDDY: Well, of course, I'm worked up! How can you say such a thing?

EDNA: I meant nothing by it. I just want you to be all right.

EDDY: Okay.

EDNA: And are you all right?

EDDY: Well, of course, I'm all right.

EDNA: Yes, of course, you are, dear.

EDDY: I forget some things now and then. It's normal for a man my age. I will admit, there are moments when I sometimes get a little mixed up. You know ... where my memories get confused with my current thoughts ...

EDNA: Yes, I know ...

EDDY: And sometimes ... I can't tell the difference. I can't tell them apart. Do you know what I mean? Have we discussed this before? We have, haven't we, Edna?

EDNA: Yes, we have. Of course, we have.

EDDY: Of course, we have.

EDNA: And is there anything else, Eddy? Is there anything that you want to talk about?

EDDY: Yes ... but maybe I've already told you this too.

EDNA: It doesn't matter if you did. What is it, Eddy?

EDDY: Have I told you ... have I told you that sometimes ... in the middle of the night ... I break out in an uncontrollable sweat. And I wake ... and my pajamas are soaked through, and my heart is pounding? Have I mentioned this before?

EDNA: Yes, the night sweats.

EDDY: Right in the middle of the night ... and then I suddenly wake with a fear ... a horrible, gut-wrenching fear ...

EDNA: Yes ... a fear. I know Eddy. But what is it from? What is it you're afraid of?

EDDY: That's what makes it so horrifying. The fact that I can't remember what it is that terrorized me. I wake up and I realize that it may be a fear based on absolutely nothing.

Because as I wake up ... as I come to ... out of my deep and horrifying sweaty sleep ... I realize there is nothing there ... There is no reason to be scared. No reason at all.

EDNA: Well, of course, there isn't.

EDDY: I look around the room. I see my things ... our things ... our furnishings. I see my eyeglasses and my wristwatch on the nightstand ... and I see you. Sound asleep. Having no idea of the horror that had been present in that room only moments before. A horror that has now vanished.

(HE goes back into a trance-like state)

EDNA: And did this happen last night? Eddy. EDDY!

EDDY: What?

EDNA: And did it happen again last night?

EDDY: Did what happen?

EDNA: Never mind Dear, Eat your breakfast.

(Pause)

EDDY: What's happened to Danny?

EDNA: *(Startled)* What!?! What's happened to who?

EDDY: Danny. The boy has gotten so big.

EDNA: *(Pitifully)* Oh, Eddy.

EDDY: And he's gotten so strong. I think the chores he's been doing around the store after school are really helping to build his arms up. His legs too. He's getting stronger every day.

EDNA: Don't, Eddy!

EDDY: I promised I'd come to his game on Saturday. It's going to be a scorcher Saturday, but I have to go. I have to support him.

(EDNA wipes a tear from her eye)

EDDY: Edna, are you crying? Did I say something that made you cry?

EDNA: Oh, Eddy, you need to stop.

EDDY: Stop what? What do you mean?

EDNA: There is no Danny! Not anymore. Eddy ... listen to me! You know this ...

(EDDY freezes up and goes back into a fog)

EDNA: Eddy?

EDDY: Huh? What happened to Danny?

EDNA: What happened to who?

EDDY: I said, what happened to ... ? What happened to ...?

(EDDY slips into his fog again as EDNA rises and clears the table. SHE brings the coffee pot to the table)

EDNA: More coffee?

(EDDY doesn't respond)

EDNA: EDDY!

EDDY: What?

EDNA: I said, do you want more coffee?

EDDY: Oh, yes. I'd like some more. But I can get it.

(HE starts to rise)

EDNA: I got it. Sit. I'm up already.

(SHE brings him the coffee)

EDNA: Are you sure you're okay? You just seem kind of ...

(The doorbell rings. EDNA exits right)

EDDY: Kind of? Kind of what ... ?

(DANNY enters left)

DANNY: Hey, old man! What's going on? You don't answer the doorbell anymore?

EDDY: Who are you?

DANNY: Dad, it's me. It's Danny.

EDDY: Danny?

DANNY: Dad, are you okay?

EDDY: But she said you didn't exist.

DANNY: She what!?!

EDDY: She said you never did.

DANNY: Well, Dad, obviously, *she* was wrong ... because here I am ... your fifty-six-year-old bouncing baby boy.

EDDY: So. you *are* Danny! You *are* my son!

DANNY: Yes! Yes, I am! So who is this *she* who has been questioning my existence?

EDDY: Edna, my wife. My wife, Edna.

DANNY: And my mother? That Edna?

EDDY: Yes, that Edna.

DANNY: And when exactly did she say these things, Pops?

EDDY: Just minutes ago. Just before you came in.

DANNY: She was here?

EDDY: Yes!

DANNY: In this kitchen?

EDDY: Yes, that's right. She made me breakfast.

DANNY: Dad, listen to me. Please try to hear what I am saying. Mom died four years ago. You need to face this.

EDDY: What do you mean?

DANNY: She's not here anymore, and she is not coming back. You need to let her go.

EDDY: No, son, that isn't possible.

DANNY: Okay. Let me get your pills. Maybe they will make things clearer.

(DANNY exits stage right)

EDDY: She was just here! Why would you say such a thing? She was just here …

(EDNA re-enters stage left)

EDNA: Who was just here?

END OF PLAY

ROAD TRIP

by Jan Probst

CHARACTERS

ALLEN T., 50s, male. Buttoned down in personality and appearance.

MARY T., 50s, female. Allen's wife. A former free spirit, her enthusiasm for life has been dampened over the years.

JACK T., 29. Their son. Still a kid at heart.

AUNT PAT, Mary's sister.

UNCLE JOE, Allen's brother.

MICHAEL, Jack's best friend since childhood.

SETTING

ALLEN and MARY's place, in a small town somewhere east of the Mississippi.

TIME

A Saturday morning, present time.

NOTE

Stage set should be minimal, allowing the audience to fill in the details with their imagination. Two folding or straight back chairs, side by side, center stage, represent the front seat of a two-door car. Back seat could be created by the positioning of the actors, as they enter the car, or a bench may be used, if needed. The actors maintain the illusion of the car while opening doors, getting in, fastening seat belts, etc., except in one instance, as noted in the text.

...   at the end of a line indicates an unfinished thought

—   at the end of a line indicates an interruption by the following speaker

PRODUCTION HISTORY

Road Trip was presented by Winding Road Theater Ensemble, Tucson AZ, as part of Eight 10s in Tucson Online, May 27–June 30, 2022. The production was directed by Annie Koepf. The cast was as follows:

ALLEN T.:	Chad Davies
MARY T.:	Peg Peterson
JACK T.:	Andres Garcia
AUNT PAT:	Rae Williams
UNCLE JOE:	Larry Gutman
MICHAEL:	Preston Campbell-Cueva

ALLEN and MARY sit center stage, side-by-side in chairs, as though they are in the front seat of a car.

ALLEN: Seat belt, Mary?

(MARY fastens her seat belt.)

MARY: Seat belt, Allen. And yours?

ALLEN: Of course, Mary.

MARY: Naturally, Allen.

ALLEN: No need to say "naturally," Mary, when I have simply responded to your query.

MARY: Of course, Allen.

(ALLEN reaches out the open window and adjusts his side mirror. Takes a deep breath.)

ALLEN: Just smell the freshness of summer, Mary.

MARY: Lovely, Allen.

ALLEN: Map, Mary?

(MARY carefully unfolds a large, paper road map.)

MARY: Map, Allen.

ALLEN: Route clearly marked, Mary?

MARY: You marked it, Allen.

ALLEN: Of course I marked it, Mary. I am merely ensuring you have the correct map.

MARY: I have the correct map, Allen. The map that has been prominently displayed on my dining room table, in lieu of a flower arrangement, for the past several months.

ALLEN: Careful planning breeds success, Mary.

MARY: So you have said. Allen.

(MARY awkwardly tries to refold the map.)

ALLEN: No need to fold the map, Mary. We will need it again soon enough.

(MARY consults the map.)

MARY: Are we supposed to be in … Nebraska, now, Allen?

ALLEN: Indeed we are, Mary.

MARY: Then why do we need a map at all, Allen?

ALLEN: Knowing exactly where you are enriches the experience of traveling, Mary.

MARY: I know exactly where I am, Allen, and I'm not feeling particularly enriched.

ALLEN: Try to open your mind, Mary, to the nuances of the situation.

MARY: I am well aware of the situation, Allen, and its nuances are not at all striking.

ALLEN: If Nebraska is not your cup of tea, Mary, there will be other states. Seven, as I recall.

(Increasingly frustrated, MARY again attempts to fold the unwieldy map.)

MARY: Why can't we just use G.P.S., Allen?

ALLEN: Because the satellites used for the Global Positioning System are notoriously inaccurate, Mary.

MARY: Are they now? Allen.

ALLEN: Whereas a traditional road map is one hundred percent reliable, Mary.

(He finally notices her frustration.)

ALLEN: If I could make a suggestion …

MARY: I am in charge of the map, Allen!

ALLEN: Of course you are, Mary. I just thought —

MARY: Stop thinking, Allen!

(A doorbell rings. MARY reacts, ALLEN does not.)

MARY: Did you hear that, Allen?

ALLEN: Ignore it, Mary.

(MARY tosses the map into the backseat.)

ALLEN: I did not mean you should ignore the map, Mary.

MARY: I know what you meant, Allen.

(Doorbell rings. MARY again reacts, ALLEN does not.)

ALLEN: Ready to go, Mary?

MARY: No, I am not ready to go, Allen.

ALLEN: Is there a problem, Mary?

(Doorbell rings.)

MARY: Stop the car, Allen.

ALLEN: I have not yet started the car, Mary.

MARY: Oh, never mind.

(MARY abruptly stands, dropping the illusion of the car, and begins to walk away.)

ALLEN: Mary! What are you doing?!

MARY: Answering the door!

ALLEN: You can't just stand up like that! In the middle of Nebraska!

MARY: Allen! We're in the middle of our living room!

ALLEN: I'm really looking forward to this next stretch of road.

MARY: There is no road! It's carpeting! *(To herself)* Same stupid shag carpet that's always been here.

(JACK enters.)

JACK: Hey Mom! Hey Dad! Door was open. What are you guys up to?

MARY:	Rehearsing for our trip.
JACK:	Again?
ALLEN:	One cannot over-plan.
MARY:	Oh, I think one can.
JACK:	So where are you now?

(They respond together.)

MARY:	*(Bitterly)* Nebraska.
ALLEN:	*(Enthusiastically)* Nebraska!
JACK:	Fun! Can I come along?
ALLEN:	Oh, I don't know, son. Your mother and I …
JACK:	Just for this leg of the trip. I have friends in Omaha.
ALLEN:	What do you say, Mary?
JACK:	Please, Mom?
MARY:	Why not. Get in.

(JACK opens the passenger side door, tilts the seat forward, and squeezes into the back seat of the car.)

JACK:	You guys should really invest in a four-door.
ALLEN:	This suits our needs just fine. Doesn't it, Mary?

(MARY ignores him. JACK picks up the map.)

JACK:	Why is there a map on the backseat?
ALLEN:	Surest way to plan, surest way to navigate, son.
JACK:	Wow! Old school!

(MARY turns downstage, again talks to herself.)

MARY:	All our friends go on cruises. London theater tours, trips to the Mediterranean …
JACK:	Get in, Mom. It'll be fun!
MARY:	I'm stuck riding shotgun. Through our living room.

(Doorbell rings.)

ALLEN: Don't answer it!

AUNT PAT: *(Offstage)* Yoo hoo! Mary!

(AUNT PAT enters.)

JACK: Hi Aunt Pat! We're headed to Nebraska!

AUNT PAT: What fun! Can I ride along?

ALLEN: Oh, well, I don't know if that's such a good —

AUNT PAT: Get over it, Allen! A chance to go to Nebraska?! Make room, Jack.

JACK: Yippee!

(AUNT PAT awkwardly climbs into the back seat, as MARY attempts to sneak away.)

AUNT PAT: Mary! Get in here!

(Doorbell rings. UNCLE JOE enters.)

JACK: Hey Uncle Joe!

UNCLE JOE: Hey gang! What's up?

JACK: We're headed to Nebraska!

UNCLE JOE: Not without me, you're not!

(UNCLE JOE squeezes into the backseat. MARY remains outside the car. Doorbell rings.)

MARY: Oh, don't get up. I'll get it.

(MARY turns to answer the door as MICHAEL enters.)

MICHAEL: Morning Mrs. T.! Jack here?

JACK: Michael! Perfect timing!

MICHAEL: What's all this?

ALLEN: Family road trip, son. Quality time.

MICHAEL: Oh gosh. My family never does anything cool like this.

JACK: Can he come along, Dad? Please?

ALLEN: Now Jack, I think we have a full car.

MARY: Of course he can! Take my spot, Michael.
             You can be the navigator.

MICHAEL: Oh boy!

(MICHAEL climbs into the front seat. JACK hands him the map.)

MICHAEL: Wow! Old school!

(MARY again attempts to sneak away.)

ALLEN: Now, I know you all mean well, but this trip was
             supposed to be just me and —

UNCLE JOE: Mary! Where are you going?! We can squeeze you in!

MARY: I'm good. Just send me a postcard.

AUNT PAT: Nonsense! Get in here, Mary!

MARY: No, really, I have a lot of —

*(She is interrupted by a chorus of encouragement to get in.
ALLEN does not join in.)*

JACK: Come on, Mom!

UNCLE JOE: We're not leaving without you, Mary!

MICHAEL: Gosh, Mrs. T!

MARY: Oh … all right.

*(MICHAEL hops out, holding the door open for MARY, who
squeezes into the center of the front seat. MICHAEL gets back in.
It's very cramped.)*

ALLEN: This isn't safe, Mary. There's no third seatbelt
             in front.

MARY: Lighten up, Allen.

ALLEN: This is not going to work.

*(ALLEN gets out of the car. MARY slides into the driver's seat,
closes the door, takes the wheel.)*

ALLEN: Mary! What are you doing?!

MARY: Taking charge, Allen.

ALLEN: But Mary! It's a stick shift!

MARY: Perfect time to learn, Allen. *(To MICHAEL)*
            Lose the map, kid. There's been a change of plans.

ALLEN: But Mary! All that preparation.

(MARY looks out the window, talks to ALLEN.)

MARY: Believe me, Allen, I know how you feel. By the way,
            if you get bored, there's a sink full of dishes, and the
            kitchen floor could use a scrub. *(Shifts the car into
            gear.)* Hang on, folks! We're goin' to Vegas!

(Engine roars to a chorus of cheers as ALLEN looks on, aghast.)

END OF PLAY

HUSK

by Erin Proctor

CHARACTERS

ABEL — 20s. A corpse.

CAIN — 20s. A farmer.

EVE — 40s. Their mother.

SETTING

A pasture.

TIME

20 years after the Fall

NOTES

//   denotes a character being interrupted.

Each line is a new breath.

PRODUCTION HISTORY

Husk premiered at The Player's Theatre in New York City on October 20th, 2023, as a part of the BOO!: Short Play Festival. The production was directed by Rose Kortrey. The cast was as follows:

CAIN: Sam Danko

ABEL: Jarrett Cordeiro

EVE: Dana Tortora

EVE waves her hand in front of ABEL'S face.

CAIN: Mom …

EVE: I've never seen such affliction.

          I'm sure it's nothing a pot of my soup can't fix.

(ABEL'S corpse slumps over and falls because gravity. He is now lying face down on the ground. There is a bloody gash on the back of his head. EVE screams. CAIN just stares.)

EVE: WHAT HAPPENED TO HIS HEAD?!

CAIN: It um. A rock hit it.

EVE: How did a rock hit it?

CAIN: I threw the rock.

EVE: Why?

CAIN: We were arguing … I … I was angry and …
          He just went down.

CAIN: He went down and he hasn't come back up.
          He's been lying there for an hour.
          And I've been trying to wake him.
          I don't feel his breath.
          I don't think he's asleep.
          I don't know what I've done.
          I don't know what's wrong with him.

(EVE starts violently shaking ABEL, who is still dead.)

CAIN: Tried that.

(EVE pulls open ABEL'S eyelids.)

EVE: It's like he can't see me.

CAIN: I don't know what I did …

EVE: He is not breathing. But everything breathes. You. Me.

          The grass beneath our feet.
          The sheep out in the pasture.

The wind blowing through the brush …
Everything has a breath

But Abel is not breathing.

CAIN: I have seen something not breathe.

EVE: What?

CAIN: It was um … It was earlier today. Before I don't know
Before all this. When Abel was up
And breathing
And walking
And getting on my nerves.
We were to present our bounties to the Lord.
I presented a basket of grain.
Abel presented the first born of his fattest ewe.
And the Lord instructed Abel to take my scythe
And quickly strike the lamb across the throat.
And so he did
And the lamb bled out
And stopped breathing.
And the Lord lauded Abel's sacrifice.
Showered him in praise.
And was disappointed in mine
Because I left the ripest grain for us to use at dinner
For your soup.
And I did not offer it to Them.

EVE: And the lamb did not breathe?

CAIN: The lamb did not breathe.
And both Abel and the Lord ridiculed me.
Abel more so after.
And that's when I picked up that rock over there
And I threw it at him
And he went down.
And I don't know exactly what I've done.
But the blood let from the nape of his neck
Just like the lamb …

EVE: Did the lamb ever get up?

CAIN: The lamb is over there. Under that cloth.

(EVE removes the cloth to reveal the dead lamb. She presses her hand on it to feel if it is breathing. It's not. She goes to ABEL and does the same. He is also not breathing.)

EVE: I don't understand.

CAIN: They do not breathe.

EVE: What happens when you hold your breath too long?

CAIN: You get light headed
And start to faint
Until your body then forces you to breathe again.

EVE: Within our breath
The soul must lie.

CAIN: I'm confused.

EVE: I think you reaped him
Like your grain.

CAIN: When you cut grain
It stops growing.

EVE: It stops breathing. When you cut Abel //

CAIN: I didn't cut him. I hit him with a rock //

EVE: It was like when he cut the throat of the Lamb
to present to the Lord.

CAIN: And now?

EVE: Abel became your bounty.
And the Lord left us with his husk.

(EVE slaps ABEL'S lifeless face.)

EVE: There's nothing inside! Just a husk!
Where are you?!
Where is my son?
Where is my baby?
You're just …Where are you?
Abel where are you?

(EVE cradles ABEL in her arms.)

EVE: If you struck me
          Would I dissipate?

CAIN: Mom …

EVE: Where would I go?

CAIN: Mom stop…

EVE: Would I see my Abel again?
          Or would I … Would I just …
          Disappear?

CAIN: He's going to wake up.
          He's playing a trick on us.
          This is just one of his tricks.

EVE: He's cold to the touch.
          He's not in there.

CAIN: And he's going to be like,
          "You should see the looks on your faces!"
          And he'll have a real laugh
          While we both scream at him
          For scaring us to bits!
          And then I'll have a laugh
          Because I can never stay mad at him for some reason
          And you'll eventually start to crack
          And give a smile.
          And then we'll all go home
          And gather around the fire
          And eat your soup.
          What you make it with
          Onions and leeks?
          And spicy peppers.
          I love the spicy peppers.
          Abel can't handle the spicy peppers.

(EVE starts to cry.)

CAIN: And we'll sit and we'll eat

And talk about our very strange days!
And Azura will pour us fresh wine
That she made in her vineyard.
While Avan will bring out the fresh fruits she harvested
in the baskets we weaved.
While Dad will complain about how hot the sun was
while he was out tilling the soil
And how we're overdue for a nice rain.

EVE: He's just a husk.
Just an empty husk.
Cain, come look into his eyes
And you'll see nothing.

CAIN: And we'll all fall asleep under the stars.
And ready ourselves for another day.

EVE: Look into his eyes.

CAIN: I can't.

EVE: Why can't you?

CAIN: It frightens me.

EVE: Look into his eyes.

CAIN: Mom I //

EVE: Look into your brother's eyes!

(EVE pulls CAIN down to her level.)

EVE: Tell me what you see.

CAIN: I see nothing.

EVE: Exactly. Nothing.

(EVE tries to sit ABEL upright. Being a corpse, he falls to the ground.)

CAIN: Will he come back?

EVE: Who are you asking?

CAIN: I don't know.

EVE: I think we both know the answer.

CAIN: We can keep waiting
            For him to breathe again.

(CAIN gets on his knees.)

CAIN: Join me in prayer.

EVE: I've no prayer left in me at the moment.

(EVE holds ABEL'S lifeless hand to her face as CAIN prays.)

EVE: My baby isn't in here.

(CAIN, frustrated, lets out a scream. EVE pulls him to her side and tries to soothe him.)

EVE: My boys.
            My sweet little boys.

CAIN: I don't understand, Momma
            I don't understand, Momma
            I don't understand I don't I don't I don't
            I don't understand
            I don't //

EVE: Shh

CAIN: What've I done?
            Did I do this?
            What is this?
            Momma
            I don't know!!

(EVE closes ABEL'S eyes. It is beginning to disturb her.)

EVE: The Lord collected another sacrifice.
            I hope Abel serves Them well.
            How They love to take.

CAIN: What?

EVE: Cain.

CAIN: Mom?

(EVE holds her son in her arms.)

EVE: I will not have any more taken from me.

(CAIN weeps onto his mother like a child.)

CAIN: I didn't know
            I didn't
            I don't //

EVE: Shh …

CAIN: It never
            I never meant!!

EVE: I know, baby.

CAIN: I'm afraid.

EVE: Me too.

CAIN: What scares you?

EVE: All of the things that are still unknown.

(EVE kisses both of her sons. ABEL begins to stir and convulse and have a seizure. It terrifies EVE and CAIN. ABEL'S eyes open. He coughs up blood. He stares blankly.)

EVE: Abel?

(ABEL laughs.)

ABEL: Abel?
            No not Abel.
            Abel's dead.
            Your other son killed the shit out of him.
            Literally.

(EVE realizes that this is not her son. She falls to her knees and bows.)

ABEL: You just couldn't just given me the best your bounty
            Could you, Cain?

CAIN: Lord?

ABEL: Yeah. Lord.

(ABEL spits at CAIN.)

ABEL: You wanna know what he did?
           Wanna know what your baby boy did, Evie?
           He killed your son.
           Your Abel.
           And he's never coming back
           Because that's how Death works.

EVE: What?

ABEL: Cain over here
           Was a little upset that I didn't appreciate his bounty
           And praised his brother.
           And he took this rock

(ABEL picks up the bloody rock.)

ABEL: Tackled Abel to the ground
           And bashed his head with this rock against the dirt
           Until Abel stopped moving.
           That's what your baby boy did.

(EVE looks at CAIN.)

CAIN: I didn't know this would happen!

ABEL: You still did it.

EVE: He can never come back.

ABEL: Nope. Gone forever.

CAIN: There has to be //

ABEL: Death can't be undone.
           At least not yet anyway.

EVE: What now?

ABEL: Go lie with your husband.
           Make another child to replace this one.

*(EVE, in a fit of rage, screams, and pushes ABEL back to the ground.
EVE exits.)*

ABEL: Ow.
           Sheesh!

(CAIN, hollow, curls up in a ball.)

CAIN: What now?

(ABEL takes his blood and marks CAIN with it.)

ABEL: Don't disappoint me again.

END OF PLAY

THE SUNSET TOUR

by Mabelle Reynoso

CHARACTERS

NAYELI, 16, surfer girl; sunny disposition but with a hustler streak. Latina.

DALE, 34, dressed in khakis and a long-sleeve button down shirt. Any race or ethnicity.

GRACIE, 50s, NAYELI'S grandmother, proprietor of kayak rental business. Latina.

SETTING

Beach Mama, a kayak rental and beach wear shop.

TIME

Present day, early afternoon.

NOTE

This script features some translanguaging between English and Spanish. Spanish is in italics. Translations are in brackets and are to be used for reference only. Coyolxauhqui is pronounced "Koy-yol-shauw-kee." Nayeli is pronounced "Nah-yeh-lee."

PRODUCTION HISTORY

The Sunset Tour was presented by The Roustabouts Theatre in San Diego, CA in February 2022. The production was directed by Ron Christopher Jones. The cast was as follows:

NAYELI: Arianna Vila

DALE: Walter Murray

GRACIE: Shirley Johnston

NAYELI is behind the sales counter, scrolling through her phone, checking out her ex's Instagram. The shop is otherwise empty.

NAYELI: "Oh look, I'm standing next to a surfboard with my shirt off." *Baboso* [dummy], you don't even know how to surf. *(Swipes)* Oh no. Please tell me that's not what I think it is. I know that ain't a picture of your *pendeja* [dumbass] girlfriend holding E.

(NAYELI spots DALE as he cautiously enters the shop — clearly an out-of-towner. He appears very uncomfortable as he looks through a rack of swim trunks.)

NAYELI: *(Voice change ... bubbly.)* Hi there. How're you doing today, Sir?

(DALE does a quick nod in her direction and then looks away.)

NAYELI: You visiting from out of town? *(DALE nods but does not look at her.)* Awesome. Where from?

DALE: *(Almost indiscernible.)* Up north.

NAYELI: Fantastic. Let me ask you something. Have you ever gone kayaking before?

DALE: No.

NAYELI: Dude. Today is seriously your lucky day. The water is amazing. Come over here. Come on, don't be scared.

(DALE moves closer with trepidation. NAYELI whips out a kayaking tours brochure and imposes it on him.)

NAYELI: We have a bunch of wonderful kayak tours that you can actually still jump on today. Are you here by yourself or with people? You got family with you?

DALE: By myself.

NAYELI: Cool. This is a great way to meet people. I feel like kayaking is a super fun social activity. Super easy to make friends. Plus, if you follow us on Insta, at Beach Mama, you get like a five-dollar discount. *(Beat.)* You

	look more like a Facebook guy. What's your username? I'll friend you.
DALE:	No.
NAYELI:	No?
DALE:	I mean, I don't have that. No Facebook.
NAYELI:	That's probably a good thing. I'm like so over social media right now. My stupid ex is posting all of these dumbass picture ... Sorry. I talk a lot. My nana says I have diarrhea of the mouth. That's a pretty gross visual, I know. *(Beat.)* Do you have any interest in kayaking today?
DALE:	*(Lost in thought.)* What?
NAYELI:	Kayaking? It really is a beautiful day for it. I'm not just saying that. It's been really hot lately and today it's cooled down a bit. Thank God. I mean it's still hot but at least you don't feel like taking a shower after just having taken a shower. You know? Of course, you're all dressed for a boardroom or something. Are you looking for some beach clothes?
DALE:	*(Concerned.)* Do I need them?
NAYELI:	I mean does anyone need beach clothes?
DALE:	I don't know.
NAYELI:	Dude, you don't need any clothes for the beach. You could run around naked. But I wouldn't recommend it unless you wanna go to jail.

(DALE looks up at her and takes a step back.)

| NAYELI: | What time is it? *(NAYELI checks her phone.)* Okay, look. I know we're already at max capacity but I'm going to make an exception for you. You say the word right now and I will get you on this afternoon's sunset tour. You get out in the water and you're there just in time to watch the beautiful sunset. It's amazing. You like sunsets, don't you? |

DALE: Huh?

(DALE is having a hard time being in this situation.)

NAYELI: *(Shakes her head)* Look at you. You're so caught up in the rat race that your mind can't even shut down. I see guys like you all the time. You're here at the beach, but your brain is still stuck at the office. Meanwhile, you're ignoring that there is a giant beautiful world outside. Seriously, when was the last time you saw a sunset?

DALE: I don't know.

NAYELI: That long, huh?

(Having a disappointing realization, DALE makes eye contact for the first time.)

DALE: I have never seen a sunset.

NAYELI: *(Disbelief.)* Come on.

DALE: At least I don't think I have. I don't ever remember seeing one.

NAYELI: Dude. A sunset is magic. No matter what crazy stuff happened during the day when that sun sets, it's like, poof. You turn the page. You start over and you get another chance to make it right. Witnessing that moment is like the greatest. Seriously, dude. Get yourself the sunset kayak tour and let this mark the beginning of a new chapter in your life.

(DALE takes a moment to think about it.)

DALE: Okay.

NAYELI: Yeah? Okay, awesome! I just need you to fill out a waiver so you can't sue us if a shark bites your leg off. I'm totally kidding. You'll be fine. Hopefully. What's your name?

DALE: Jensen.

NAYELI: Jensen. Cool. Last name?

DALE: Oh, last name is Jensen. First name is Dale.

NAYELI: Great. Dale Jensen, please sign here.

(NAYELI hands him a sheet of paper. He scribbles his name and hands it back to her. She looks at the paper.)

NAYELI: Dale Jensen, do you know what you and my two-year-old have in common?

DALE: Two-year-old?

NAYELI: Yeah, my son. Your signatures look exactly the same. Dude, you write like a toddler. *(Beat.)* I'm sorry. That was rude. I don't even know why I said that. Diarrhea of the mouth.

DALE: How old are you?

NAYELI: Sixteen.

DALE: And you have a baby? Just one?

NAYELI: What's that supposed to mean?

DALE: I don't know. I just —

NAYELI: Look, dude, you can think whatever you want about me but I'll have you know I'm on track to graduate next year. I work. I pay rent. I feed my kid and pay for his Pull-Ups all by myself. And it ain't easy and I don't care because he's the best thing that's ever happened to me. So, you can go ahead and judge me if you want, but I am not ashamed.

(DALE starts to tear up.)

NAYELI: Oh Jesus. I didn't mean to make you cry.

(NAYELI gets a tissue and hands it to him.)

DALE: I have to go.

NAYELI: Wait, no. Don't go. You gotta take the tour.

DALE: I can't.

NAYELI: Yes, you can. Look dude, I'm not gonna lie. Part of me needs you to take the tour because I make ten bucks extra every time I get a booking. And honestly, the sunset tour is totally not at max capacity. But man, we're at the beach. It's a beautiful sunny day, and you haven't smiled once. What the hell dude? I can feel your energy. You've got some heavy stuff going on in that head of yours. Newsflash. The stock market will be fine.

DALE: Stock market?

NAYELI: Or whatever you're tripping on. Let it go. Smell the ocean air. Feel alive.

(DALE pulls money out of his wallet and sets it down on the counter.)

DALE: I'll pay. I'll pay for the tour.

(GRACIE walks in from the back door with a shopping bag. DALE sees her and moves away, pretending to look at board shorts.)

GRACIE: They didn't have those nasty kale chips you like but look what I got Emilio.

(GRACIE pulls out a plastic sand pail and shovel.)

NAYELI: *Nana, ya te dije.* [Grandma, I already told you.] He does not need any more sand toys.

GRACIE: *Ay no seas así.* [Oh don't be like that.] It was only a couple of bucks. How are things going here?

NAYELI: This fine gentleman is about to book the sunset tour. *(to DALE)* That's my grandmother. This is her place. She's the OG Beach Mama.

(GRACIE starts tidying up and doesn't look at DALE.)

GRACIE: Wonderful. You're gonna love it.

(DALE picks up the toy shovel and sets it back down.)

DALE: His name is Emilio? Your son?

NAYELI: Yep. Named after my tata. I call him E. *(NAYELI finishes up the paperwork.)* Okay, Dale Jensen. You are all set.

(GRACIE looks up from what she is doing.)

GRACIE: Dale Jensen? *(She looks at DALE.)*

DALE: Gracie.

GRACIE: What the hell are you doing here, Dale? When did you get out?

DALE: Two weeks ago.

NAYELI: Nana, do you know this guy?

DALE: I should go.

GRACIE: The hell you will. You're here now.

NAYELI: Nana, what's going on?

GRACIE: You gonna tell her or will I? *(DALE looks like a deer in headlights.)* I guess I will. Nayeli, *saluda a tu papá.* [Say hello to your father]

NAYELI: *¿Cómo que mi papá?* [What do you mean my father?] My father's name is Thomas Wolf.

GRACIE: Dale Thomas Wolf Jensen.

(NAYELI looks at him. She starts to speak but then catches herself. She takes a deep breath and resets.)

NAYELI: What do you want from me?

DALE: Nothing. I just wanted to see you.

GRACIE: Okay. You've done that. You can go now.

(DALE looks to NAYELI. She looks away. DALE makes his way toward the exit.)

NAYELI: I wrote you once. When I was ten. You never wrote me back. How come?

DALE: I don't know.

GRACIE: Great answer, Dale.

(DALE turns back.)

DALE: I was in a really bad place for a long time.

GRACIE: That's your excuse?

DALE: You wouldn't have wanted to know me. But I … Your mom sent me a picture of you and I got this made.

(DALE rolls up his sleeve and reveals a tattoo of a baby's face.)

GRACIE: You think a tattoo is gonna make up for everything?

NAYELI: Looks kind of like E.

DALE: *(To GRACIE.)* No. I don't know how to make things right.

GRACIE: You can't. Nothing you can ever do will make things right. The amount of damage you've done to this family. To this girl. To *my* girl.

DALE: Gracie, I'm really sorry about Tilly.

GRACIE: Don't you say her name. You don't get to say her name. My baby was a good girl until she got mixed up with you. She died with a damn needle in her arm and this poor child over here *(looks at NAYELI)* was the one who found her. Nayeli was nine. God damn you, Dale.

(DALE nods and starts toward the door. NAYELI watches him leave.)

NAYELI: So that's it? You're just gonna go?

(DALE looks back at her, resigned.)

GRACIE: Let him go.

NAYELI: *No puedo, Nana.* [I can't, Grandma] *(Calling out.)* Hey Dale, tour starts at 5:30. You have to be here at 5 for a safety briefing.

DALE: You still want me to take the tour?

NAYELI: You paid for it. I gotta pick up E from daycare. Be here by four forty-five if you wanna see him.

DALE: I can meet your son?

NAYELI: You can *see* him. That's gonna have to be good enough. For now.

GRACIE: Nayeli, *se te fue la onda?* [have you lost your mind?]
He's why your life has been one mess after another.

NAYELI: One mess after another. That's me. *(To DALE.)* You see
a mess, Dale?

DALE: No.

NAYELI: Lot of people think I'm a mess. They have no problem
coming up to me and telling me so. Especially when I
got E with me.

DALE: They don't know what they're talking about.

NAYELI: You think you're a mess?

DALE: I'm pretty worthless.

NAYELI: Worthless? *(Beat.)* They made us watch a video in
health class ... how babies are made. Like a scientific
video, not, you know, people doing it. It's basically
a miracle. The odds of the exact combination that
made us is like really a miracle. How can any of us be
worthless if we're all miracles?

GRACIE: Don't do this, Nayeli.

NAYELI: Nana, I'm not inviting him to live at our house. But
he's got a right to know his grandson.

GRACIE: He's got no right —

NAYELI: Well *I've* got a right to know him. He's my father.

GRACIE: And I raised you. *Yo te crié.* [I raised you.] *(GRACIE
locks in on the sand toys and grabs them.) Voy por Emilio.*
[I'm going to pick up Emilio.]

(GRACIE gives DALE a deadly look as she exits.)

NAYELI: She'll cool down. She always does. *(NAYELI raises
her sleeve and shows her own tattoo.)* You know what
this is? Coyolxauhqui. It's kind of a long story but
basically she was gonna kill her mom and then her
brother stopped her and chopped her up. Chopped
off her arms and legs. And her head. And then he took

her head and threw it up into the sky. She became the moon. Why am I telling you this crazy story, Dale? Because in this world, we can do really terrible things and then become the most beautiful version of ourselves. *(Beat.)* So we'll see you back here in a bit?

DALE: Thank you, Nayeli.

NAYELI: I want this to work, Dale. But a lot of things have to happen before you become a part of our world. I think you know that. You can start with taking in the sunset.

DALE: I'll be back at 4:45.

(DALE walks out, almost smiling.)

END OF PLAY

ORIGINAL SQUEEZEBOX

by Steve Serpas

CHARACTERS

ERIN, female, late 30s, real estate agent, determined.

TOMAS, male, late 30s, Erin's estranged professor husband, on disability.

AGILAR, male, late 60s, a 10th Century Norse Viking. Alpha but tender.

SETTING

Los Angeles. Silverlake. The bedroom in ERIN and TOMAS' house.

TIME

Winter morning.

NOTE

A few years back, I noticed the etiquette of giving and receiving hugs appeared to be changing. Instead of being an act of freely given affection amongst trusted parties, the hug became governed by rules, hesitations and doubt. Even if the occasion warranted one, we were giving hugs to each other less and less. Also, there's this: some of us don't like to be touched. Then a worldwide pandemic made hugs broadly prohibitive. Yet somehow, we needed them more than ever. It had me wondering — what was the origin of the hug? Who historically gave the best one? Who needs a hug the most? Herein lies a few comic answers to these questions, and I hope a lot of playful playmaking for those who *embrace* it!

PRODUCTION HISTORY

Original Squeezebox was first read as part of The Antaeus Company's Playwrights Lab in April 2022, with Antaeus Producing Executive Director, Ana Rose O'Halloran and Artistic Director Bill Brochtrup. The cast was as follows:

ERIN: Avery Clyde

TOMAS: Luis Kelly-Duarte

AGILAR: Harry Groener

Morning light finds ERIN squared-off at the foot of a king-size bed, dressed for work. She looks down on TOMAS, her husband, who peeks out from under the covers, frazzled.

ERIN: That flash of lightning in the cold, dark night spoke *volumes*. It sent valuable service from centuries past. But most of all, it reminded me why I hate you. With the heat of a thousand suns. I hate that you've become a rancid magpie chronically suffering because it's the only way you get your needs met, the constant whining.

TOMAS: The shoe has been on the other foot.

ERIN: You've been in bed for eight months!

TOMAS: Seven.

ERIN: You smell like garbage. Sitting here watching garbage.

TOMAS: I love THE CROWN.

ERIN: Last chance. Get out of bed and sign the divorce papers. Then get out of my house.

TOMAS: That's not what the lightning was telling you. Lightning is about awakening.

ERIN: Medieval pressure is coming. Along with a check. You can say, "thank you" at any time.

TOMAS: I can barely breathe, I'm suffocating.

ERIN: I've heard it all before.

TOMAS: I'm highly sensitive.

ERIN: I need things to work! I need a schedule beyond taking care of you. I need my assistant here to manage stuff so I can sell houses and pay the bills for this one. Remember? When I was working and you were just reading books or whatever it is you do.

TOMAS: You have no interest in me anymore.

ERIN: I have an interest in you being better than this.

TOMAS: Dante scholar. The Divine Comedy. There's only a handful of us left in the world who teach it.

ERIN: That's not even a job.

TOMAS: You're so untreated.

ERIN: And around we go again! … Okay, that's it.

(ERIN exits, then quickly returns with AGILAR, an elder warrior dressed in full Viking regalia. He stands between them. TOMAS reacts.)

TOMAS: There's a ghost in the room.

ERIN: Tomas, this is Agilar.

AGILAR: Agilar the Retriever.

TOMAS: Strangers in our bedroom? You know I have a condition.

ERIN: We're at DEFCON One. You need a new place to live.

TOMAS: I'm a scholar in transition!

AGILAR: He goes off like a harpy.

ERIN: Since you have been unable to comport yourself, I went to Kathy for help.   .

TOMAS: Kathy's a massage therapist.

ERIN: As well as a Reiki master and a conjurer. She's had to double-up on modalities she could perform over Zoom. I told her about your "condition."

TOMAS: H. Pylori with acute anxiety, possible PTSD from my childhood, and I'm susceptible to all the current strains and sub-strains of EVERYTHING.

ERIN: Treatment-resistant, agoraphobic, you need to touch grass. Kathy already diagnosed you.

TOMAS: Just give me this side of the house. And Door Dash.

ERIN: Kathy prescribed you "intense physical enclosure." That's right. You need hugs. To rid you of your paralysis so you can move out. So I said, "What's the best hug we can get? Like the best hug ever. I have cash." She did a little digging. Turns out: Norway, 1066 A.D.

TOMAS: The Viking era.

ERIN: She whipped up a conjuring spell and *viola!* Lightning struck, and Agilar appeared in her driveway this morning. *(To AGILAR)* You invented the hug?

AGILAR: *(Pronounced "WHO-ga")* Hugga.

ERIN: Perfect.

AGILAR: When are we to eat?

ERIN: As soon as you squeeze the daylights out of this one.

TOMAS: He's not touching me.

AGILAR: I cannot complete my mission without a proper meal.

ERIN: Lasagna in 10 minutes. But first.

AGILAR: I have traveled through time against my will, spanning many seas and mountains and glowing, vibrating tunnels, as if I had just drank goose fat mixed with henbane tea. I was told I passed through a — how did she call it? — "time warp."

TOMAS: What were you doing before you came here?

AGILAR: Beheading Tostig and taking Stamford Bridge with 800 warriors. We were triumphant and began to roast a deer.

TOMAS: You're probably really hungry.

AGILAR: I have some constitution. Only some.

ERIN: Go to him now. Hugga!

AGILAR: *(Summoning power from the heavens)* By the hands of Freya —

TOMAS:	No! I forbid you!
AGILAR:	Oh come on, man!
TOMAS:	You've really lost it.
ERIN:	You didn't want to deal with me, now you're going to deal with him.
TOMAS:	I might be on the spectrum. Can't you just get me that machine from that movie, *TEMPLE GRANDIN*? The squueezebox?
ERIN:	They just give people weighted blankets now.
TOMAS:	They don't work.
ERIN:	It wasn't heavy enough. This guy, though. The original. The source.
AGILAR:	Come on now.

(AGILAR steps towards TOMAS.)

TOMAS:	He's coming in. *(To AGILAR)* You're coming in!
AGILAR:	Come on future boy. You've, who has been separated from the birds and the trees.
TOMAS:	I'm from Tenafly, New Jersey. I hate the outdoors.
AGILAR:	Come on man!
TOMAS:	I can't.
ERIN:	TOMAS!
TOMAS:	He can't just do this, he's got germs and everything. He needs my permission.
ERIN:	It's fine, he's fine. He could hug me anytime, it's FINE. He came all this way.
AGILAR:	I cannot delay anymore. I hunger.
ERIN:	Two more minutes.
AGILAR:	M'lady, no.
ERIN:	Just —

AGILAR: I have kept my word but the subject is not willing, and I cannot move him to receive.

ERIN: You could break him in two and serve him to your men.

AGILAR: What an insult to believe we eat each other.

ERIN: We only have a small window of time to send you back. I've given up everything to try and help him, I have done everything right. I'm even giving him half my land and money because that's the law. But he is still stuck somewhere in his mind. This is why we conjured you.

AGILAR: Are you sure you are not stuck somewhere, too?

ERIN: Kathy does Reiki on me every Thursday.

AGILAR: Just as I am stuck. In this house with big chairs and obscene paintings.

ERIN: It's all from West Elm.

AGILAR: I am stuck no longer.

ERIN: You can't go.

AGILAR: Move.

ERIN: You have to go back through the portal. I'll lose my deposit.

AGILAR: M'lady.

TOMAS: Careful. This is when she escalates.

ERIN: It's true. I'm not backing down. I was on the high school varsity team for volleyball, we went to state twice. I've been top agent four years in a row, I sold 26 homes last year.

AGILAR: M'lady.

ERIN: I've done an Ironman and I've got a black belt in Kuk Sool Won. I could stop you physically but I won't have to because I'm commanding you to stay!

AGILAR: *(To the heavens)* By the hands of Freya, EMPLOY ME!

(AGILAR promptly embraces ERIN and gives her the biggest, longest hug. Electricity shoots visibly through both of their bodies for 10 seconds, then he releases her.)

AGILAR: I led hundreds of warriors to battle over the bridge. We were outnumbered. There were many bodies strewn across the land, many souls who were leaving us or just about to leave. Surgeons and wise-people went about shutting the eyes of the departed across the field. I would walk around, pull them up to me and hold them in my arms until they came back. Until they found their way home … That is Hugga. It is not for the dying. It is to make sure the survivors keep living … And now I must feast. I saw a small wild boar running around out there … Bless.

(AGILAR exits. TOMAS gets out of bed to attend to ERIN, who's catching her breath, slowly regaining her strength.)

TOMAS: Darling. You're going to be okay.

ERIN: … you got out of bed.

TOMAS: I was concerned.

(ERIN becomes distracted, suddenly moves toward the window.)

ERIN: *(Shouting out the window)* Agilar, no! That's not a wild boar, that's Kathy's Doberman Pinscher! Don't eat him please! *(A beat)* He's right. I was stuck. I stopped living.

TOMAS: Because of me?

ERIN: You came close to dying. I didn't want to die. So tried to motivate you. I got mean.

TOMAS: You started doing what you do.

ERIN: I crank shit up.

TOMAS: Your shit gets sophisticated. Mine too … I don't know what happened to me these last few years, but I turned inward … I'm better now. I'll be better … Listen, I'll

just go. I'll find my own place. I mean if you really are
sick of me. Are you?

(ERIN goes over and embraces TOMAS deeply. He accepts the hug.)

TOMAS: This doesn't suck.

ERIN: I'm sorry, too.

TOMAS: This is a good start. But it's going to take a few
           more hugs.

*(ERIN hugs TOMAS again. Then, a CRACKING of thunder starts,
building up to a white-hot CLAP of lightning that strobes above of
the bedroom scene, washing it out until it disappears.)*

END OF PLAY

SNOWMAN

by Leda Siskind

CHARACTERS

IVAN, a man, 30s, middle class merchant, could pass as Swedish or not.

LARS, a man, 60s, a professor, friend of IVAN, could pass as Swedish or not.

PETTER, a man, 30s widower, friend of IVAN, could pass as Swedish or not.

INGRID, a woman, 30s, IVAN'S wife, could pass as Swedish or not.

SETTING

Outside a forest area, snow on the ground, rural Sweden.
A snowman — perfectly built with top hat, red muffler, coal eyes and smile, complete with a pipe in his mouth and outstretched branches for arms — stands just outside the forest.

TIME

Winter, late 1800s.

NOTE

This one's for Strindberg.

PRODUCTION HISTORY

Snowman was presented by the Alliance of Los Angeles Playwrights, in the Dramalicious Festival, on October 9, 2022. The reading was directed by Leda Siskind. The cast was as follows:

IVAN: Dan Perry

LARS: Steven Wollenberg

PETTER: Akshaya Pattanayak

INGRID: Brittany DeLeon

Three men, bundled in 1800s winter wear, stare at the snowman opposite them.

IVAN: I just can't believe it's back. I … I really don't know what to do.

LARS: Incredible. I wonder if it will be the same as last winter.

PETTER: I'm sure it will be … and if we chop it down, it will just appear again, just like before.

(They stare at it.)

IVAN: Maybe … it's *not* the same. *(Beat.)* We could test it out.

LARS: *You* want to do that? *(Laughing)* I mean, are you in *need* to see if it — ?

IVAN: No, no! I am perfectly satisfied at home! Ingrid — I mean — we — you *know* what I mean!

PETTER: Well, since I'm the only bachelor here, due to my widower state, *I* will test it out.

(PETTER walks briskly toward the snowman and then stops just within a foot of it.)

PETTER: Oh … oh, oh, no… I feel the tingling, the tightening … !

LARS: Stop!

IVAN: Petter, stop! For God's sake — !

(PETTER throws himself onto the snowman.)

PETTER: Ah! Ooooh! Ohhhhhh!

(PETTER slides downward, obviously in a state of sexual climatic ecstasy, and crumples face downward at the foot of the snowman.)

LARS: That's disgusting!

(PETTER rises, smiling.)

PETTER: That was *great!*

IVAN: Obviously, it still works.

(INGRID, IVAN'S wife, appears.)

INGRID: Ivan! *Here* you are! We received a post this morning from the Lutheran Council and I ... *(sees the snowman)* Oh good heavens, it's *back?*

LARS: Yes, sadly.

IVAN: I wanted to shield you, my dear, so I arranged for Mr. Svendsen and Mr. Oganspool to meet —

INGRID: Whatever for?

IVAN: So that we could quietly decide —

INGRID: No, I meant, shield me from what?

LARS: Well, from ... from what the snowman *does.*

INGRID: Oh, I know what it *does.*

IVAN: You *do?*

INGRID: Well, that can't be *helped,* can it? I mean, one sees a perfectly built snowman mysteriously appear one day in the forest and one innocently walks toward it to get a closer look ...

IVAN: Ingrid!

INGRID: ... and one suddenly enjoys the rapture one's own body can give one!

IVAN: Ingrid! I had no idea!

LARS: Mrs. Bunsenbrik!

PETTER: *(To LARS)* You needn't appear so shocked, professor. You, of all people, should know that women have ... shall we say ... physical desires, too.

INGRID: Thank you, Mr. Svendsen. Nicely said.

LARS: That's all very well in *theory,* in the back bedroom of a consecrated *home,* perhaps, occasionally, for *holidays* and so on — but what about out here in the bloody *forest*?

INGRID: Well, didn't you all try to demolish it last winter?

PETTER: Yes, groaning all the way — my poor testi —

LARS: No details, please.

PETTER: Sorry.

INGRID: And it just popped up again, eh? So …

IVAN: What are you suggesting, my dear?

INGRID: That we just accept it. That it's here for a reason.

LARS: What "reason" could there possibly be?

INGRID: Well, we Scandinavians aren't exactly known for our sensual, erotic ways —

LARS: And a good thing too, my wife Gudrunn always says.

PETTER: Is it? I mean … Lars! Have *you* ever run to the snowman?

LARS: What a question!

IVAN: *(To LARS)* Well, *have* you?

INGRID: *(To IVAN)* Have *you*?

| IVAN: | Yes! | LARS: | No! |

(Beat.)

| IVAN: | *(To LARS)* | LARS: | *(To IVAN)* |
| | I thought so! | | I thought so! |

INGRID: Ivan!

IVAN: What? You were all the way over in Klingenhoten taking care of your sister!

INGRID: For *five days.*

PETTER: Well, as you have *often* said, Ingrid, we *all* get to enjoy the, um, bliss our own loins can give us.

LARS: You're calling Mrs. Bunsenbrik "Ingrid?"

IVAN: Ingrid has *often* said … ?

PETTER: Well … yes … we — we've become close —

IVAN: "Close?" *How* close?

INGRID: I can explain. Mr. Svendsen, being a widower …

PETTER: Needed encouragement —

LARS: Are you two having a tryst? A tete-a-tete? A liaison? An aff —

IVAN: *(To LARS)* Lars, please. *(To INGRID)* What do you mean "encouragement?"

INGRID: Petter was achingly lonely after Julia — Mrs. Svendsen — passed on last winter. So, when the snowman appeared, and I discovered its … uh, *use*, I encouraged Petter to meet me here so I could, umm, *demonstrate* the correct way to achieve —

IVAN: Say no more! *(He stops to collect himself)* Well, all right, Ingrid, as you pointed out, we *all* have, er, physical, instinctual longings, and perhaps you did a good deed, a Christian act of charity, by introducing Petter to a *singular* way of, ummm, satisfying those *solitary* needs.

PETTER: We *did* hold hands.

INGRID: Petter!

IVAN: What?!

PETTER: *(To INGRID)* We have nothing to be ashamed of. *(To IVAN)* We ran to the snowman together.

IVAN: The *two* of you?

PETTER: And it's amazing! That … that *thing* over there causes simultaneous —

IVAN: I don't want to hear it!

INGRID: I have never been unfaithful to you, Ivan! Other than our clasped hands, Petter and I have never touched! It's just that the snowman induces —

IVAN: You've never asked *me* to venture out in the moonlight and gallop toward the snowman!

INGRID: It's difficult to do that when you are away trading herring in Oslo most of the winter! And besides, I want to ... to ... uhm ... share my ... ummm ... tactile orifices with the sensate, umm, muscles of another human body... not with a frozen ball of snow wearing a top hat and a muffler.

IVAN: Aww, my kitten!

INGRID: *(As she motions, with a hand behind her, for PETTER to step away.)* Meow! Meow!

(INGRID and IVAN touch noses and snuggle.)

LARS: Well, I say, however you may personally feel about this ... this ... *aberration*, it is best if we attempt to destroy it once again ... or at least, cover it up so it will not be found.

INGRID: Oh, Mr. Ogenspool, I fear it is too late for that! Last night I looked out my back window and noticed a *line* of people waiting patiently... now I know why!

LARS: Degenerates, surely!

INGRID: I think I saw your university chancellor, Dr. Hartzen there!

LARS: Exactly!

PETTER: Well, in any case, we tried to rid ourselves of the snowman last winter and here he is again. No doubt he will remain, whatever we do, until the winter thaws.

INGRID: As I said, I think the snowman is here for a reason ... perhaps to enlighten ourselves or to learn how to appreciate what our mortal bodies are capable of ...

(IVAN takes INGRID'S arm and they stroll off. PETTER tips his hat to LARS and leaves the opposite way.)

(LARS waits a few beats for them all to leave. He stares at the snowman, looks away, looks down at himself, places his hand on his heart and closes his eyes. He opens his eyes and rushes toward the snowman.)

LARS: Ohhhh! Oooooh Mine Gott!! Yes, yes, yes, *yes!*

(He collapses in front of the snowman in spent sexual pleasure.)

LARS: Oh! Gudrunn!

END OF PLAY

MISSED DISCONNECTIONS

by Samara Siskind

CHARACTERS

BEN, male, early thirties. A hopeless romantic.

SLOAN, female, late twenties. A girl with her guard up.

MARGOT: female, mid-twenties. Just wants to be noticed.

SETTING

A city park, anywhere.

TIME

The time is now.

PRODUCTION HISTORY

Missed Disconnections was first produced by Lakeshore Players Theatre, White Bear Lake, Minnesota, June 2022. The production was directed by Daniel Stock. The cast was as follows:

BEN: Jesse Villarreal

SLOAN: Alicia Ehleringer

MARGOT: Laura Trudell

A park bench. A man sits, smiling to himself. Woman enters.
He stands.

SLOAN: *W4M — 27. We locked eyes for a second this morning at*
Whole Foods. I was wearing a red polka dotted sundress,
you had on jeans and a hipster sport jacket. There was a
banana in your basket next to a pint of chocolate milk,
like a child's lunch. I thought that was adorable.

BEN: *M4W — 32. I noticed you sniffing and fondling half a*
dozen grapefruits at Whole Foods on 14th. Your red dress
and little white sneakers destroyed me. I was the guy with
the fogged up glasses in the freezer aisle. I hope you read
these things.

BEN: *(Holding out hand)* Ben.

SLOAN: *(Nervous)* I can't believe I'm doing this.

BEN: First timer?

SLOAN: Missed Connection virgin. I mean, I've written dozens
. . . in my head. This is the first time I've been brave
enough to post one. Do people even use this anymore?

BEN: I'm pretty sure it's mostly personals now. But hey, we're
here.

SLOAN: Strange, isn't it? I mean, good-strange, not freaky-
strange. Two people posting about each other, *to* each
other.

BEN: I looked for you at every checkout lane that day.
I circled the parking lot twice, but you disappeared.
I was kicking myself for not talking to you.

SLOAN: Why didn't you?

BEN: Let's see. Good old fashioned fear? Fear of rejection.
Fear of a jacked up boyfriend appearing out of
nowhere . . . Fear of coming off like a creeper
interrupting a magical moment between a girl and her
produce. *(Beat)* Why did you write to me?

SLOAN: You look like a boy who broke my heart in 6th grade, all grown up. *(Beat)* I made a New Year's resolution to be more spontaneous so, I finally threw my message in a bottle into the ocean. Way more romantic than asking someone for their number, right?

BEN: Missed Connections *are* safer than Tinder.

SLOAN: We've already seen each other in the flesh.

BEN: No fear of being catfished.

SLOAN: The initial spark is already there.

(Beat)

BEN: You're wearing it, the dress.

SLOAN: I thought I'd make it easy for you to spot me.

BEN: I spotted you in a sea of over a hundred organic food shoppers.

(A few beats. Fleeting glances. Half smiles.)

SLOAN: So, I'm going to hit the coffee cart over there and text my friend that I'm still alive. Would you like a coffee? Chocolate milk?

BEN: No thanks. I just had a Lunchables.

(SLOAN smiles and exits, giving him one last head turn. BEN sits as before, pleased. A woman enters. BEN does a double take, then stands.)

BEN: *(Flustered)* M4W — 32. You were wearing a short denim skirt and a green shirt with puffy sleeves. You stood next to me in the red wine aisle eating from a bag of chickpea snacks. You looked amazing. I hope you see this.

MARGOT: Hi. Ben? Sorry I'm a little late, I've never been to this park. The layout is confusing. *(Reaching her hand out)* Margot.

BEN: Margot. Hi, uh. Wow, you look great! *(Looking off)* Weren't we supposed to meet Sunday?

MARGOT: It's not — ? Wait. *(Checks her watch)* Oh no. I'm a day early. Oopsies!

BEN: No, no worries.

MARGOT: Well since we're already here. *(Plops down)* I guess subconsciously I wanted it to be tomorrow. Can I just tell you, I like, loved what you wrote. It just made me feel so, like *(Fanning herself)* flattered you know? Like, *noticed*. Being admired from afar. I can't stop thinking about it. I didn't even think people used Missed Connections anymore. Don't they use TikTok now? I've never posted, I'm a horrible writer, but I still read it sometimes. I always hoped someone would write to me.

BEN: Well, I'm, I'm, glad it, it did all that. Look, I —

MARGOT: So, did you end up getting the Cab or the Zin?

(BEN just looks at her, confused.)

MARGOT: The wine. Did you end up going for the Cabernet or the Zinfandel?

BEN: Oh, ah, huh. You know, I — I don't remember.

MARGOT: I hope you went with the Zin, it would've gone great with the feta.

BEN: The feta?

MARGOT: In your basket, silly.

BEN: The cheese! Yes! So, uh, you know I think tomorrow would be better.

MARGOT: Better for what?

BEN: For this, this meeting.

MARGOT: Tomorrow? You want me to come back here tomorrow?

BEN: It looks like it's going to rain.

MARGOT: My Smartwatch says it's sunny with low chance
of showers.

BEN: Yeah, well, I have another . . . I was headed to my
mom's house, actually.

MARGOT: But it took me *(Checking watch)* 2,668 steps to get
here from my car.

BEN: I'm really sorry. She's old and I need to help her ...
walk.

(SLOAN enters.)

SLOAN: Hi.

BEN: Hey.

MARGOT: Hi.

(Painfully awkward silence. Finally —)

SLOAN: I'm sorry. Am I interrupting something?

MARGOT: *(Blissfully unaware)* It's our first date. Missed
Connection at Whole Foods. He liked my puffy
sleeved top. Isn't that romantic? *(To SLOAN)*
You look familiar. Do you two know each other?

SLOAN: Really? You double booked a Missed Connection?

BEN: No, no!

SLOAN: I can't believe this. You're, you're — Mason Mayfield
all over again!

BEN: Sloan, I — Let me —

SLOAN: My first middle school dance. My first date, ever! I go
to get some punch and BAM! There he is making out
with Shari Snipes behind the DJ table. You even look
like him!

MARGOT: I got the day wrong. We're supposed to meet
tomorrow. Ooohhh. That's why you wanted me to go.

SLOAN: He wanted you to go?

MARGOT: To come back tomorrow. He said he needed to help his mom . . . walk.

SLOAN: Okay, wow. I knew I shouldn't have come. Just when I finally find an ounce of courage to put myself out there.

BEN: Please, can I just —

SLOAN: It's all about the chase for you, isn't it? You find it entertaining to manipulate women's feelings?! Lead them on and, and lie to them?!

BEN: No! I don't! I didn't lie, or lead anyone on! I met you after I met ah,

ah —

MARGOT: Margot.

BEN: Margot, right!

SLOAN: And then you wanted to ditch her?!

BEN: I didn't want to ditch her! I just wanted to see her tomorrow. As planned.

SLOAN: Unbelievable.

BEN: What's unbelievable? I never said it was my first time posting. I never said it was my only time. Did you know men on average fall in love 19 times a day?

MARGOT: I believe the statistic is men think about sex 19 times a day.

SLOAN: Does this mean 17 other women are going to show up?

BEN: It means I've thrown a lot of bottles into the ocean.

MARGOT: That's not very eco-conscious, Ben.

BEN: So, what? I'm not allowed to have two dates in the same weekend?

SLOAN: It's not that. It's you approaching both of us in the same exact way. Me in my red dress, her in her puff sleeves. Like, like a formula. Sending us these parallel posts cheapens it all. It's the equivalent of rotating the same pick up line at a bar.

BEN: Well, it's hard for guys too! I don't do this just to hook up. None of these things have ever worked out for me. Like the cute Uber driver who ended up stealing the silverware from my favorite diner. Or the flirty bank teller whose entire Instagram account was pictures of her cat wearing doll clothes. There's more.

SLOAN: Oh, cry me a river. You just didn't want to put all of your Whole Food eggs in one basket.

BEN: Well, what about you?

SLOAN: Me?! What about me?

BEN: At least I try! Fine, maybe I try too often, but you don't try at all!

SLOAN: You don't know anything about me!

BEN: I know that Mason Mayfield guy sure did a number on you. I know you don't take chances. You bury moments that could turn into something beautiful. You sit on the sidelines instead of throwing your hat in the ring.

SLOAN: Yeah, except for this time! And look what happened!

BEN: Look, let's just take a moment. *(Beat)* I, I saw . . . *(Lost. Looks at Margot for help.)*

MARGOT: Margot.

BEN: Margot. I saw Margot and took a shot in the dark. Most people don't even know the Missed Connections section of Craigslist exists. She responded. We made plans. Then I saw you with the grapefruits, so I took another shot in the dark. Then *you* posted to *me*! How amazing is that? What was I supposed to do?

SLOAN: You could have changed locations.

MARGOT: At least he picked different days.

BEN: Look, my only crime here, if it can even be considered a crime, is finding the both of you attractive and seeing potential for something more. You'll never win the lottery unless you buy a ticket.

(Beat)

BEN: Or multiple tickets.

(SLOAN turns to MARGOT.)

SLOAN: How do you feel about all this?

MARGOT: We only have one life. I think Ben was just being realistic about his needs and accepting that a moment of intimacy between two strangers doesn't always evolve into a deep, long lasting connection. It's hit or miss, and timing is everything. If I hadn't shown up you two might be seeing a movie together or making plans for dinner. He hasn't forgotten your name.

BEN: Sorry about that.

MARGOT: You remembered Mason Mayfield.

SLOAN: So you think he deserves a second chance?

MARGOT: No.

BEN: No?

MARGOT: After scrolling my Smartwatch, I see a few more trademark Ben Whole Foods posts and two at Trader Joe's, which leads me to believe . . . you're just a serial poster. *(Shrugs)* Sorry Ben. *(Beat)* Wait. Did I just feel a drop? *(Looking up)* Oh no! My Smartwatch said no rain!

(MARGOT reaches into her bag for an umbrella. As she takes her umbrella out a hat falls to the ground. SLOAN and MARGOT both reach down to pick it up and lock eyes. Beat.)

SLOAN: *W4W — 27. Cute girl in the yellow bucket hat. We reached for the same copy of FRANNY AND ZOOEY at Second Chance Books. You let me have it. I love your smile and the star tattoos on your wrist.*

(MARGOT holds up her wrist, revealing her stars.)

MARGOT: You wrote that? About me? I never saw it.

SLOAN: I never sent it. I wrote it . . . in my head.

MARGOT: You were wearing cat-eye glasses and had a reusable farmer's market tote with a whole wheat baguette in it. I knew you looked familiar.

(They slowly stand.)

SLOAN: Thanks again, for the book.

MARGOT: You're welcome.

(A few beats.)

BEN: Well, this is an exciting turn of events. *(Hopeful)* Maybe the three of us can find a nice spot for brunch?

SLOAN: It's not happening Ben.

MARGOT: I think you need a time-out.

SLOAN: Do yourself a favor. Find a new venue.

(MARGOT holds her palm out to the sky, looking up.)

MARGOT: False alarm. *(Gestures to Sloan's coffee)* Would you like a refill?

SLOAN: I'd love one.

(SLOAN and MARGOT exit, together. BEN sighs and returns to bench. He takes out his phone and makes a call.)

BEN: Hi there, beautiful. I'm at the park. Want some company? . . . Okay, great. I'll see you in a few, Mom.

END OF PLAY

BENCH

by Katherine Swan

CHARACTERS

BENCH

LIGHT

MOTH

All characters are open to any age, gender, race or ethnicity.

SETTING

A park on a summer night.

TIME

Around 8 PM.

NOTE

Movement in the play can be very stylized, incorporating dance, or very simple, depending on one's preferences.

PRODUCTION HISTORY

Bench was presented by Arc Stages in Pleasantville, NY as part of their first annual *New Voices Festival* on April 30, 2022. The reading was directed by Jeff Raab. The cast was as follows:

BENCH: Nancy Jane Blake

LIGHT: Arnie Toback

MOTH: Phoebe Dunn

BENCH and LIGHT are onstage. LIGHT stands and BENCH sits,
maybe on the floor, or maybe on a bench. They are near each other,
but do not touch.

BENCH: You're quiet tonight.

LIGHT: You don't say?

BENCH: Normally you would have turned on by now. Aren't
you going to turn on?

LIGHT: No.

BENCH: No . . . ?

(Beat.)

LIGHT: I'm not the same anymore.

BENCH: Since they . . . upgraded you?

LIGHT: Don't call it that.

BENCH: Since they changed you?

LIGHT: Yes. I'm ugly now.

BENCH: You're different, it's true. Being different doesn't mean
you're ugly.

LIGHT: HA. They took my essence from me. My glance: swirl
of gold in a glass of blackness. I was like the moon,
emerging from dark curtains of cloud. Now I'm just
some cold eye, perpetually open. A blight on the night
world. Who would shelter beneath me? All creatures
that love the dark will shun me. I'm a surveillance
beam, irradiating all mystery from the night.

BENCH: They're trying to conserve energy. They're saving
the world!

LIGHT: This sweet, sick world will never be saved. From
darkness to darkness; our lives are a journey charted
by stars that have already gone out.

BENCH: Okay . . . Well, you know, we're all just trying to get by, just living, right? There are some things we don't get to choose.

Remember two years ago, what happened to me? The kid who ate two orders of McNuggets and a strawberry shake and was sick all over my lap? And the Mom just left the mess on me and ran off with him? And then. Then the pigeons came. Remember how people looked at me? How they turned away in disgust and sat on the *grass*? "Oh Chad, don't sit there, that bench is covered with bird shit." It was July. The best month to be a bench. I was alone, I had never been more alone. Sometimes a rat would come by and eat some of the mess. Even you, even you were embarrassed to be associated with me.

LIGHT: That was a hard time for me too. No lovers sat beneath my light.

BENCH: But then August came. And a hard rain came. A rain so hard it peeled some of my paint. It washed away the remains of that day in July. After that, I wasn't the same. I looked older: no longer shiny and green. But the people came back. And they liked being with me. My touch was softer; strangers sat in my lap and felt held again. Since that rain I've grown softer and softer. I'm even beginning to splinter over here.

LIGHT: They'll fix that when they come to repaint you.

BENCH: Maybe. Maybe they'll just saw me in half and haul me away. Put in someone that's all metal. Someone tougher than me. More modern.

And when they do, you know what I'm going to miss? More than anything?

That moment each night when it happens. When darkness seeps into the air like tea staining water and your light clicks on and touches me all over. That's the moment I live for.

LIGHT: I'm ashamed for you to see me like this. What you
           remember. The memory will always be better.

BENCH: But if you just stand there, extinguished . . . we'll never
           touch again. Just.

           Show me. Once more. Just once.

(Pause. LIGHT considers.)

(LIGHT turns on. A physical gesture.)

BENCH: Ahhh. You're radiant. Thank you. Thank you.

(MOTH enters.)

MOTH: Moon, moon

(MOTH circles LIGHT, coming closer and then moving away.)

LIGHT: You've come back

MOTH: Moon, moon, moon

BENCH: Always

MOTH: Moon

BENCH: Be careful

MOTH: Moon

(MOTH goes to LIGHT. They kiss. MOTH falls on BENCH, dead.)

(LIGHT and BENCH stretch towards each other.)

LIGHT: My love

BENCH: My love

END OF PLAY

BONUS

by Lolly Ward

CHARACTERS

KATE, female, a great employee.

JACKSON, male, a great employee.

GREG, male, the company's Chief Executive Officer.

SETTING

An office holiday party.

TIME

Night. When people are starting to let loose.

PRODUCTION HISTORY

Bonus was presented by the Playwrights Union in the Atwater Theatre in Los Angeles, CA, May 19, 2023.

Sounds of an office holiday party. KATE and JACKSON feel their way through the dark to her empty office.

KATE: *(Hushed, laughing)* Come on, you, get in here.

(She flips on a lamp. A dollhouse and a shoebox sit on her desk.)

JACKSON: I gotta close the door!

KATE: Close it. And lock it!

JACKSON: I'm gonna lock it so hard.

KATE: Yes, you are. You're gonna lock that door so goddamn hard.

JACKSON: Do you think people know about us?

KATE: How would they know? We're discreet.

JACKSON: Mainly . . .

KATE: It's a party! Everyone's having fun. We can tell them when we're ready.

JACKSON: You're right.

KATE: Blow their minds.

JACKSON: You said it.

KATE: It's not like we're breaking any laws —

JACKSON: Just company policy.

KATE: Which is fake anyway. I read the employee handbook. It's not enforceable.

JACKSON: I love it when you talk tough.

KATE: What else do you love?

JACKSON: *(Getting into it)* I love when we run meetings together.

KATE: *(Getting into it)* Yeah, you do . . .

JACKSON: I love how we're such a badass team with clients.

KATE: That's right . . .

JACKSON: I love how we clinch the deals. You get in there with the data, and I show them the charts until they're eating out of all four of our hands . . .

KATE: We closed that last deal eighty thousand dollars higher than anyone thought we could!

JACKSON: And that's why I'm going to take my bonus and splurge it all over your —

KATE: Hold on, your what?

JACKSON: My bonus.

KATE: Your what??

JACKSON: My . . . bonus?

KATE: How big is your bonus? What'd you get, like twenty dollars?

JACKSON: No, my holiday bonus.

KATE: Yeah?

JACKSON: It's way more than twenty bucks. What'd you get?

KATE: Twenty bucks.

JACKSON: Nah.

KATE: Yah.

JACKSON: But we were in the same meetings.

KATE: Yep.

JACKSON: And met the same clients.

KATE: Hm.

JACKSON: And closed the same deals.

KATE: Uh huh ...

JACKSON: It doesn't make any sense. There's no difference between us . . . that I can think of . . . at all . . . Hold on! What about a work perk? Did they tell you about some cool new thing you could do?

KATE: They said I could use the gym on Mondays.

JACKSON: Only Mondays?

KATE: What does that mean?!

JACKSON: They said I could use it every day. That's so weird.
            Why wouldn't they want you to be fit?

KATE: I don't know, I want to be fit.

JACKSON: I know . . . you love to work out! Wait a sec. Besides
            the cash, the bosses gave me a funny animal gift.
            Did you get a weird pet?

KATE: *(Pointing out the shoebox)* Yeah, I got a guinea pig.
            What am I supposed to do with a guinea pig?
            I don't even have a cage.

JACKSON: Tell me about it, they gave me a gator.

KATE: Stop it. They gave you a live alligator?

JACKSON: Right? Like I have time to feed that thing between
            meetings. Or when we're traveling.

KATE: Why wouldn't they give us both guinea pigs?

JACKSON: Or both gators? Then we could share the live meat.

KATE: I don't get it. They never gave any indication that they
            were unhappy with my work.

JACKSON: No, they love you. Like I love you.

KATE: Well, not like you love me.

JACKSON: No, but close. They're always going on and on about
            how great you are. I kind of thought they guessed
            about us because they gush about you so much.

KATE: When?

JACKSON: . . . When? Whenever. All the time. Like, when we're
            out together.

KATE: When are you and the bosses out together?

JACKSON: Oh —

KATE: At drinks?

JACKSON: No when they took me house-hunting.

KATE: For . . .

JACKSON: *(Holding up keys)* A house? Didn't they get you a house?

KATE: Yeah, they sure did.

JACKSON: Oh good. You scared me!

KATE: *(Pointing to the dollhouse)* You're looking at it.

JACKSON: Is that the model of the one you picked?

KATE: That's the whole house.

JACKSON: Why would they give you a dollhouse for a bonus?

KATE: I don't know, Jackson, you tell me.

JACKSON: Look, Kate, let's not lose our heads. The great part is that we love each other. This company can't take that away! They may not treat us equally, but the joke is on them, because I'm going to share it all with you! The gator and the house and —well, not the gym, unless I take you as a guest, which could be hard to coordinate — but all the rest of it, for sure! *(He hands her the keys.)* What's mine is yours!

KATE: You're going to share your house with me?

JACKSON: Of course! Here's the deed. *(He pulls out the paper and signs it.)* For Kate, the perfect home for us. Love, Jackson.

KATE: But we should have two houses!

JACKSON: Hey, at least I got a house — a really, really nice house — so I'm starting to believe that we're missing something here.

KATE: You think?!

JACKSON: Do our CEO and CFO do a good job?

KATE: Yes, in general.

JACKSON: And this company is a nice place to work —

KATE: It's been a good ride —

JACKSON: And it has a solid reputation in the field?

KATE: Yes, Jackson, what's your point?

JACKSON: So, the only other possible explanation is that I deserve the bigger bonus. They know what they're doing, and they found me worthier. They're wise people who move in not so mysterious ways.

(There's a knock on the door. KATE and JACKSON spring apart. JACKSON opens the door while KATE pretends to play with the dollhouse. The CEO, GREG, enters.)

GREG: There you are! We've been looking for you everywhere. Oh good, Kate, I'm so happy you like the dollhouse. Our CFO wanted to get you a car, but I said, if I know Kate, she'll get a kick out of something esoteric like this. Right again!

KATE: Hi, Greg, I'm glad you're here. Jackson and I were talking, and —

GREG: I bet you were, you wacky dealmakers! And I will rush right back to finish this chat, but first we have a big announcement at the party, and everyone's waiting. Come on, Jackson.

KATE: That's fine, we can walk and talk —

GREG: *(To KATE)* You're welcome to come if you want or stay here. We're announcing promotions, so Jackson needs to say a few words.

KATE: You're promoting him over me?

GREG: It's not a competition. But that's right.

KATE: We do the same job.

GREG: Also right.

KATE: So, why?

GREG: I discussed it with our CFO, and we just feel more comfortable paying him more, you know? He might want things, and need to pay for them, like gas for his new car.

JACKSON: It's gorgeous, by the way, thank you again.

GREG: No problem. The red really suits you.

KATE: I have bills, too!

GREG: Little bills.

KATE: I have needs!

GREG: But smaller. That's why, after you'd been here awhile, we brought Jackson in at double your salary.

KATE: (*To JACKSON*) You make twice as much as I do?!

JACKSON: I thought you knew.

KATE: How would I know?

GREG: We really frown on sharing salaries among our corporate family. It's so gauche. But he — and I — do make a lot more.

(*KATE picks up the dollhouse and raises it over her head.*)

KATE: That's it. I QUIT! If you don't value me and the job that I do, then I don't want to be here anymore!

JACKSON: Don't do it, Kate!

KATE: Thank you, Jackson. Are you going to quit instead?

JACKSON: Me? No . . .

KATE: Or quit with me in solidarity?

JACKSON: No again . . .

GREG: Listen, this is all riveting, and quite possibly a human resources fiasco, but Jackson and I have to rush over to that celebration. Can't leave everyone waiting for the guest of honor!

JACKSON: Shoot, Greg, I forgot to feed the gator.

GREG: *(With good humor)* Oh, you . . .

JACKSON: *(Also laughing)* That's how it's gonna be, I guess!

GREG: I've got you covered. I grabbed a tray of sushi from the party. Is that big boy still in your office?

JACKSON: Sure is. Oh man, you're a lifesaver!

(The two men leave. KATE holds the dollhouse, unsure of her next move. Suddenly there are sounds of a scuffle and screams from the next office.)

GREG: *(Off)* Jackson, help me!

JACKSON: *(Off)* I don't know how!

GREG: *(Off)* It wants the sushi!

JACKSON: *(Off)* So give it the sushi!

(More screams and thrashing and carnage. Alas, they are consumed by their own greed.)

KATE: *(About the dollhouse)* I wonder if I could modify this into a guinea pig dream house. I bet I could, after I drive my new car . . . to my new home . . .

(She picks up the house deed and jingles the keys.)

(The end of income inequality. And . . .)

END OF PLAY

GOWN

by Robert Weibezahl

CHARACTERS

LYNN, female, 50s. Any race or ethnicity.

ANNIE, female, LYNN's daughter, late 20s – early 30s. Any race or ethnicity.

COURTNEY, female, late 20s – early 30s. Any race or ethnicity.

SETTING

A bridal shop.

TIME

Present day.

PRODUCTION HISTORY

Gown was presented by Lakeshore Players Theatre in White Bear Lake, Minnesota, June 2–12, 2022. The production was directed by Audrey Johnson. The cast was as follows:

LYNN: Maggie Diebel

ANNIE: Audrey Johnson

COURTNEY: Katie Rowles-Perich

A bridal gown shop. LYNN, a woman in her fifties, sits on a bench or chair. She looks tired but is serene.

LYNN: *(Calling offstage)* I liked the last one.

ANNIE: *(Offstage)* What?

LYNN: The last one. I liked it.

ANNIE: *(Offstage)* The Vera Wang?

LYNN: Was that a Vera Wang?

ANNIE: *(Offstage)* Yes.

LYNN: Yes, I liked that one.

ANNIE: *(Offstage)* You don't think it was to ... froufrou?

LYNN: Froufrou can be nice ... in a wedding dress.

ANNIE: *(Offstage)* Not really me.

LYNN: I guess not. *(Beat)* What's next?

ANNIE: *(Offstage)* Coming. Just a sec.

(After a moment, ANNIE enters from the dressing room. She is in her late twenties, early thirties. She is wearing a relatively simple wedding gown. She is trailed by COURTNEY, the saleswoman, who is about ANNIE's age.)

LYNN: Oh ... that I like!

ANNIE: It's nice, no?

LYNN: Who's the designer?

COURTNEY: It's one of our better-priced dresses.

LYNN: The price doesn't matter.

COURTNEY: Oh. Okay. Nice. It's from one of our exclusive suppliers. It's sort of a Stella McCartney-inspired — *(Whispers)* — knock-off.

ANNIE: Well, it's beautiful.

LYNN: Yes.

COURTNEY: It really does suit you.

LYNN: *(Working hard not to tear up)* It's what I always imagined.

COURTNEY: And that company makes some beautiful bridesmaids' dresses as well.

(ANNIE gives LYNN a knowing look.)

ANNIE: *(Hesitant)* We don't need bridesmaids' dresses.

COURTNEY: No?! Will they all be wearing something different? I know that's being done more and more. Personally, I prefer a more ... *collective* look.

ANNIE: No bridesmaids.

COURTNEY: Oh. Well. Your maid of honor should come in. Once you've chosen your dress. So we can coordinate something nice for her.

ANNIE: *(Looking at LYNN)* No maid of honor.

COURTNEY: What a small wedding! Private?

LYNN: Are there more dresses to look at?

COURTNEY: *(Lightly)* There are *always* more dresses to look at. Let me go see what else I think is right for you.

(COURTNEY exits into dressing room.)

ANNIE: Mom, I feel terrible. Should we tell her?

LYNN: We will.

ANNIE: We're wasting her time.

LYNN: No one else has come into the shop the whole time we've been here. What else does she have to do?

ANNIE: I don't know. She may have *something*. Take inventory? Place orders?

LYNN: I'm sure she's happy to have customers. It can be very boring working in a little shop on a weekday afternoon. It's a nice distraction.

ANNIE: Technically, we're not customers.

LYNN: Of course we are. Every customer doesn't
            buy something.

ANNIE: People don't typically window shop in a bridal shop.

LYNN: Sure they do. And we're not window shopping.

ANNIE: Still, I feel guilty.

LYNN: You do look lovely in that dress.

ANNIE: It is perfect, isn't it?

LYNN: You'll make a beautiful bride.

ANNIE: *(Tearing up)* Oh, Mom —

LYNN: Stop that! This is a happy day. Our special day.

(COURTNEY pops her head back into the room.)

COURTNEY: I found three more you might like. Do you want to
            come back and try them on?

(ANNIE hesitates.)

ANNIE: Sure.

(ANNIE looks pleadingly at LYNN.)

COURTNEY: What?

LYNN: Courtney, we have to be honest with you —

COURTNEY: Is something wrong? Are you unhappy with my
            service? I thought —

LYNN: It's not that, it's —

COURTNEY: I haven't worked here very long. I try to do my best.
            It's my aunt's shop and —

ANNIE: Everything's great, Courtney.

COURTNEY: I'm still learning, I know. But I work hard to make
            everything special for the big day.

LYNN: That's just it. *(Beat)* There isn't one.

COURTNEY: Huh?

LYNN: A big day.

COURTNEY: Oh! You haven't set the date yet? Well, that's okay. You can never plan too far ahead, right? And when you and your groom do pick a date —

ANNIE: There isn't one of those, either.

COURTNEY: One of what?

ANNIE: A groom.

COURTNEY: Oh, I'm sorry. There I go again. Making assumptions. You and your bride, then.

ANNIE: Courtney, I'm sorry. This is getting out of hand. The truth of the matter is there's not a bride or a groom ... or a wedding. I'm not getting married.

(COURTNEY, confused, doesn't know what to say.)

ANNIE: We've been wasting your time.

LYNN: We have not been wasting her time. It's her job. You don't mind, do you?

COURTNEY: *(Baffled)* I'm afraid I don't —

ANNIE: Let me try to explain. *(Deep breath)* You see, my mom here is ... sick.

LYNN: Technically, I'm dying.

ANNIE: Mom, don't make this any harder.

LYNN: Just a fact.

ANNIE: My mom has cancer. Stage four. She's had all the available treatments. Even went to Mexico for an experimental one. Nothing has worked and, well —

LYNN: Oh, for Chrissake, Annie. She doesn't need to know all that.

ANNIE: I just —

LYNN: Courtney … dear. What Annie said — those are the facts. I'm not going to be around much longer. A month, maybe. Three. Six at the outside. I've tried it all. I've lost my hair. I've made my peace. We all have to go sometime, right? Sooner than I planned, sure. But I've stopped raging against the dying light. Didn't see the point.

COURTNEY: I'm so sorry, I —

LYNN: Thank you, dear. I know you are. People have been wonderful. So kind. *(Pause)* So, you're wondering what this is all about? Well, it's quite simple, really. This morning I woke up and I realized that I wasn't going to live long enough to see my Annie get married. I'd never see her walk down the aisle. I'd never see her in a wedding dress. At first that made me want to cry and I was feeling sorry for myself again, and then I thought, well hell, screw that. I texted Annie to take the afternoon off and pick me up. I've often seen this shop, but never had a reason to come in. Now I had a reason. And now I've seen my Annie as the beautiful bride I know she's going to be someday. When she meets the right person and falls in love and begins the next chapter of her life. And I may not be at the wedding, but at least now I've had the chance to see her in the dress. And she's going to a beautiful bride, isn't she? Just like I always knew she would be.

COURTNEY: I, I … don't know what to say. I'm going to cry.

LYNN: No tears! I told Annie, and now I'm telling you. This is a happy day. *(Beat)* And you will always be a part of it whenever Annie thinks about it. Next year. The year after. Hell, ten years from now.

COURTNEY: I'm … *(Beat)* Thank you.

ANNIE: Thank you, Courtney. Thanks for understanding. *(Beat)* Let me get out of this dress and then we can get you home, Mom. You must be tired.

COURTNEY: But ... no. Wait. There are those three other dresses I picked out for you to try on.

ANNIE: I —

COURTNEY: And if those are not quite right, there are at least a half dozen more.

ANNIE: Courtney, I don't want to waste any more of your time.

COURTNEY: I have some that may not be in your size, but we can pin them up if we need to and make things do.

LYNN: That would be wonderful. I'd love to see some with more lace.

COURTNEY: One of the ones I've already set aside has a beautiful lace bodice.

LYNN: Sounds perfect.

ANNIE: Aren't you tired, Mom?

LYNN: I have plenty of time to be tired.

COURTNEY: Oh! And what about *your* dress? We have a nice selection of mother-of-the-bride gowns, too. Are you thinking floor length or cocktail?

LYNN: *(Smiles)* Let's see a few of each.

END OF PLAY

RIGHTS & PERMISSIONS

PLAYS FOR ONE ACTOR

FLAT MEAT SOCIETY © 2023 by Tom Coash. Reprinted by permission of the author. For performance rights, contact Tom Coash, thomascoash@sbcglobal.net

CARRY ON © 2023 by Jennie Webb. Reprinted by permission of the author. For performance rights, contact Jennie Webb, jenniewebbsite@gmail.com

PLAYS FOR TWO ACTORS

SIX FEET © 2023 by Claudia Barnett. Reprinted by permission of the author. For performance rights, contact Claudia Barnett, clodilla98@gmail.com

POCKETBOOK © 2023 by Cris Eli Blak. Reprinted by permission of the author. For performance rights, contact Cris Eli Blak, crisblakwrites@gmail.com

MOLLIE and HARRY© 2023 by Tom Block. Reprinted by permission of the author. For performance rights, contact Tom Block, thomasablock@gmail.com

ONCE REMOVED © 2023 by Jami Brandli. Reprinted by permission of the author. For performance rights, contact Jami Brandli, jamibrandli@gmail.com

A MAN WHO KNOWS HOW TO HOLD A BABY © 2023 by Hal Corley. Reprinted by permission of the author. For performance rights, contact Hal Corley, corleyhal@gmail.com

THE MOST PRECIOUS THING © 2023 by Amy Dellagiarino. Reprinted by permission of the author. For performance rights, contact Brian Sherman, bts@ipexartists.com

THE PITY MOURNER © 2023 by Paul Donnelly. Reprinted by permission of the author. For performance rights, contact Paul Donnelly, paul@pauldonnellyplays.com

INTIMATE MATTERS © 2023 by Mikki Gillette. Reprinted by permission of the author. For performance rights, contact Mikki Gillette, mikkigillette@gmail.com

SOULMATE © 2023 by Deirdre Girard. Reprinted by permission of the author. For performance rights, contact Deirdre Girard, deedeegirard@gmail.com

הבהא | AHAVAH © 2023 by Dana Hall and David Lipschutz. Reprinted by permission of the author. For performance rights, contact Dana Hall, magnoliawrites120@gmail.com or David Lipschutz, david.lipschutz@gmail.com

PLAYS FOR THREE OR MORE ACTORS